So You Want to Be a Political Journalist

So You Want to Be a Political Journalist

edited by Sheila Gunn

First published in Great Britain in 2011 by
Biteback Publishing Ltd
Westminster Tower
3 Albert Embankment
London
SE1 7SP

Copyright © Sheila Gunn and the individual contributors 2011

Sheila Gunn and the individual contributors have asserted their rights under the Copyright, Designs and Patents Act 1988 to be identified as the authors of this work.

All rights reserved. No part of this publication may be reproduced, stored in a retrieval system or transmitted, in any form or by any means, without the publisher's prior permission in writing.

This book is sold subject to the condition that it shall not, by way of trade or otherwise, be lent, resold, hired out or otherwise circulated without the publisher's prior consent in any form of binding or cover other than that in which it is published and without a similar condition, including this condition, being imposed on the subsequent purchaser.

ISBN 978-1-84954-085-8

10 9 8 7 6 5 4 3 2 1

A CIP catalogue record for this book is available from the British Library.

Set in Sabon LT Std
Printed and bound in Great Britain by
CPI Mackays, Chatham ME5 8TD

Contents

Acknowledgements

When pulling together this book, I had one particular audience in mind: those I meet at university and elsewhere who are determined to become confident and competent journalists. Yet while politics impinges on so much media coverage, the level of knowledge among student and trainee journalists of how our political and parliamentary systems work seems to be alarmingly low.

So I am immensely grateful to Shane Greer at Biteback Publishing for offering me this opportunity to produce a book that looks at politics from the point of view of a journalist. And a huge thank you to Sam Carter and Hollie Teague for their efforts in helping to edit the final results.

Any reporter should benefit from the contributions from journalists, lecturers and others, writing about their own specialities, their own experiences and giving their personal advice on identifying, tracking and reporting political stories. My heartfelt thanks go to them: Chris Moncrieff, Michael White, Peter Riddell, Ann Treneman, James Landale, Joy Johnson, Nick Jones, Andrew Pierce, Adam Holloway MP, Richard Osley, Ivor Gaber, Steve Schifferes, Colin Brown, Amanda Brown, Andrew Hawkins, Carolyn Quinn, Sam Macrory and Jonathan Isaby.

My gratitude goes also to those journalists who, whether they know it or not, I regarded as my mentors over the years, especially: Chris Moncrieff (PA), Phil Webster (*The Times*) and Alan Kirby (*Coventry Evening Telegraph*). And the editors who either employed or tolerated me over the years, including the late Harry Pigott-Smith (*Stratford-upon-Avon Herald)* and editors of *The Times*, the late Charles Douglas-Home, Charles Wilson, Simon Jenkins and Peter

Stothard. What they all had in common was to encourage and trust me to pursue 'stories', to beat me up when I made mistakes and to support me without hesitation whenever politicians complained. That is the best that any political journalist should expect.

Finally, I doubt if this book would have been possible without the unwavering confidence in the results of my children Ben and Kate, and their spouses, Inger and Martin.

Sheila Gunn

Part I:

So you want to be a political journalist

1: The front page

Sheila Gunn

When students say that they want to be a political journalist, my first question is: why? This is perhaps slightly unfair given that I have probably just described some aspect of life at Westminster, peppered with anecdotes, which makes it sound as if it is all fun and games.

Since I do not want to sound pompous, I don't talk to them about 'writing the first rough draft of history' or 'you'll have a seat in the front row...' Instead, without meaning to be unkind, I ask if they have been to a meeting at their local council and identified any stories. This is an essential first step. If they bother and it does not put them off completely, then maybe they are considering a reasonable career choice. Alternatively, I suggest they attend a select committee or Westminster Hall debate in Parliament. They are easy to access, more intimate and focused events which discuss issues in some detail, without the usual ya-boo associated with MPs. At the very least I would expect them to have watched elected representatives at work via the BBC's excellent Democracy Live website or the parliamentary channel. If none of this attracts them, I presume that they have a totally starry-eyed, misguided vision of life as a political journalist.

The first task set for students when I arrived at journalism college in Cardiff – and is still set on some courses today – is to go into the local city and come back with a number of good ideas for stories. A wonderful test, as it drives home the point that journalists need to view the world in a different way than other mortals. For some, such an experience is unsettling, if not downright uncomfortable. Hopefully they will find a different, more conducive career path.

News v. comment

Political journalism in particular seems to be open to misunderstandings about what the job actually entails. Perhaps you thought it was all about standing in front of that famous black door and giving the world your view on what was happening behind it? A big mistake. Just read James Landale's description of his working week if in doubt.

You will soon learn that there is a distinction between reporting and commentating. Do you want to communicate your views on the comprehensive spending review, the proposed schools reforms or the war in Afghanistan? Then, OK. Join a campaign, set up a blog, start out on the long road to becoming a politician. But it is a very bad idea to use this as a basis for becoming a political journalist.

Any confusion is understandable. Too much of what is called 'news' – which should be about the reporting of facts – is now tainted by personal comments. Oddly enough, the puritans at *The Independent* must bear some of the blame for accelerating the trend of weaving opinion into news stories. And talking of puritans, painting all politicians as criminals – while jolly good fun for a lot of journalists for a couple of years – is not actually in the interests of journalists or their audiences in the longer term. Yes, let's punish those who broke the criminal law. But if you start out on a career in political journalism with the objective of humiliating as many politicians as possible, do not be surprised if your reputation sinks alongside theirs. There's a world of difference between challenging, scrutinising, criticising – all of which you should be doing – and sneering cynically at our elected representatives. When on *Desert Island Discs,* the *Channel 4 News* presenter Jon Snow described his role as: 'I am simply someone who questions.' A near perfect description of a journalist's role.

You may tell me that you regard covering politics as the most important job in journalism. Perhaps. Although the role has diminished to some extent as the differences between the political parties have narrowed. This means that more of the focus tends to be on the analysis and impact of particular policies, which is covered in greater depth by specialist reporters.

'So, why did you become a political reporter?' you are justified in asking. Rather than pretend that I had some grand ambition, I tend to tell you the truth. We all need a USP – unique selling point. I managed to beat off competition to get my first job in journalism, on the *Stratford-upon-Avon Herald,* because I already had good shorthand and a clean driving licence. Not very exciting, I know. The paper had never employed a girl before because, as the editor put it 'there are certain jobs I just cannot send you out on'. I kept silent but made a point of quickly proving him wrong. As I moved up via a regional evening and a regional daily to the Press Association, that shorthand gave me an important advantage. I could be trusted to cover any council meeting or criminal court and sprinkle my stories with a reasonable amount of accurate, direct and relevant quotes.

Never underestimate the value of this type of practical skill. For instance, I joined the (then) *Surrey Daily Advertiser* in Guildford as deputy news editor five days before the Provisional IRA bombed two pubs in the town, killing five people. I was a natural to cover the subsequent Old Bailey trial of the Guildford Four (later, of course, cleared), with myself and a colleague filing virtually a full broadsheet page a day.

On moving to PA, I had to decide whether to specialise in crime or politics. A senior colleague pointed out that, if you cover politics, your byline is more likely to be on the front page. That persuaded me. Maybe not the most honourable of motives, but one which is immediately attractive to a journalist.

History matters

You need to be interested in politics. As Peter Riddell makes clear in his chapter, you should develop a good understanding of what has happened in politics in the past thirty or forty years. It is too easy to sound ignorant or lazy if you do not. I make absolutely no excuse for the fact that there are similarities in the advice given by several contributors about monitoring and absorbing political stories on an almost hourly basis.

Another great advantage is to regard politicians neither as friends nor foes, but as a group of people who can influence the lives and livelihoods of all of us. That is what makes them worthy of your interest. Most of them may look uninspiring or boring, but luckily for journalists they are capable of doing the most extraordinary and unexpected things. Just think back to events over the past twenty years. A novelist could not make it up!

Are you party political? That is, do you feel strongly about a particular party? Its politicians? Its policies? This is not a sin. But what if you were given a good story that would damage any of these entities? Any hesitation at all, should make you think twice about political journalism as a career choice. There are plenty of roles within the parties, think tanks and campaigns which may be more satisfying for you. Because what should turn you on is the scent, the tracking and the development of a good story. 'Good', of course, is not used in any moral sense; to a journalist, it means a story that will be featured high up in the running order.

A 'normal' life

Observing politicians at crucial times is fascinating. And you may be seated only a few yards away from them. Or you may even – like many of the contributors – have a role in the events that determine their future. You will often be bored; you may occasionally be scared when a deadline looms and the story is not evolving as expected; and you should have plenty to laugh about. But your job, essentially, is to report stories within a tight timescale. You do not have the benefit of hindsight, of mulling over all the implications. You must churn it out.

This does not mean that, on any day, you can predict what you will be doing. Do you regard this as an advantage or a problem? We are all creatures of habit to a certain extent. But unless the idea of not quite knowing what you will be required to do within the next twenty-four hours appeals to you, then perhaps a more dependable job would suit you better. Chris Moncrieff wisely advises you to have your up to date passport with you at all times. You never know when you might need it. I am taking as read that you are not looking for a desk job? Although for too many reporters, life today means a computer screen. Please try to escape as often as possible. You can be the eyes and ears for your audience only if you witness key political events and are in regular contact with politicians. This usually requires spending time outside your formal working hours to develop your knowledge and your contacts.

The very uncertainty of political life makes the job a poor companion to life outside Westminster. Booking theatre tickets (unless it is essential political viewing), arranging dinners, attending that PTA meeting all become more of a challenge. Too many of us have let down loved ones at the last minute because of some drama. To say that politics is a form of addiction is, hopefully, an exaggeration. But beware. It can take over your entire life.

Top political jobs are among the most sought after in journalism, up there with foreign postings. It is a highly competitive world and there will be plenty of other journalists lusting after your job. New editors and producers have an unsettling habit of wanting to shake up the political team they inherit or even, as I have actually witnessed, offering a Westminster posting to someone they meet at a party. It is not a lifestyle that suits everyone.

Different voices

This book is not designed as an examination of all the political processes. Instead it describes the political processes and players from the point of view of a working journalist. What and who is important? How do you operate? Who do you need to know? And, most of all, where are you most likely to find the stories? In other words, it aims at stripping away any mystique surrounding life at Westminster and offering very practical help in reporting the actions and decisions of our politicians and public servants.

All of the contributors to this book have been highly successful in their different roles in politics. Most work or have worked for a wide variety of media outlets and specialised in different forms of political journalism. Others, such as Adam Holloway MP and the pollster Andrew Hawkins, will give you a different, but essential perspective.

Hopefully their advice and experiences will help you make your own decision about the next steps in your career. Much of it, of course, applies to whatever sort of journalism you embark on. For whether you are at Westminster, or anywhere else these days, you can dig out excellent, significant and unexpected stories. And really that should be all that matters to you.

2: The best job in journalism: political reporting

Michael White

One Saturday in the late 1980s I attended a party political conference staged at an American-owned hotel in the small Central American republic of El Salvador. The country had been going through a brutal civil war and the star of the day's show had been associated with right-wing death squads. No, I don't speak Spanish, but I got the point of the occasion.

That's why I love being a political reporter, why it's the best job in journalism, why it's the best job in the world. What, even now, I hear you ask? When the British Empire has evaporated and our Lilliputian MPs, more social workers than legislators, sometimes shrink before the power of executive government and the lash of a media emboldened by the shame of the expenses scandal and newspapers which break the law?

It's a fair heckle, but only as far as it goes. In our own time and place, slowly emerging from a nasty recession in early twenty-first-century Britain, just as Asia dramatically reasserts its central role in world history, politics is widely despised – though an exception is usually made for Nelson Mandela, a wily man as well as saintly.

But the lip-curling response is always a mistake, as Aristotle could – and did – explain. Bernard Crick put it simply in his evergreen and much reprinted volume, *In Defence of Politics* (1962). People who prefer to ignore politics in the hope of being left alone, he wrote, usually find themselves an 'unwitting ally' of those who think a state is better off without politics or politicians. In the process of cleansing it that sort leave nothing – and no one – alone. Did I hear you murmur 'Putin' there, or 'Palin'?

Cheers and jeers

That was the point I revalidated in that air-conditioned hotel in a steamy Latino republic. Every time the party star's name was mentioned everyone stood and cheered. This wasn't a political conference in any meaningful sense of the word, it was a rally for someone for whom politics was a cloak for military-backed authoritarian rule.

As such it reminded me of a story told by the late Mark Arnold-Forster, one of my *Guardian* heroes, admirably modest but also a twice-decorated veteran of World War II. At the start of the Cold War, Mark and a correspondent from the communist *Daily Worker* had been the only British reporters present at a congress of the Polish United Workers Party (PUWP), which ran Poland after Stalin had consolidated the Soviet grip on eastern Europe. As with the right-wing thugs in San Salvador, every time Stalin's name was mentioned at that Warsaw Congress everyone rose to applaud – including the chap from the *Daily Worker*. 'Why are you doing that?' asked Arnold-Forster. 'Why not? It's a free country,' replied his irony-lite colleague.

Which, of course, it wasn't, not until the trade union politicians of the Solidarity movement called the Soviet bluff in the 1980s – no military invasion this time – and the fall of the Berlin Wall in 1989 triggered the final collapse of the PUWP. The mighty Soviet system which had suppressed open politics across the Iron Curtain countries of eastern Europe – and in the USSR itself – collapsed like the proverbial domino to the astonishment even of those who had long predicted such a climax to the 40-year Cold War stand-off.

It wasn't that there were no politics in Soviet Russia, of course not. But they were the politics of a Kremlin court, of a rigid, increasingly unresponsive bureaucratic network, more concerned with protecting its own power than addressing the ever-more urgent challenges of economic, social and political modernisation. It was a world of whispers and intrigue where rumour (often wrong) thrived and the party controlled the courts and press: a recipe for disaster and backwardness.

China's Communist party has adapted to the challenge much more effectively, though many predict that its *political* rigidity will eventually prove its own downfall too. Left, right and centre – as Hosni Mubarak's regime reminded us again in Egypt – sooner or later regimes which suppress politics prove too brittle to resist internal or external shocks which shatter them if they cannot adapt. Thus did Mogul India fall so easily to the British in the eighteenth century, the Aztecs and Inca civilisations to (even fewer) Spanish invaders in the sixteenth and half the Middle East (the half which most hated Roman rule) to Mohammed's holy warriors almost a thousand years before.

Changing times at Westminster

Forgive the civics lesson. What has any of this to do with the parochial, sometimes grubby politics of the Palace of Westminster where I have loitered on and off for thirty years? Everything to do with it. Whether a state and wider society – there is an important difference – are in confident expansion, in terminal decline or (as ours is) struggling to adapt to a new role in a fast-changing world, we have to settle our differences. The most effective way to do so (usually by compromise), to divide up the national cake as fairly as possible (not easy at present) and to decide how best to move forward is via open politics, responsive and accountable.

Put simply, we elect people to make decisions on our behalf – from parish pump to Edinburgh Parliament and Brussels ministers, but chiefly still at Westminster. If we don't like what they do (or fail to do), we sack them and try another lot. No one is imprisoned or tortured, murdered, dispossessed or exiled in the process. In Britain these ground rules have been developed over centuries and is a miracle of liberty which we neglect at our peril. Though hard-won democracy is more easily lost, as Aristotle's beloved Athens discovered.

In my lifetime, the political process in Britain has never been revolutionary but frequently dramatic. In July 1945 – three months before my birth – British voters ejected Winston Churchill, the right man to win the war, but not the peace, they rightly judged. 'Will you be shot?' a woman admirer asked the sacked great man. Worse than that, he replied, I will have to sit on the opposition benches. And so he did: lose touch and you lose power. Harold Macmillan (handing over to a thirteenth earl in 1963 did not save his party twelve months later), Harold Wilson, Ted Heath, Jim Callaghan, Gordon Brown in 2010, all were unceremoniously ejected. Voters usually did the job, but Margaret Thatcher and Tony Blair – both triple election winners – were deemed over-stayers by their party and cast out. Anthony Eden, whose 1956 invasion of Suez makes Blair's Iraq adventure look a model of openness and wisdom, was forced out by a palace coup: the Tories were much less open in those days, no leadership elections for them until 1965!

Amazing! And I had a ringside seat for half of it, from the bit where Callaghan took over from the exhausted Wilson in early 1976. Late one night just three weeks later young Michael Heseltine picked up the ceremonial Mace after a narrow, slightly dodgy, Commons defeat and virtually hurled it at Labour MPs. I know, I saw it – as few did in the pre-TV era. Old lags in the press gallery had seen nothing like it. But there I was, watching open-mouthed in the pre-TV lights gloom. Magic! I was there next morning too, when Hezza apologised.

Trivial? Yes, of course, but the underlying issues were serious in that crisis-torn decade. The three years of the Labour minority government (1976–79) which preceded Mrs Thatcher's arrival at No. 10 were like that: a nightly drama when the government could lose a 10 o'clock vote and fall at any time, as it eventually did. When they were in danger of losing by 300–299, ministers sent the 299 home early, lost 300–0 thereby nullifying the defeat's meaning. They really did that too!

What followed was different; Margaret Thatcher was different. No more trimming, no more compromise or muddling through. After the industrial winter of discontent the unions must be DEFEATED! Along with inflation, the Argentinians, assorted terrorists (including that Mandela man), Communism and 'wet' liberal Tories. The white-knuckle ride worked for almost a decade, but ended in tears, as it usually does, in 1990. They stay too long, they think themselves indispensable, they run out of luck and excuses and – this one's important – the voters get BORED. Thatcher, who compromised quite well to start with (you have to in politics), made the mistake of believing her own Iron Lady propaganda and lost touch over the poll tax.

Daily life

What was it like reporting all this? Wonderful. I was a member of *The Guardian's* four-strong lobby team, the group of political reporters entitled to hang around in the members' lobby outside the Commons chamber – then the great crossroads of Parliament – to speak to MPs, as well as attend the mysterious twice-daily briefing from the No. 10 spokesman. But I was also the paper's parliamentary sketchwriter, recording the dramas, the jokes, the folly in the chamber itself.

Hard work, but gripping. In the days before the 24/7 cycle of relentless rolling news, of fax machines, mobile phones and parliament live on *radio*, let alone the internet, blogging, tweeting and spin doctors, life was often more leisurely – and more reflective. Westminster was much more insulated from voters and political reporters more independent from those pesky newsdesks a couple of miles away in and around Fleet Street.

If you were a junior, you came to work by 11am and read select committee reports or talked to any MP you could find. You read the papers, perhaps attended the 11 o'clock briefing, perched on Bernard Ingham's sofa in the window to the right of the big black No. 10 door. Or you might pop into Annie's Bar or the Strangers' for a pre-lunch drink in the hope of meeting a minister.

Ah, Annie's. It had been revived in the 1970s as a watering hole where hacks and MPs could meet on equal terms and my old boss, Ian Aitken, *The Guardian's* political editor from 1975 to 1990, made it a basic principle to be there after 5 o'clock so MPs who wanted to tell him something (no mobiles in 1975) knew where to find him. On a good day they queued up!

By late afternoon decisions must be made, stories discussed with patient news editors, copy typed or mapped out as points one to five on an envelope with a view to being dictated over one of the phones dedicated for the purpose in the rabbit warren of press rooms known as 'the Burma Road'. Did I say dictated? Yes, no laptops then. You mostly phoned all out-of-office stories to men and women wearing headsets and known as 'copytakers'.

Some were rude ('is there much more of this?' and 'you've already made that point'), others delighted. Old Joe with the smoker's cough had serious left-wing politics. 'That's complete rubbish, you know, Mike.' Or 'I knew Denis Healey when he was a Communist, Mike.' Annoying but better than 'Thatcher? Can you spell that please.' And at least at Westminster you weren't dictating for half an hour from the only red payphone on the council estate with grannies tapping the window with 10p coins, mouthing 'are you going to be much longer?' That would have been the polite grannies.

Twenty-first-century Westminster

It's all gone and it won't come back. Earlier deadlines; the intrusive demands which the internet makes on reporters and MPs alike (they used to get an average twelve constituency letters a week, they now get 300 plus emails, I get 100 daily emails from strangers); the so-called 'family-friendly' hours regime which sends parliament home long before midnight. All have helped make the Palace of Westminster more efficient, though not necessarily wiser than in the 1970s (when many ministers were World War II veterans) and certainly not friendlier or more fun. Even the modern craze for sensible eating has combined with the curb on expenses to make chips a rarity on the health-conscious menus and the good old TBL (that's a Two Bottle Lunch with a good contact) virtually as dead as Mr Gladstone. Indian arm-wrestling at midnight on the floor of the SNP whips office? It wouldn't happen now. Or would it? Perhaps I am too old to know.

Either way, contacts, how to make them, keep them, cherish them or lose them, remain much as they were. Yes, 'Westminster village' is a cliché but, like many clichés, an accurate one. Write something nasty, nice, wise or foolish about a politician and Sod's Law dictates that you meet them in a corridor next day. All MPs, peers too, officials and spin doctors (they're only press officers with attitude) have their favourites and their enemies in the press. And vice versa. I have often found myself liking people whose politics I don't much approve of (Alan Clark?) and approving of dull, decent types with whom I would not want to be stuck in a lift.

That's life. Some MPs expect to be lunched and quoted by name, not necessarily accurately if they are rent-a-quote types who love the tabloids and believe (wrongly) that there is no such thing as bad publicity. Each to his own. Reporters were once playing a 'Ten Biggest Shits' game with a list of MPs names when Gordon Grieg, naughty-but-nice political editor of the *Daily Mail*, intervened: 'But they're all my best contacts.' Gordon once forced a Tory minister's resignation (unfairly I thought), but the ex-minister was seen buying him a drink that evening. He liked him; nothing personal.

Are there different ways to do the job? Of course. Some political reporters like my old *Guardian* colleague, David Hencke, specialise in reading the small print and trying to unearth scandal. Others are diligent students of policy who wouldn't look at gossip, even if some MP's love life was all over the tabloids. Yet for some reporters – and MPs – gossip (who's up, who's down) is the essence of politics. In one sense they're right too. In politics, personality is inseparable from policy and the exercise of power. Tony Blair and Gordon Brown were different, right? John Major was definitely not Mrs T and we were grateful, for a while anyway.

In the fast-moving world of today, when Britain is experiencing its first peaceful coalition in eighty years, Gordon Brown already feels like history. He was Prime Minister as a boom turned into bust. The public mood is different. And Asia – China and India, not forgetting distant Brazil – are on the rise. David Cameron, Nick Clegg and their teams are struggling to guide Britain through an economic storm, but in a world changed forever.

What now?

I am close to retirement, but I find the dynamics of coalition politics refreshingly different too. Suddenly it's OK for Cabinet members to disagree publicly over policy as Tories and Lib Dems do. Well, up to a point it is, Vince. And electoral reform, will that make a new kind of politics? No, says me! Europe, an issue which ruined so many careers, seems to have gone quiet. Or is it only sleeping? And will the coalition last until 5 May 2015, as it promises to do, cheeky fellows? Or will it split – as British coalitions did in the past? We know about Nick Clegg (we think we do), but which way would Vince Cable jump?

So many questions, so many possibilities, and I haven't even mentioned the biggest of all: Will the coalition's economic strategy kickstart us into prosperity again or mire us in stagflation? The next scandal to rock the government? How can I tell? It may be in tomorrow's Sunday papers, meaning that people like me will be bashing the phones tomorrow afternoon, asking ministers and MPs 'is it true about old X and the model?' and – even more importantly – does it matter?

How exciting, how trivial, how important. The show must always go on, through dull patches and times when you think nothing worse could happen, whereupon it immediately does, through tumultuous times and squalidly inadequate ones. I have seen parliament's performance improve in my time, but also seen it get worse – much like the voters really.

But I cling to the romance of an incident recorded at the dangerous height of World War I when Winston Churchill, then in disgrace as so often, took a Liberal MP into the darkened Commons chamber and predicted that, though the German war machine's 'brilliant efficiency' was clearly superior to our own, we would win through in the end because we thrashed our disagreements out openly 'even in war-time, this little room is the shrine of the world's liberties', he said.

Self-centred, overblown, ridiculous? Of course, but remember Churchill was also a journalist. They need us, we need them, locked in a love-hate relationship, circling each other suspiciously. Beat that.

Michael White was parliamentary sketchwriter of The Guardian *from 1977 to 1984 and the paper's political editor, 1990 to 2006. He currently writes about politics in Westminster and beyond for the paper.*

3: What it takes to be a political journalist

Peter Riddell

Political reporting is one of the most challenging and rewarding branches of journalism. Challenging in the range of personal skills required, and rewarding in the opportunity to observe at close hand the way we are governed.

Many of the skills and qualities required are exactly the same as for any journalist: curiosity, interest in the outside world, tenacity, determination, resilience, working fast without sacrificing accuracy, a simple and clear writing, or broadcasting, style, detachment (though without cynicism), an ability to get on with a wide range of people and a sense both of proportion and of the relative significance of events. That applies to all journalists.

But there are also crucial differences in the degree of closeness between reporters and politicians. As a financial and economic journalist, I obviously cultivated my sources, but it was at one remove. I worked from a newspaper office, and phoned and arranged meetings with my contacts at their offices. But national political journalists, in the modern jargon, share the same space as their sources. They work in the same building, and use the same cafeterias, and even bars. They can get to know politicians very well over the years. That underlines the central challenge of being a political reporter: how to balance the necessary closeness to politicians in order to understand what is going on, with the detachment required to provide a balanced account.

Consequently, one of the most frequent criticisms against political journalists is that they are too much insiders, that they are part of the Westminster village, and are captured by its habits and culture. That is usually linked with attacks on the closed world of lobby journalists with their secret, unattributable briefings, and allegedly arcane rituals and language. Such charges had a lot of truth when I first became a political journalist thirty years ago. But this closed world is long gone, destroyed by a combination of a new generation of younger political journalists, the arrival of 24-hour news and, in the past decade, the internet and blogging, and even Twitter. And a good thing too. More transparency is highly desirable.

Working with politicians

The real issue is different. The very closeness involved in working alongside politicians imposes its own opportunities and risks. The opportunities are the chance to understand what makes an MP tick – his or her ambitions, background and attitudes. Just after the 1983 general election, I asked the late John Smith who out of the reduced band of new Labour MPs I ought to get to know. He replied Gordon Brown and Tony Blair, and it was in that order then, and for some time afterwards. I followed Smith's advice, and got to know them both, to my and, above all, my readers' benefit over the following twenty-five to thirty years. So when both rose to the top in the 1990s, I was in a better position to write about them, not only because they were more willing to see me, but also because I understood the way they thought, and were therefore likely to react. The risks are of getting too close, of becoming too much a part of the political scene which you are covering. There is a tricky balance between a long-term contact and a friend. You must always be in a position to write critically about politicians. There is a danger of institutionalism, of seeing events through the lens just of Westminster, and not that of the readers, viewers and listeners whom you are meant to be serving.

Political journalism is in many ways a form of high-grade voyeurism denied to most people. During over thirty years as a political correspondent and commentator, I observed, and wrote about, some of the most fascinating leaders of the past generation: Margaret Thatcher, John Major (still greatly under-rated), Tony

Blair and Gordon Brown, and – during and after three years in Washington – George Bush senior and Bill Clinton. And, as a result of covering them, I saw Margaret Thatcher with Ronald Reagan and Mikhail Gorbachev and George Bush with Deng in the Great Hall of the People in Beijing. What you should offer readers is your knowledge and insight based on such a privileged access to the powerful, your job is to convey to the public what happened, and why it matters for them, as voters and as taxpayers.

So the first quality you need is a sense of excitement – a feel for a great story. There is a real buzz when something important is happening – on the night of, and even more the day after, a general election, or, even more, when something completely unexpected has happened, such as a ministerial resignation or a Cabinet reshuffle. So you need to avoid a world-weary, seen it all before attitude. I well remember sitting in the Winter Gardens in Blackpool late on the Friday afternoon after the end of the Conservative Party conference in October 1983 writing up the splash story about Cecil Parkinson's resignation from the Cabinet after a week of drama. I was then political editor of the *Financial Times* and my opposite number on *The Times*, the deceptively languid Julian Haviland looked up and said, 'Well, I suppose it beats being a bank clerk.'

Exactly a year later, in Brighton, on the Friday of the Conservative conference, the challenge was to write the story on the bombing of the Grand Hotel which killed five people and nearly caught Margaret Thatcher and much of her Cabinet. This was the most damaging attack on a British government ever, comparable to the failed Cato Street conspiracy in 1820 or even the Guy Fawkes plot in 1605.

Getting the right balance was hard: between the drama and tragedy of the day, and putting it in historical perspective. I remembered reading the account by Tom Wicker of the *New York Times* about how he covered the assassination of John F. Kennedy in Dallas in November 1963 – keep it simple and don't over-elaborate. Some stories tell themselves provided you have assembled the facts correctly – and they should be facts, not rumours. Never be reluctant to check. I always hated colleagues who said a story was too good to check. That debases them, and journalism.

A journalist, not a politician

Second, remember that you are not a political player yourself. If you rise to become political editor of one of the big national dailies or, now even more illustrious, for one of the main broadcasters, you will certainly be influential. Your words will be followed closely. But never get above yourself. You are reporting on politicians, and interpreting them; you are not one yourself. Of course, some illustrious journalists do become politicians, like my old *Times* colleague Michael Gove – and quite a few move the other way, like Matthew Parris and Michael Portillo. But if you are a reporter, as opposed to a columnist (and never confuse the two), you should not be too partisan or, else, you will risk being in the pocket of one party or another. Successful reporters have to develop good contacts, but these should be in all parties, not just one. Your job is to report on what politicians do and say, with a sceptical eye and ear, but not to impose your own personal opinions in news stories. There is an opposite danger of being too cynical, regarding all politicians as scoundrels and rogues. The behaviour of quite a few MPs recently has given plenty of ammunition to the anti-politician school. But that can result in entirely negative and destructive journalism.

Third, apart from the basic journalistic skills noted above, you need to be interested in politics – not as a partisan but you have to care about what is happening. The best political reporters never really switch off, apart from when they are on holiday. They get up listening to the *Today* programme, look at all the main newspapers and, now, the main political internet sites throughout the day, and they go to bed after watching *Newsnight*. Almost none of their readers or viewers will be so obsessive. But that is how a successful political reporter keeps ahead of the news – sensing small changes that might develop into bigger stories.

Who does what

Fourth, it is also vital to understand how politics and government work. You are not an academic – fortunately since few political scientists know how to write in a clear manner. But you should grasp the essence of how the British constitution works – how

Whitehall and Westminster interact. If you are a parliamentary reporter, you must have some understanding of procedure – the way that bills are considered, relations between the Commons and Lords, and the like. Unless you do, your contacts will not take you seriously. A knowledge of political history is also important, both in the conventional sense of appreciating who was Prime Minister when and, personally, about the background of particular politicians. If you know that x and y were rivals or close friends in their early twenties, it may explain a lot about their relationships now. A depressingly large number of new political journalists have not bothered to learn about these matters – and it shows in naive and error-prone stories which are noticed by well-informed MPs and civil servants.

Fifth, the best political journalists have been around for some time. Nothing beats experience. Few journalists take a top political job without working their way up the ladder – either covering a local council/devolved government or as a junior member of a political team. I personally benefited from my period as economics correspondent of the *FT* – both in familiarising myself with the overriding political issues of the time and in developing contacts with politicians and civil servants. Both served me well when I moved across to Westminster. Moreover, my colleagues who had worked on a local paper were often able to take their contacts from there to Westminster as someone who had been a leading figure on a local council became a prominent MP or minister. Time enables you to build up a contacts book and a reputation among MPs as someone who is worth getting to know. Countless times a contact made a few years or even a decade or two ago will come in useful again. It is vital to have an excellent memory since, under the pressure of deadlines, that will enable you to place an event or a person in their proper context.

Tough but fair

Sixth, you need to be resilient and have a strong constitution. The hours can be very long, reporting on a slowly developing story or responding quickly to a late development. You always have to be ready to file a report immediately. When I was posted to Washington as the US Editor of the *Financial Times* to cover the elder George Bush's administration, I found it very useful to have been a political correspondent at Westminster where speed is of the essence. That is for the simple reason that Washington is five hours behind London which means you are filing at lunchtime local time for the first editions, so there is little time for reflection.

Seventh, like all journalists, you must have a plausible charm, as well as cunning and determination. You need to win politicians' trust, which they will not give immediately. I was helped by the fact that I looked older than I was, a process that I now hope is in reverse. Taking over as political editor of the *FT* just before I was thirty-three was a challenge when most of my contacts were a decade or two older: the cult of relative youth among leading politicians came later. Looking rather older than my years was a help. One important change over the past thirty years – and it is wholly for the better – has been the growing number of women political journalists and, of course, women MPs. Back in the early 1980s it was hard for the very few women reporters who tended to be patronised by the often chauvinist older generation of politicians. That still happens but it is much less prevalent.

Eighth, you must be a team player. It is possible to operate successfully as a loner. But most political reporters are part of teams, so you have to get along with people of very different ages and temperaments. I always found that fun and rewarding, not least because of the opportunity to share experiences and knowledge. If you work at Westminster, or for that matter, at any of the devolved parliaments, you will be in constant contact with your main competitors. As Adam Smith pointed out 230 years ago, there are always dangers when people in the same trade get together (he was talking about the monopolistic practices of businessmen). They can collude for an easy life. It should be the first instinct of any journalist to get the story first. That may produce tension from time to time with your competitors. But they will do the same to you. Personal cordiality and professional rivalry can exist side by side.

Ninth, remember who you work for. It is easy for national political journalists to feel more loyalty to their colleagues at

Westminster than to their employers. You can often feel irritated and, indeed, furious with editors about their demands, which you feel are ill-informed and based on the last person they met or watched on television. You may be correct but they determine whether your stories get in the paper, or are broadcast. So considerable tact is needed. Unless something has gone seriously wrong which could damage your future work and relations with contacts, count to ten and never moan to the newsdesk in the morning. No one likes a moaner, however justified. There is always another day.

Both in order to get a job in the first place and in order to rise up the ladder, try and identify gaps in the coverage and/or new areas which editors want to develop. Also do not underplay any distinctive selling points which you may have, such as strong contacts with a leading politician or party. If you have been, say, an economics or business journalist, or have reported on local politicians, these experiences could be a big asset.

That magic ingredient: judgement

Tenth, the most important single quality for a political journalist is independence of judgement. There are always pressures from the newsdesk, from your colleagues, from your competitors to take a particular line. Be your own man or woman. It is not always easy to resist the conventional wisdom. Having seen reports on 24-hour news and listened to the *Today* programme, the newsdesk and editorial executives will often be convinced of what the line is on a story. They may be, and often are, wrong. It is hard for a junior reporter to resist these pressures. But your job is to say what you think the story is and, over time, you will gain respect if you are shown to be right – provided that you do not gloat.

Similarly, it is too easy to be swayed by journalists from other papers not to rock the boat on stories and to follow the conventional wisdom on the line to take. That way no one will be asked to justify their individual line. Again, trust your judgement. That means injecting some excitement into a story but also not losing perspective. Beware of superlatives. Few events are the most humiliating, most embarrassing and most damaging ever.

The resignation of a junior minister or even more a parliamentary private secretary seldom matters and is usually not even a 24-hour wonder. So do not exaggerate. Judgement is what counts in the long term. If you have developed that, you stand a good chance of being a successful political journalist.

Peter Riddell worked on the Financial Times *for twenty-one years, including periods as economics correspondent, political editor and US editor; and then for nineteen years on* The Times, *mainly as chief political commentator. He has written seven books on British politics, including* In Defence of Politicians *in 2011, and has been a presenter of the* Week in Westminster. *Since leaving* The Times, *he has been a Senior Fellow of the Institute for Government, a member of the privy counsellor inquiry on the treatment of detainees, and chair of the Hansard Society.*

Part II:

The Westminster and Whitehall village

4: Early lessons

Sheila Gunn

I arrive in plenty of time. Through the door. Lots of people milling around. Who are they? They clearly know each other and turn towards me with looks that say: 'Is this someone I need to know?' 'Friend or foe?' Cringe making. This pretty much describes my first experience of walking into the environs of Henley-in-Arden parish council, Rugby Borough Council, Surrey County Council and the Houses of Parliament.

The next challenge: where do I go? Probably best to ask someone who looks official – often a wrong assumption. Why didn't I carry out a recce beforehand? I'll have to tell someone I'm 'from the press' and ask for directions to the press seats. 'Where are you from? Do you know the rules?' someone asks.

Most journalists must experience similar dilemmas when they start out. If this does not totally turn you off, you may find your job becomes more enjoyable. But not immediately. After finding out where to sit, the next questions in any of these environments are likely to be: Who are these people? What language are they using? What are they talking about? What should I report? When can I leave?!

There may be some sort of order paper or agenda. Local authorities usually place names in front of councillors at the key meetings open to the public and the press. That does not necessarily help you when people are popping up and down talking in a language you do not understand.

In Parliament, of course, there are no place names but the Speaker or one of his deputies will call them out. That does not always help. This very nearly led to my job covering politics at *The Times* lasting two weeks rather than twelve years. There had been a fiery intervention by a female Labour MP on the backbenches. I asked the doorman for her name, 'Short,' he whispered. I looked up 'Short' in my *Times* guide and wrote up the exchanges, attributing the quotes to the Labour MP Mrs Renee Short. It wasn't. I had confused her with another Labour MP, Clare Short (no relation). The subsequent dressing down, plus the inevitable correction in the paper, was horrible. Luckily I had the good sense not to whine that, with very few women MPs at that time, it was extremely bad luck that two had the same surname.

All that sitting around

One of the things that people don't tell you about is the hours spent in tedious meetings. You're almost always convinced that it could have been done within one hour rather than three.

The best introduction, as Richard Osley says in his chapter, is to go to a meeting in your town hall. Sit in the public gallery during, for instance, a planning or licensing committee meeting of a local council. These are decision-making bodies with councillors from different parties, debating and voting on applications for such issues as new buildings or extended opening hours of pubs and bars. You would not believe how strongly some local people will feel about these applications. Unless, that is, you happen to live nearby and can see thousands of pounds shaved off the value of your home because it is next to a noisy pub, disgorging drunks and low lifes at 2am – who then throw up in your front garden.

A trawl through your local newspaper should reveal coverage of the 'rows', 'controversies', 'protests' these applications provoke. Full council meetings tend to be less productive affairs these days, as they are not decision-making bodies.

Your first experience of, say, a planning committee meeting is likely to be uncomfortable. Councillors and officers talk a different language to the rest of us: all those S106s, UDPs, sub-section this or that. But it should not take long before you gain a sense of what is being talked about. A little like listening to Shakespeare, do not struggle too much to translate each word. Watch the body language, sense the atmosphere. I cannot in all honesty say that any council meeting can compare to Shakespeare, even while working on the *Stratford-upon-Avon Herald*. But, occasionally, it can provide good theatre and, more often, acceptable farce. And let's face it, if you really cannot stand sitting through such sessions, perhaps journalism is not for you.

Once you move from covering a local council to Westminster, you find the language changes again. There's standing order this and beg to move the motion that. Again, it does not take too much experience to translate. Just remember that your audience is probably expecting you to then translate for them. Do not fall into the mistake of adopting the jargon and assume your readers, listeners or viewers can decipher it. It is a delicate balance between expressing yourself in the simplest of terms and yet not patronising your audience.

When I went for an interview to join *The Times* parliamentary team, I had to report Northern Ireland question time as my 'test'. In spite of being half Scottish and a quarter Irish, I struggled to understand what some of the MPs were saying – let alone take a note. Points made by the Rev. Ian Paisley and Enoch Powell were delivered with the speed of a machine gun. Somehow I survived. But from then on, NI questions were an event which made me shiver. (Not least because Enoch Powell spoke with the speed and rattle of a machine gun and would always complain if you did not report him verbatim.)

Eyes open wide

How to stop yourself falling asleep? No one warns you about this when you embark on your career. You have worked all day and now you must sit through three or four hours of a meeting or cover a late night debate in Parliament. The challenge remains: you must suss out some stories to justify your existence and most of all, you must not be seen to fall asleep. It fails to inspire confidence.

One unfortunate incident occurred at a party conference in the days when the press tables were situated between the audience and the platform. A TV camera zoomed in on a national newspaper reporter clearly fast asleep during a Cabinet minister's speech. The obvious, televisual message was that 'even the reporters are bored by the speech'. In truth, the reporter had already written up the speech from a copy he had been handed by the press office. Nevertheless he was given a hard time by his editor who spotted the shot on his TV in the newsroom.

There are a few tricks to survive this challenge which are useful in journalism – and in many other jobs. A lot depends on the research you have done into the items on the agenda or order paper. You know the items which are most likely to be productive. In town hall meetings you can probably risk leaving the press seats for a time to stretch your legs but also, more importantly, to mix with politicians, officials and residents interested in particular items. Some of your best contacts can be made this way – as well as picking up ideas for stories and quotes. This is much harder to do in Parliament as there is a long walk from the press gallery to the lobbies.

During the exchanges and speeches, keep at least half an ear open to what is being said. Meanwhile you can use the time to write up other stories in your notebook (sometimes, I would even write letters). When not doing this, learn to form your features into an expression of, at least, vague interest – even if your mind is a million miles away. With some experience, you should develop a sense of impending trouble, that is, a half-decent story.

Perhaps it can best be described as tuning your antennae. When they start to twitch, you instantly drag your mind back to what's happening.

One of my early reporting memories is of dozing gently – and not too obviously – through a long parish council meeting while councillors heaped praise on the design and durability of a new bus stop. Then one sighed that: 'It's a great pity it's not on the main bus route.' The other councillors started shuffling their papers and the chair immediately moved them on. But I had my story!

As soon as my 'scoop' appeared in my paper, a colleague showed me how to sell it as a 'most beautiful bus stop – but sadly no buses' story to a national newspaper. It earned me more money than I received in a fortnight as a graduate trainee reporter. Perhaps to you it does not sound that exciting. But I can still recall my delight, not least because of the ultimate praise from my editor, Harry Pigott-Smith: 'Maybe we'll make a journalist out of you yet!' Worth all those hours of tedious meetings.

What do I write?

If only there was a norm. I tend to write too much, partly because I have reasonable shorthand (160 words per minute was the minimum requirement when I joined the Press Association's parliamentary staff) and can actually read it. It's the notes jotted down in longhand I can struggle with. In the early years I used my shorthand as a comfort blanket and perhaps should have listened a little more. Others take fewer notes, but have formidable memories. That's wonderful. But I believe that our audiences still trust direct quotes more than a journalist's version of what a politician has said.

Whatever your style, it is essential to develop a reliable note-taking skill. It is no coincidence that the political journalists who have survived decades at Westminster can take down a few sentences verbatim without panicking. Tape recorders are all very well, but they put news reporters immediately at a disadvantage. It takes time to run the tape back and forth to check the quotes you want to use.

Yes, of course I prefer Pitman's to Teeline. But that is only because Pitman's is phonetic. I am not sure of the science behind it, but it is possible to write in Pitman's, think, ask questions and analyse at the same time – whereas I don't think this is so easy with inferior methods. But I am hopeful that within a couple of years, we will all have a button on our mobiles to record and type out any conversations in any language at the touch of a button.

Why is note-taking so important? Apart from the obvious reasons, it disconcerts politicians. They see you making these hieroglyphics with no understanding of what you are writing. It gives you a little more influence. Well, usually. I had a most disconcerting experience early on in my days in Parliament. A Conservative MP started reading my fairly scrappy shorthand notes back at me. Apparently he had learnt Pitman's as part of his national service. Occasionally it pays not to take a note during a conversation. A politician will feel less inhibited. You then have no option but to rush into a corner to regurgitate the gist of the conversation into your notebook.

In taking notes, it is an excellent idea to distinguish between the important and the boring as you go along. That makes the writing up much quicker. Phoning over your story to copy directly from your notes used to be a valued skill. Perhaps the stress levels of today's journalists are lower as they are less often required to do this. But those aiming for higher echelons of journalism would do well to practise it.

Many journalists draw a vertical line about three-quarters of the way across the page; that gives them scope to make notes beside them in the remaining quarter. In addition, I have a three line system – not dissimilar to the whipping system described elsewhere. Three lines scratched vertically beside a sentence or two means this is headline material; two lines, indicates worth reporting; one line, paraphrase or useful facts. Unmarked, then you can usually ignore it. This, of course, is handy for any type of reporting.

Demands of HQ

More frustrating are those political events which fail to live up to the expectations of your newsdesk or producer. They are expecting a good story or, at the very least, enough to fill an allocated space or time slot. It is on the editorial schedule, therefore it must happen – is their mantra. Your standing will quickly slump if you start claiming 'there wasn't a story'. It is your job to find one. Management of media space (either by time or word count) would be even more chaotic if there is little correlation between what is anticipated by your boss and what you deliver.

But there are many times when the expected story does not materialise. Hence you need to hunt around, use your ingenuity. Often it is by engaging with those on the fringes of meetings, asking questions, being visible – in other words, make it clear you're in the market for a story! If there is no way that story is going to materialise, it is an excellent idea to keep a few solid leads under your belt that you can offer to your newsdesk as alternatives.

How to behave

You are face to face with a politician, whether it is a councillor, MP or government minister. Do you smile? Look serious? Treat them like a defendant in the dock? The answer is obvious. You treat them like any other human being, in a courteous manner. Even if you are planning to ask them if it is true that they have transferred a few million into a secret Swiss bank account. Good manners are one of the strongest weapons in your armoury.

Most of the time you want to elicit information and quotes from politicians. So a polite introduction, a good morning, even a little small talk does not go amiss. It is many days since a BBC reporter greeted a Prime Minister on his return from a trip abroad with the words: 'Good morning, Prime Minister. Is there anything you would like to say to the British people?' The answer was: 'No thank you.' The reporter thanked him and left. But greeting a politician with an attitude that says: 'OK you lying bastard…' is unlikely to be helpful to either of you. After all, quite a few men and women did turn out to vote for them at some point.

If possible, give some thought to your questions and precede them with some sort of introduction. It helps even more if you demonstrate that you have done your research. For instance, if you mention that 'I was interested in the comment you made in the … debate/meeting about the need for…' you are far more likely to gain the politician's attention.

For ten years, I would take politicians to lunch with John Williams, who was then on the *London Evening Standard* – a common pairing arrangement between journalists. John was assiduous in searching out a few points from the politician's recent speeches to mention. Apart from showing that he had done his homework, it was a touch of ego-massaging which very often led to a reasonable story.

What to wear

It may seem frivolous to mention your clothes, but they matter. You are, in a way, an ambassador for your media outlet. So how you appear can reflect this. One of the great attractions of being a journalist is that you have little idea of what is going to happen to you during the day. Are you going to trudge around the streets, asking people questions about their voting intentions? Will you have to doorstep – that is stand outside – in a thunderstorm or heatwave, waiting for that key moment when you can ask a politician for a comment? Or will you be mixing with prime ministers, presidents, leaders in business, the arts or charities?

The answer is generally an innocuous suit. It covers a multitude of sins – just think of the former German Chancellor Helmet Kohl if you have any doubt. Ties are still seen around Westminster and Whitehall, even though they are quickly dying out elsewhere. No trainers please. Smart casual is wonderful if done properly. Just remember that it can feel far less smart if, on a slow Sunday, you are suddenly invited into Downing Street or the Foreign Office for a briefing with a Head of State. The wily often keep a spare suit in the office, just in case. Remember that you and your turnout are not meant to be the story. This is not your Lady Gaga moment.

But what if you have to run after a disgraced minister? Stand in the rain outside No. 10? Never underestimate the amount of walking involved; smart but comfortable shoes are a must. A reasonable mac is useful. Umbrellas are a nuisance, but a waterproof hat which can be squashed into your bag or pocket can serve the purpose.

As Chris Moncrieff makes clear, it is always wise to have your passport on you. Few things are more debilitating than missing out on a sudden trip abroad because you do not have time to go home and pick it up.

Work–life balance

While I hesitate to actively encourage you to break the law, anyone keen to do a 35-hour week is unlikely to make it as a senior political journalist. But then it depends on what you think of as 'work'. Listening to the *Today* programme, going through the papers, watching news political programmes, keeping up to date with the latest political books. Is this work?

Then there are political events, such as elections and party conferences which can take you away from home for weeks at a time. Very hard work and, hopefully, some fun. But not often appreciated by your family. Nor is it a wise idea to tell them all about those 3am conversations in some bar and the many incidents of bad behaviour.

As Peter Riddell points out, there are now more women political journalists. Luckily the days when I had to share the same loo as the men in the House of Lords' press room are long gone. I was one of the few when I first went to Westminster. It took a little time to persuade MPs to take me seriously. Initially they would chat amiably to me and then give a story to a male colleague. That soon changed as I gained in knowledge and experience. Then I and other female journalists had a distinct advantage over our male colleagues. The MPs and peers were more likely to remember us and more willingly offered up their stories.

Combining the work with parenthood is a real challenge. Inevitably it is harder for mothers. That's just a fact of life. What can be unfair is the lack of opportunities for women to step off the career ladder for a few years and then make their way back. But that is the same in most jobs. I took nearly five years off paid work to see my children through babyhood. My old PA boss said I could always come back. But when I applied, the then editor said they had a firm policy of never re-employing people.

PA did not like to be used as a stepping stone by journalists who then go on to newspapers and, if it does not work out, try to return to PA. The editor said they had never had the experience of a woman going off to have children and then wanting to return. Nowadays such treatment would lead to outrage or even legal action. Back then, while feeling both hurt and angry, I knew it was not that unusual.

After doing a few Saturday night shifts on the *Mail on Sunday*, I was lucky enough to hear that *The Times* needed temporary help on its parliamentary staff. And once in, that was it. As some of the stories in this book confirm, if you manage to get inside the door in the first place, you're halfway there.

That magic ingredient: judgement

One of my four editors at *The Times* was Charles Wilson, one of the most brilliant newsmen of his generation. Early on in my time as political correspondent, he said: 'The thing about Phil [Webster] is that he has judgement.' I knew what he meant. Phil, one of the longest-serving political editors, and still on *The Times,* is a class act. At the merest whiff of a story, he would start to categorise it: Interesting? A real problem? A crisis?

At whatever level you are covering politics, you need to develop the judgement to gauge the level of importance of a story. I do not believe anyone is born with this, although following the news and politics from an early age could help. This is not something anyone can teach. But close scrutiny of political stories, examining the entrails to see why some disappear and others have a lasting impact, is a good starting point.

5: A week in the life of a broadcast political journalist

James Landale

Preparing for the story

My former colleague on *The Times*, Matthew Parris, once began a sketch along the following lines: 'Sunday is no day for politics. So what better day then to start the Liberal Democrat party conference.' It was a good joke and a great piece. But it was written a long time ago. For these days, Sunday is no longer a day of rest for the political world. In fact, it is the start of the week.

There are the Sunday newspapers to read. They are not what they once were, but they are still important. There are fewer hot, breaking political news stories in the Sundays, but they are packed with comment, context, background, juicy nuggets and they need to be read. Then there are the political programmes. From *The Andrew Marr Show* to *The Politics Show*, from *The World This Weekend* to the *Westminster Hour*, there is a feast of political viewing and listening to keep an eye and ear on. You miss them at your peril. Sunday is also a day for telephone calls. It is one day in the week when the political world sits back and catches its breath. Ministers can speak to each other in private, chewing the cud with colleagues away from their civil servants or advisers. For some, it also means the chance to talk privately with journalists. So Sunday is a day of preparation which sets the tone for much of the rest of the week.

The story of the day

An average day. Get up. Listen to the *Today* programme. Read the papers. Read the blogs. Follow Twitter. Make some calls. Discuss with colleagues who is doing what story. With luck, *decide* who is doing what story. Go to press conference. Listen in on select committee hearing. Answer phone constantly. Gossip with sources. Go to the morning Downing Street lobby briefing. Discuss with colleagues how to tell the story. Interview ministers and MPs for clips. Go to lunch with contact. Discreetly read emails on BlackBerry when contact goes to loo. Think about script. Write script. Go into edit suite and rework script entirely. Stay calm while technical problems threaten disaster. Enjoy buzz as deadline approaches. Make 6 o'clock deadline by skin of teeth. Celebrate with tea and unhealthy chocolate. Do it all again for 10 o'clock. Go for drink with politician. Learn about story you wish you had been told four hours ago.

Choosing a story

The most significant difference between broadcasting and print in political journalism is that the broadcasters must be far more selective in the stories they run. Newspapers, with their large pages and infinite websites, can run everything and anything. Broadcasters have a much smaller prism through which to shove their journalism. The main network television news bulletins will in practice have space for only one or two political stories each day. In other words, political broadcasting is essentially about front page stories – big, forceful, important stories that muscle their way forward. The subtle change, the nuanced development, the arcane but intriguing political background, all of that is for the commentators, the blogs, the websites, page ten of the newspaper. It is all interesting stuff but for the aficionados, not for the general mass audience.

So broadcasters must be selective. They must choose wisely. And not just because their outlets are limited. Their resources are limited too. Print journalists can tell their stories simply by knocking out a bit of copy on their computer or dictating a few words to a copytaker (I am told one or two still exist). It is all quite low tech. Radio is a little more complicated, with the additional factor of recording someone saying something, choosing a clip from it, inserting the clip, recording the whole piece, and then sending it to the right computer so it can be checked at head office and re-transmitted to the nation. All that can still be done by one man or woman with a recording device and laptop. But it still requires a bit of effort.

Television is even more time consuming. You need pictures. That requires at the very least a cameraman or woman physically to have witnessed stuff. Their footage needs to be transported or transmitted from where they are to where the correspondent is editing. The correspondent needs to see all these pictures. He or she needs to do what is called a piece to camera, a few remarks said into the camera that gives a sense of place to the report. That, of course, requires another camera. All the footage needs to be edited and then sent to London. That normally requires a satellite truck. With an engineer. And a picture editor. All these resources are expensive and finite. Broadcasters can't send trucks to all locations. So they need to choose. And choose early.

Telling a story

Telling a political story on the radio is simple and effective. Parliament has its own sound and mood that can be captured quite easily. There is normally enough time in the report to include a fair amount of detail. There is often time for a second piece, such as some analysis giving context to the news of the day and its potential impact. Television is much harder. A lot of political news centres around a man or a woman standing up saying stuff. This makes for boring television. The daily challenge of political television news is to make it visually interesting. How do you make a complex issue understandable? How do you get across the essential point of the news? The answer is normally a mixture of several things, above all, planning. You need to pre-film pictures before the story happens. So if you know a health story is coming up, get to a hospital, film some general views – known as GVs. Do a piece to camera. Knock off a few interviews. But all that works only if you know a story is coming up. Spot stories that you have to do on the day normally require a little imagination, such as good use of archive, graphicised sequences, and a few tricks of the trade by cameramen and film editors. And of course, good writing can often do wonders to dull pictures.

Getting a story

Getting a story is the same for any journalist. But how you tell it depends on your medium. Political stories can sometimes be simple. Minister announces something. You report it. Minister resigns. You report it. It is like any reporting: you witness something or listen to something and you get it onto the network. But what makes political journalism different is that often you have to report a story that is not fully formed. A hint from one minister, added to a lunch with an official, mixed up with gossip from a press officer can a good story make. How hard you go with a story is a matter of judgement, editorial cojones and, ultimately, the attitude of the company or corporation you work for. If you work for the BBC, you think long and hard before you run a story. The audience has high expectations; they want informed judgement, not a casual punt. If you are merely speculating about something in a blog, the threshold is perhaps somewhat lower. In broadcasting terms, one way of telling rolling, developing, partially formed stories is through the live two-way interview with the newscaster. It is flexible, live and the story is utterly in the hands of the correspondent who got it.

Another way of getting stories is through pre-planned edited packages. You persuade a politician to give you an interview in which they make the news. They agree to give it to you exclusively. They give you access to film them doing something relating to the story. This is the televisual equivalent of the big newspaper interview in which both sides agree discreetly beforehand what the story is likely to be. The upside is that you get a story first and tell it well. The downside is that it involves a substantial level of cooperation with the politicians.

Telling the story live

The 'live' is now a stable part of broadcast news, whether the ubiquitous on the hour, every hour turn for the 24-hour news channels, or the highly edited one minute twenty seconds of added value on the main network bulletins. On the news channels, lives can seem to go on forever – I once had to speak without stopping and without question for more than seven minutes due to a technical failure. Seven minutes does not sound long. But in broadcasting terms, it is an aeon. The key to political lives on the news channels is maintaining freshness and impartiality. You can be on air for a long time and the risk is that you end up repeating yourself. The remedy is simply to stay on the phone all day, getting updated so that you are ahead of the game and have something new to say. And as for balance, broadcasters have an absolute requirement to be impartial. You should just stick to straightforward analysis. Why is something happening? Where has it come from? How is it likely to end up? What is everybody saying about it? What is the context? You should answer all of those questions. What you should never say is whether something is right or wrong. That is for the audience to decide themselves.

The edited live is another thing altogether. It is not scripted but the content is discussed with programme editors. It is short and to the point. And in political terms, it adds context and last minute news to the edited report. Keep it simple, strip out the extraneous detail. You may have spent all day on top of the minutiae. Just bank it all and broadcast the one thing that really matters to the audience.

Finding out about the story

In politics, as in any other area of life subject to journalistic scrutiny, stuff sometimes happens fast. The key task of television journalism is to tell the story quickly. That means having at your fingertips a stable of smart websites, clever boffins and informed sources. What you want from them is not necessarily the story itself, but the explanation behind the story. You want them to tell you quickly what it means. Political journalists are essentially general reporters who happen to operate in the field of politics. That means they may suddenly have to become experts on anything from arcane procedures in the House of Lords to MPs' expenses rules, from the minutiae of a tax credit to the operation of the monetary policy committee, from the constitution of the Liberal Democrats to the mysteries of the civil service. So much news passes through the prism of Westminster that it is almost impossible to master it all. It is not like being an education or health correspondent. The focus is too broad. And that is why you always need to have people close at hand who can explain stuff to you, so that you can then explain it to the audience.

Making the story relevant

Westminster is a village, its currency gossip. But it is the role of the political correspondent to sort the wheat from the chaff. It is all too easy to get wrapped up in the fast-moving events within SW1 – the local postcode in central London – and forget there is life outside. Most of the gossip – who is up and who is down – is utterly irrelevant. But sometimes the gossip does matter if it could affect policy; if it could change ministers who hold different priorities. The key is always to find a moment every day to lift your head above the fray and ask yourself some hard questions about what it is that really matters about the story and what the audience would want to know. Quite often even that is not enough and you have to get out of London physically to maintain a broad perspective. Much of the journalism that pours out of Westminster is far too London-centric.

Friday

Friday used to be a day to pause, a moment in the week when Westminster was deserted. The House of Commons occasionally sits on Friday, but mostly MPs are back in their constituencies nurturing their majorities. And this is the moment when MPs say something they regret to their local media. In times past this would have become a story on Saturday morning and picked up by a fleet-of-foot Sunday newspaper. But things move faster these days and gaffe stories often blow up out of nowhere dominating the weekend's news agenda. All of which takes me back to where I began, namely Sunday, which definitely is a day for politics.

James Landale is the deputy political editor of the BBC. He joined the corporation in 2004 and spent five years as the chief political correspondent for BBC News 24. Before that he worked for The Times *for a decade as the paper's political correspondent, Brussels correspondent and assistant foreign news editor.*

6: A week in the life of a PA reporter

Chris Moncrieff

There is no such thing as a routine week for a political reporter at Westminster. Sometimes there are days which promise little or nothing in the way of stories: no big events scheduled, the likelihood of hours of tedium in the Commons chamber, with peace and serenity abounding. Then suddenly out of the blue, something tremendous hits us like a thunderbolt. The peace and serenity is quickly dissipated and the press gallery starts to throb with excitement.

But whatever happens, there are certain chores which have to be tackled every day. Failure to do so can mean missed stories and angry telephone calls from your newsdesk, who may have heard an item on the radio which you have not covered.

All this is particularly important for an agency reporter. The Press Association, where I have worked at Westminster for nearly half-a-century, provides blanket coverage for all the newspapers and broadcasting outlets. The PA has no views, it does not campaign nor does it write editorials. It simply puts out stories, fast and accurate for the rest of the media.

For instance, the PA has a reporter in the chamber of the Commons – and the House of Lords as well – during the entirety of the sitting. Most of the other journalists and broadcasters leave the chamber after the busy periods, like Question Time and important statements, in the knowledge that the PA will always be on the watch.

Breakfast fodder

For most political reporters (and certainly for those at the PA) the day starts at 6am, with BBC Radio 4's *Today* programme. This is the programme which reputedly sets the agenda for the political day – and it is essential listening for Westminster journalists. Usually there are two or three ministers on, as well as leading opposition politicians, plus other MPs who, for one reason or another, happen to be in the news. The main interview, which is invariably political, is normally just after the 8am news bulletin.

The huge advantage of this programme is that it gives you an early story, which is just what the evening papers want. This is all the more vital as edition deadlines, oddly, are now much earlier than they were, say only ten years ago.

In addition to this, other broadcasters, both radio and television, usually make a point of telling you if they have anyone interesting or topical on their early morning programmes. You might well ask why the writing press does not do its own interviewing, instead of leaving it all to the broadcasters?

The answer is that we *do* interview people but unfortunately a lot of politicians, particularly ministers who are nervous about deviating from the government 'line', have an unreasonable fear of being misreported or quoted out of context by newspapers. They have no control over the way the interview is subsequently written up and that makes them fearful. They prefer to go on live radio or television when they know they cannot be misquoted and when they can actually keep some control over the interview and, in some cases, even dominate it.

First tasks at Westminster

Although the *Today* programme goes on until 9am, the Press Association always ensures that at least one other reporter is at Westminster before 8am. The task of scanning the daily papers has usually been done late the previous night when the first editions emerge, but the later editions now need to be perused to see if there are any new stories which have not been covered.

One of the first tasks of the reporter at Westminster is to go down to the members' lobby and collect from the Vote Office, which issues all the parliamentary documents, the order paper for the day as well as 'the blue pages'. These contain all the questions to be asked in the Commons that day and new questions that have been tabled in the previous twenty-four hours for answer on future dates.

These questions, especially the new ones, should be gone through with a toothcomb. A check with the MP who has tabled what you would consider a quirky question, can often reveal a good story. Once the late Labour MP Gwyneth Dunwoody tabled a question demanding the return to Britain from a New York museum of the original Christopher Robin dolls, Winnie the Pooh, Piglet, Eeyore, Tigger et al. I telephoned her and put out a story which ran, in one form or another, for nearly a week. It culminated, to my great joy, with a statement from the President of the United States, Bill Clinton, no less.

You will also find in these documents lists of so-called 'early day motions', which never, or very rarely, get debated, but which are nevertheless often newsworthy. Since they are printed in official documents, you are at liberty to say 'Joe Bloggs today raised in Parliament the question of...' even though it will never, or hardly ever, reach the floor of the House.

These motions also carry parliamentary privilege and might say things which in other circumstances would be grounds for a libel action or contempt of court.

I remember once when during an Old Bailey paedophile trial a high-ranking Canadian diplomat was referred to as 'Mr X' throughout the case. We all knew who he was but were not allowed to print the name. I managed to persuade a friendly MP to include the name in a House of Commons motion, which immediately enabled it to become public property, because of the parliamentary immunity accorded to Commons motions.

You should also ask the Vote Office for any new documents that have arrived. In fact, it is advisable to do this several times during the day. You will normally be given White Papers (which set out government proposals on a particular issue), reports of Commons committees and other material.

More often than not these documents are given to the press gallery twenty-four hours or more in advance of their official publication to give the reporter sufficient time to do them justice. But the reporter is bound by a strict embargo on the time of publication.

The best way to handle these documents – occasionally you do not enjoy the luxury of having a reasonable amount of time in which to study them – is to start not at the beginning, but at the end. Often these papers are long and wordy, but you will find at the end a summary which will, within the space of three or four pages, tell you what you need to know.

The summary will also refer you to the page of the main document if you are looking for more detail on a particular aspect. And remember, White Papers are those which set out what a government actually plans to do. A Green Paper is a consultation document that reaches no firm conclusions – a big distinction between the two.

And don't forget, political stories can turn up in the most unlikely places. I remember Ann Widdecombe writing an article in *Good Housekeeping* saying that she was considering leaving Parliament because, at the time, her mother was not in good health. We picked up the story and ran it on PA. Miss Widdecombe was cross. She said that she had deliberately written it for a woman's magazine because she did not want national coverage.

We had to tell her that unfortunately for her, whatever appears in *Good Housekeeping*, or the *Beano* for that matter, or even the parish magazine or any other publication, however obscure, is by virtue of that fact deemed to be in the public domain.

We're journalists, not typists

You must also beware, especially on an agency, of those MPs and political party officials, who regard organisations like the Press Association as though they were the Post Office or a nationalised industry. They seem to think they have a right to have their material on the wire and that we have a duty to print it. When they, as they do sometimes, ring up to ask why some item is not running on the PA they have to be gently told that it wasn't newsworthy enough and that it is for PA, and not them, to decide what goes out on the wire.

Once, a Liberal press officer charged into the PA office at Westminster, armed with a tape measure, can you believe it? He complained that, whereas over the previous week items concerning the Conservative and Labour parties had each occupied some two feet of the PA tape, there was only about three inches devoted to the Liberals. How fair is that? He too was gently told that 'fairness' was not the issue, but news value. He learned very quickly that political parties have to compete for space on the PA tapes.

The advent of the computer means that you are liable to get 100 or more emails each day from political parties, pressure groups, charities and other organisations. Most of them are of no use whatsoever, but unfortunately they all have to be scanned. There may just be a pearl among the mountain of dross.

Lobby briefings

The first lobby meeting of the day with the Prime Minister's press secretary is held around 11 o'clock. This used to be unattributable and off-the-record and held in 10 Downing Street itself. Now it is on-the-record and more often than not held in some other government building.

The Prime Minister's spokesman lists his engagements for the day and then submits himself to questioning by reporters on current issues. This meeting is usually fairly brief because evening paper reporters, whose journals are by this time almost at their 'bedtime', need to hurry away. A digest is then posted on the PM's website.

A second such meeting is held at 4 o'clock, but in the small lobby room high up steep spiral stairs in a tower in the Palace of Westminster. This is usually longer than the morning session, since morning paper reporters tend to ask more detailed questions. It can become quite heated.

When the Prime Minister, or any other minister for that matter, holds private meetings with, say, their foreign counterparts, very often a bland statement is put out afterwards telling you virtually nothing. The talks, they say, were 'fruitful' and 'constructive'. If they say they were 'businesslike' you know that is a euphemism for a flaming row, and report it accordingly.

You need friends or contacts in very high places (they can be cultivated) to find out what really happened behind those closed doors. Never be afraid, incidentally, to resort to clichés once in a while. Phrases like 'a bolt from the blue', for instance, can breathe life into what otherwise may be a drab piece of copy.

There are also party meetings, usually held behind closed doors, which have to be monitored and reported on. We usually 'doorstep' those meetings, (ie, hang around outside in all weathers), and when they are over, you try to nobble a friendly MP who, for the price of a pint of bitter, may agree to tell you what happened. That is why it is so important to cultivate MPs at all times.

Trawling the lobby and watering holes

The best place to do that is the members' lobby of the House of Commons, to which political reporters have access. Whenever you have a spare moment, it is always a good idea to pop down there and wait for stories to come your way, which they will, once your face is known. Some have somewhat inelegantly likened this to behaving like a flypaper, waiting for flies to be trapped. Others have suggested that hanging about in the lobby is no more than an upmarket form of prostitution. Whatever it is, it invariably produces profitable results.

There are some rules about the members' lobby: reporters are not allowed to sit on the green benches which surround it. They are the exclusive preserve of MPs. Once you were not allowed to take out a notebook and write things down, but that rule seems to have fallen into desuetude. You cannot run in the lobby and you must never barge in on a conversation (which is normal courtesy anyway). But the most important thing of all is never argue with an MP. I try to give the impression, without actually saying anything, that I agree wholeheartedly with everything the MP has to say. MPs will be far more forthcoming if they believe you are sympathetic to their cause.

It is also useful to trawl the bars of the House of Commons. MPs who have taken a dram or two are often more garrulous and obliging than the strictly sober ones. I was once dragged from my bed in the middle of the night by a shadow Cabinet minister, who was, shall we say, well refreshed, telling me that he had resigned from his post, and hadn't even bothered to tell his party leader. On another occasion, an MP I interviewed at about midnight was, as a result of what appeared on PA, called up by BBC's *Today* people to appear on their programme. He had to ring me up before the radio interview so I could remind him what we had been talking about, and to tell him what his own view was!

Making it into a story

Often political stories need a peg to hang on. One way to 'sex up' (a dangerous phrase if ever there was one) a run of the mill story is to persuade the MP who has given you a fairly bland statement to table a question or a motion about it. This gives it legitimacy. This also enables you to write: 'The issue (of so and so) will be fought out on the floor of the House of Commons...' or similar.

Equally, when the Sunday papers come in late on a Saturday, you may find yourself confronted with a long and legally sensitive story on which the paper it appears in may have been working for several months. It is plainly not a story you can check in a matter of minutes. So telephone a relevant and friendly MP, describe the story to him, and then invite him to give you a quote about it, but above all to table a parliamentary question on the subject.

If the first MP you contact won't play ball, ring another, and if necessary yet more, until you find one who will cooperate with you. When all that is done, you can go merrily on your way although, of course, parliamentary privilege does not operate at that stage so you have to proceed with common sense and care. If in any doubt at all, at least note on your copy that it should be 'legalled' – i.e. passed by your organisation's lawyers.

These people called MPs

At the risk of committing a gross generalisation, I would say that MPs, as a body, are not necessarily the brightest stars in the firmament. That is why it is only in recent years that they discovered they have a captive audience in the press gallery. Whereas, some time ago, there were very few press conferences called in the House of Commons, now they are a daily practice, often with several each day. Because they are now so prolific, and with the Commons itself often sitting in the mornings, you have to cherry-pick those you think might be most productive and ignore the rest.

For a print journalist on these occasions, asking questions, particularly of a minister, is not as easy as it might sound. It is not like a broadcast interview where the interviewer can press the minister for long periods. You, as a print reporter, will have just one bite of the cherry.

If possible, hone the question in advance. Seasoned politicians, given half a chance, will fob you off with a bland, uninformative reply. Remember that they have probably been rehearsed by their press officers on how to deal with the most likely negative or hostile questions. That is why you must try to frame your question in a way which virtually forces the minister to give you a substantive answer.

Sometimes it is even possible to ask a question which, in itself, upgrades the story. I remember once asking the then Prime Minister Harold Wilson, who had just recovered from a bout of flu, whether he 'felt fine'. He replied in the affirmative. That was just the time when the Beatles' hit 'I Feel Fine' was at the top of the charts. The following day no fewer than three national newspapers splashed the 'I Feel Fine' headline across their front pages. That is what I consider a fair way of putting words into a politician's mouth.

Political reporters should also be aware that some politicians and their aides will try to put you off the scent of a good story by devious means, or they will try to 'hide' bad news in a torrent of information, or by other means.

For instance, on 9/11 a departmental press officer sent a notorious memo round to her colleagues saying that this was 'a good day to bury bad news'. She was caught out – but in fact she was advocating a common tactic used by press officers. On the last day before a recess, government departments will issue hundreds of written answers. Among these may be some 'gems' which the government would rather the journalist did not notice amid all the other welter of material. That is why written answers, generally boring, have unfortunately to be carefully scanned at all times.

On one occasion, Peter Mandelson put out a statement suggesting that Chris (later Lord) Patten had breached the Official Secrets Act in his book about his time as governor of Hong Kong. This proved to be erroneous. However, it was seen at the time, perhaps wrongly, as an attempt by Mandelson to divert attention from the then current story about the discovery of the late Robin Cook's (then Foreign Secretary) mistress and the consequent marital difficulties. If that was the object of the exercise, then it did not work. Mandelson should have realised that nothing would knock the Cook story off the front pages.

But politicians of all parties will try to spin you a line. It is never very subtle and should not fool you. But it is important to be aware of this danger.

As a story evolves...

Some stories, described as 'rolling' stories, change in emphasis several times in a single day. There is no short cut here. You simply have to keep updating them. This is not done by simply tacking new bits on the end of the original story, but by rejigging the intro and putting all the new facts near the top of the story. Then by judicial use of that useful little word 'earlier...' you can add the older bits of the story to what you have written.

Covering debates in the chamber of the House of Commons is normally the task of parliamentary reporters – a dying breed – as opposed to political reporters. The difference between the two is that parliamentary reporters do not have the same access to MPs, in the members' lobby and elsewhere, as do political reporters.

However, there are occasions when political reporters do have to report the Commons, because often what is said there is an integral part of what would otherwise be described as a 'lobby story'. Let me say at once, at risk of accusations of being old-fashioned, that good shorthand is the key to successful reporting on the Commons. Electronic recording devices are now allowed in the press gallery, but my advice is to use them purely as a back-up in case of emergency.

Writing or dictating a story straight from your shorthand notebook is far quicker than twiddling knobs and finding the relevant passage on a tape. So if you work for a newspaper, agency or broadcast channel where speed matters, this is one place where Victorian-type shorthand wins the race any day in competition with cyberspace. It is no coincidence that most of the longest-serving political journalists have reliable shorthand skills.

Even so, most political stories occur outside the chamber. Remember, that when somebody has 'MP' after his/her name it adds something, from a journalistic point of view, to the weight of what is being said.

There is nothing so passé as an ex-MP. Once those magic letters have been removed from his name, then he is, in political terms, very much yesterday's man, politically dead in the water. So don't waste your time on ex-MPs, however useful they may have been while at Westminster. Some ex-MPs cannot live with the fact that they are, so to speak, no more use to Fleet Street. For years after the 1997 general election, which resulted in a wholesale clearout of many MPs, mostly Tories, I was getting plaintive calls from people who still thought they were important.

I always take the view that when an MP talks to you it is because he wants something to appear in a newspaper or on the air. It is generally fair then to assume that the MP is talking on the record, especially if he sees you taking a shorthand note of his words. However, there are times when the MP will say that what he is telling you is off the record or non-attributable. You have to honour that request. If you dishonour it, the word will soon go around and MPs will cease to trust you, which means far fewer stories will come your way. However you can expect MPs to make it clear at the start of a conversation whether it is on or off the record. It is acutely irritating when an MP gives you acres of brilliant quotes – and then adds that 'of course, this is all off the record'. You are perfectly entitled to make this point forcibly.

Another important rule is never to make assumptions, however 'obvious' something may seem to you. If you get a story criticising, for instance, a government department, or an individual MP, you must contact them for their response. If there is no response forthcoming after a while, you are entitled to say that so-and-so 'was not available for comment', thus demonstrating that you have at least tried. Government departments that promise to ring you back with a response to something may deliberately refrain from doing so.

And remember, too, to collect MPs' and other contacts' telephone numbers with the same enthusiasm that a squirrel collects nuts. Occasionally, a little-known and obscure MP will suddenly find himself in the headlines. If you have his phone numbers you are halfway there.

Much to remember maybe, but you will find that as you gradually gain experience, everything will fall into place. Like the old song, you will be 'doing what comes naturally'.

Chris Moncrieff is the former political editor of the Press Association.

7: A week in the life of an MP

Adam Holloway MP

There is no such thing as a standard week for an MP, and the things that individual members do with their time vary considerably. Obviously, the weekly pattern while Parliament is sitting means that Monday to Thursday is spent at Westminster. Most spend the Fridays and the weekend in the constituency, but I am sure there are some who visit much less frequently and many more who have events in their diaries pretty much seven days a week. It is variable, though. I think I do something around a 65-hour week when Parliament is sitting and about thirty as an average across the recesses.

Likewise the life of an MP representing an inner-city marginal seat will be rather different from one representing rural Gloucestershire. Some live primarily in London, some in their constituencies; some 'commute' – which can involve the MP spending less than seven hours at home on Monday, Tuesday and often Wednesday nights. Contrary to press reports, most MPs spend much of the parliamentary recesses in their constituencies. For me, the only thing that is always the same whether an ordinary Monday, or on Christmas Day, or if I am overseas, is the daily deluge of emails.

The week in Westminster

On Mondays to Thursdays the thing in common for all MPs is the requirement to vote. Virtually everything else is up to the individual member, and how they want to play it. The taxpayer funds around three full-time staff. Mine pretty much exclusively focus on 'casework' – that is helping to sort out the problems of constituents.

That's anything from housing issues, child support, benefits issues, immigration, crime and anti-social behaviour, to arranging the removal of radio-active implants from the body of a constituent awaiting cremation this coming Friday, to the endless round robins sent to constituents to forward to us by lobby groups.

I have been in Parliament for nearly six years now, and my office and I have helped just under 20,000 individual people, many multiple times. Most of the issues are for things that should be the preserve of local councillors – but my team and I take the view that if someone has taken the time and trouble to get in touch with me, I am duty bound to do my best for them rather than pass the buck to others.

My team and I remind ourselves that, while it is routine for us to deal with exactly the same issue multiple times, it is a very big deal to the individual person with the problem. I would say that about half my time in the week is concerned with constituency casework, so in my office there are effectively three and a half people doing it full-time. In this last week I have not done much else other than sitting in the chamber for seven hours a day debating the EU Bill. It's a bit like a flight to the US without the stewardesses and miniature wine bottles – and if you are waiting to make a speech, you are wise to ask the Speaker's permission even to nip out to go to the bathroom, lest he think that you are skiving out and therefore not serious about speaking.

The week before last I had a school from my constituency come to London for a tour of Parliament, interviewed possible new interns (critical in order to free up full-time staff to go the extra mile on specific casework cases), had a meeting of the Council for Arab/British Understanding, did a talk at the Defence Academy down in Wiltshire, rang someone who thought they were going to jail the next day, saw a British Ambassador, was visited in Parliament by various constituents, missed a Parish Council meeting because I was in London, drank wine with a General who was complaining about the disaster of the Afghan war, saw an Arab with ideas for a peace deal in Afghanistan, impotently banged my head against the wall over rises in ticket prices of nearly 14 per cent by South Eastern trains, lobbied a minister about the crazy queues at the Dartford crossing, lobbied another on something secret I had heard about our airborne surveillance aircraft and signed the usual 100 or so letters my office send out each day. With those letters and the emails I receive, I no longer think people who complain of Repetitive Strain Injury are whingers.

Of course, there are others who spend their mornings in law firms, in a bank, a PR firm or in a barristers' chambers, and then there are the 100 plus who have much more than full-time jobs as ministers. I don't have a problem with people having 'second jobs', as long as they put the hours in for their constituents: there is already the problem that we end up with a Parliament full of people who for ever increasing years have done nothing but be MPs.

On a given evening there are any number of lobby groups, charities and special interest groups holding events around Parliament. Then each day you might have been selected to ask a question of a minister in the chamber, or you might have written a speech and be waiting all day to deliver it. Some people spend a lot of time worrying about the websites that track things like 'How Often Your MP Has Spoken In Parliament', and make insight-free speeches that add nothing to keep their statistics up on such websites. I try only to speak when I know something about the subject, but remain sceptical that my speeches add much either.

When I have something that I think is important to say, I tend to write it for a Sunday newspaper – sadly it is much more likely to get noticed there than through a speech in Parliament. And you get paid for it, which helps offset the very large amounts of money I spend each month sponsoring constituents who email me about sponsored bike ride x or y, or entertaining constituents or others in connection with my job – entertaining comes out of your own pocket. Of course, you don't have to do it, but the fact that I often spend somewhere approaching 25 per cent of my monthly pay-cheque doing so, suggests that I think I have to.

To the constituency

On Thursday evenings I head down to the constituency. I might go and do a home visit to a constituent in difficulty, or go and speak to a community group, before drinking too much wine while watching *Question Time* and then *The Week*.

Fridays I will have a full programme in the constituency. My record was twenty-nine appointments in one day, ending with some charity event last thing in the evening.

This Friday I am spending the whole morning with the police to find out how they would deal with a major terrorist incident in Kent, seeing an engineering company, meeting the chairman of governors and headmistress of a secondary school, meeting, on behalf of some residents, their evil landlord, meeting a theatre company of whom I have been patron for three years and have somehow failed to meet up with until now, having a drink with a policeman to discuss his rather good idea for a public statue of a Sikh Battle of Britain Squadron Leader who died recently and then have a former CIA officer to stay to discuss the 'War on Terror'.

In the gaps in the programme, I will go and visit constituents with problems. I do what I call 'home visits' rather than 'surgeries' as you can give people the time they need, whether that is two minutes or two hours. Once I ended up going home to collect my Dyson to clean a lady's flat for her. A couple of years later, my team and I were the only people at her funeral service, with a local friend who runs an undertakers firm doing the funeral for nothing. We also took responsibility for clearing out her council flat and visiting her on each of her final days in the hospice.

Most Fridays I will take someone to the fish and chip shop for lunch. Last week it was a lady who is thinking of starting her own business. The point about Fridays, and most days really, is that you can pretty much do whatever you like. Sometimes – not often – I will bunk off for the afternoon to avoid the Friday night traffic if I am going somewhere for the weekend.

Most weekends are spent in the constituency. This Saturday I have a light day: lunch at the rugby club (I always disappoint them by not staying to watch the match), part of the afternoon visiting the rehearsal for the choral concert that I can not go to in the evening because I am having supper with friends and someone from the army coming in for tea as he drives down the neighbouring motorway.

On Sunday I have a meeting at 10.30 to discuss the upcoming local elections and then nothing else all day, so I will visit my elderly aunt in Sussex. Quite often on Sundays I will end up being invited to a church service or to one of the two Sikh temples in the constituency. But I am being much more ruthless about accepting things on Sundays, otherwise the weeks just seem to merge into one.

Dealing with the press

You are reading this because you want to be a political correspondent. Dealing with the press is time consuming for an MP, because you need to get the facts right for any encounter. Let's start with the local press. I used to write a column for one of my local papers which took me a couple of hours most Sunday afternoons. I would also send out press releases most weeks, so that the papers could remind my constituents that I exist and try to get things done. Then there was 'the expenses scandal'.

My two local papers decided that the MPs in the two constituencies they cover provided them with opportunities to 'reveal' that we were local clones of Derek Conway and Jacqui Smith. Week after week they published stories suggesting I was some sort of crook, when my Labour neighbour and I had done nothing more than use our job package for the purposes it was intended. So I now don't write a column, don't do press releases. But while still quietly raging about their coverage and the hospitality I showed them, I do now help when they get in touch with me for a story. I don't know how many other MPs are in the same position, and it is a shame because people don't hear much about what I do (or don't do) here any more via these sources. That said, only 5,000 or so people read these papers and I have stopped buying them.

Before I became a very, very junior member of the government I had quite a lot to do with the national press, and enjoyed dealing with most of their reporters. One of the things that amuses me (yet still fills me with contempt) in Westminster is the way that some MPs use the press to get back at political rivals. I also find it surprising that those political correspondents whose year in year out narrative is that we are all the time a bunch of sleazy crooks, manage to get

MPs to talk to them at all. The MPs I consider to be media tarts irritate me.

Then there is the rather frenzied way that people are always looking for division. For example, once on the BBC's *Today* programme I was interviewed by a rather wonderful former girlfriend. Rather than being interested in what I'd found out on yet another self-funded trip to Kabul, she seemed only interested that what I was saying was not the policy of my party leader. Or today *Newsnight* were onto me with a high-quality piece of investigative journalism (I used to be the reporter running the news investigations at ITN), that the government would have known nothing about. They wanted me to go on their programme to blame the government when ministers would have wanted to know and do something about it. This said, I am consistently wowed by the quality of so much coverage. Unfortunately I don't watch *Newsnight* very often these days as I usually arrive back in my constituency well after the programme has ended.

I write this bit in the early hours of a Friday, having watched the two Thursday evening programmes referred to above. I get 95 per cent of my insight into what is going on in Westminster from programmes like these. If I was more organised I would read the newspapers every day, but instead rely on the subscription my mother buys me for *The Week* instead.

If I was not going to bed most nights after 1am I would listen to the *Today* programme. I also get the *Spectator* by mail, and the *New Statesman* send me a free copy each week, which is good for my soul, though they were insane not to do anything at all to hang on to Martin Bright.

A few ideas

If I had any tip for reporters, it would be to always call MPs on their mobile phones, or text them from your own: MPs usually can't answer their telephones and the reporter has to leave a message. The reporter is far more likely to be called back if the MP can simply press five or whatever number to automatically return the call. Leave a number from your office phone on their voicemail and you are less likely to be called back. And while we are on tips – remember that your average MP, especially when away from Westminster, will have to make some logistical effort to appear on your TV show. I invariably turn down opportunities to appear when it involves cost to me or irritating logistics like organising potentially free time spent travelling – so make it easy. Finally, remember that you would not want to be typecast yourself.

After leaving Cambridge, Adam Holloway spent five years in the army before working in television, first with the award-winning World in Action *programmes and later as a senior reporter at ITN. He was elected to Parliament in 2005, served on the Defence Select Committee until the 2010 election and is now a Parliamentary Private Secretary in the Foreign Office.*

8: Who's who at Westminster

Sheila Gunn

Sitting in the Commons press gallery at busy times, there's a sea of faces a few feet below me. Who are they? Why are they there? How do I pick the ones to talk to? Not only is there a roll call of 650 MPs, but 750-plus peers, thousands of civil servants, political party figures and the countless others involved in some way around Westminster and Whitehall. All and every one may be of interest to a journalist at some time. A good starting point is to examine who has the most power and where the best stories are likely to come from.

Our Head of State is the Queen. Unless you are a royal correspondent, you are unlikely to come into contact with her, and Her Majesty, other members of the Royal Family or their officers are unlikely to provide you with many, if any, political stories. From your point of view, the most important person is the Prime Minister.

The role and powers of the Prime Minister

Most would agree that we have been fortunate in our monarch and the string of decent and largely honest men and one woman who have been PM during her reign. Luckily for journalists, they all face crises of some sort on a fairly regular basis.

The Prime Minister is the leader of the party which wins the most seats in a general election. In other words, the UK electorate does not vote directly for their choice of PM, although the PM is also a constituency MP and must face his or her own 70,000 or so voters in a constituency at general elections. This means that there can be a change of PM without a general election, as when James

Callaghan replaced Harold Wilson, John Major took over from Margaret Thatcher and Gordon Brown succeeded Tony Blair. But the standing and character of party leaders keenly affects where voters make their cross. While a significant percentage of the electorate may struggle to name more than three or four ministers, hopefully all will know who is Prime Minister. And please remember that the PM's role extends through the four nations of the United Kingdom and not just the three nations of Great Britain.

The role of Prime Minister effectively started with Robert Walpole in the early eighteenth century, even though it is rarely mentioned in constitutional statutes and most of the powers are not set by law. In the early part of the nineteenth century, Walter Bagehot, in examining the British constitution, referred to the PM as 'primus inter pares' or 'first among equals' – a term now better remembered as the title of an enjoyable political thriller by Jeffrey Archer.

There is a debate about whether our PM is, in effect, the President of the UK or is acting in a presidential manner. This was provoked largely by Tony Blair's premiership and implies a lack of respect for the sovereignty of Parliament. While Her Majesty does not have executive powers, most PMs have the good sense to ask for and listen to her advice. In addition PMs usually have a weekly audience with her and spend a weekend at Balmoral in the autumn.

In practice, the powers of a Prime Minister are impressive. He or she also carries the titles of First Lord of the Treasury and Minister for the Civil Service.

The powers can be classified as:

The Royal Prerogative: Prerogative powers (formally powers of the monarch, but exercised by the PM) include the power to declare war, control the armed forces, control the workings of the civil service, annex and cede territory, use emergency powers (these are not written powers, but the PM is expected by the public to act, as in the banking crisis).

Foreign Role: The PM is the de facto head of state and represents the country at crucial foreign meetings, such as the EU and G7. He is also involved in numerous bilateral meetings with foreign premiers and, particularly in recesses, will make regular trips abroad. UK-based journalists will usually accompany him.

Patronage: The PM has the power to make numerous appointments, such as his own ministers, senior members of the armed forces, Bishops, senior judges, Privy Councillors and the top civil servants. He will also recommend peerages, although his nominees have to be cleared by a scrutiny committee and approved by the Queen.

Control of Cabinet: The PM decides who sits in Cabinet (in 1962 Macmillan sacked twenty-four ministers including seven Cabinet ministers in one day), controls the timing of the Cabinet – when it sits and for how long (under Blair it was often less than one hour per week). And importantly, he controls the agenda.

Given a PM's considerable powers, what are the constraints?

The state of the country and the economy

Intertwined with the factors below is the impact of policies on the country as a whole and its individual citizens. This ranges from the reputation of the UK internationally and the concerns of citizens, such as the cost of living, job security, level of crime and opportunities for the next generation. These may seem to be the most crucial issues, but they tend to influence a PM's standing through the other channels mentioned.

The party

A PM is also a party leader and needs the support of at least the majority of his ministers. Political journalists spend many happy hours trying to detect signs of unrest within ministerial ranks. Of course, these ministers and their aides will rarely be prepared to be quoted on the record. Hence a PM's office will dismiss such stories as 'tittle tattle'. This sort of game can go on for months before the true extent of unrest is confirmed.

This was the case when many ministers were whispering their fears about Margaret Thatcher's polices on the poll tax and Europe. Similarly, Tony Blair was subjected to a bitter campaign from those working for his next door neighbour, Gordon Brown – but very few would ever go on the record. All these stories were strongly denied by both No. 10 and No. 11 Downing Street. Yet recent memoirs from the key players revealed that the media actually underplayed the extent of the hostilities between the two tenants. It takes a strong stomach for a political journalist to shrug off such categorical denials.

One would expect most ministers to support the person who appointed them. But, as in the TV series *Yes Prime Minister,* PMs often fear that some of their colleagues are angling for their job and undermining their own position. It is not uncommon for a majority of Cabinet ministers to believe they can do the top job better.

A PM, especially after some time in office, is bound to face unrest from others in his own party. The reasons vary: some MPs may be disappointed at their lack of ministerial office or other jobs; they resent being sacked from office; or they disagree strongly on a particular policy. Then there are those holding position within the party, both employees and, even more importantly, the voluntary wing of the party. Serious unrest among those who fill the envelopes, deliver the leaflets and raise the funds cannot be ignored.

Parliament

If a government has a large overall majority in the Commons, a PM may be tempted to spend little time there. This generally turns out to be a mistake. Certainly the gradual erosion of support among MPs and peers damaged Margaret Thatcher and Tony Blair during their premierships. PMs will be advised to attend a reasonable number of votes, so that they can be seen and chatted to in the division lobbies. They may also invite groups of MPs to No. 10 on a regular basis and, as importantly, be seen to listen to their views (something Gordon Brown neglected to do). If there are signs of unrest, a PM may be advised to 'trawl the tea rooms', which journalists interpret as a sign of trouble brewing.

MPs and, to a far lesser extent, the peers will also carefully monitor a PM's performances within and outside Parliament. Whether the PM or the Leader of the Opposition 'win' the weekly bouts at prime ministerial questions affects morale on the green benches. Hence the balance between showing leadership and acting prime ministerial, while showing respect for Parliament and all its players, is one that all PMs will aim to achieve – and political journalists will closely monitor.

Vested interest groups

There will always be various organisations or groups of people who oppose a government policy or the current Prime Minister. This goes with the territory. But it is unwise for a PM, especially within two years of a general election, to offend too many people too often.

For instance, a Labour PM would try not to upset the big trade unions and a fair percentage of the business world at the same time. This is especially true when party leaders need money to fight elections. A Conservative PM will take care not to antagonise business leaders and too many in the professions within two years of a general election. At the start of a premiership, most PMs can risk criticism if they are confident that their policies will be seen to be the right ones well before the next election.

The media and the general public

Monitoring the standing of a PM 'in the country' at any one time, often described as 'feeling the public's pulse', is an industry in its own right. In his chapter, the pollster Andrew Hawkins describes the reporting of opinion polls. But there are other ways this sentiment reaches and affects a Prime Minister and his team.

Most PMs claim that they do not read the newspapers or watch the TV news. And this is rarely true. It is common practice for all senior ministers to receive from their press office daily digests of relevant news stories in the mainstream media and on BBC Radio 4's *Today* programme. It would be an unwise PM who totally ignored this information, because at any point it may be mentioned by those he comes into contact with during the day.

Conversely, some PMs face criticism for spending too much time monitoring the media. John Major was often accused of paying too much attention to what was in the newspapers. This was not my recollection. Although, early on in my time with him, he asked if I had read the second leader in that day's *Daily Telegraph*. I replied truthfully that I had not and added, rather unfortunately, that 'nobody reads the second leader in the *DT*'. 'I do,' he replied.

Speculation about and reporting of which national newspaper supports which political party generates a great deal of hot air. But there are some general observations. New party leaders and incoming governments are usually given a honeymoon of variable length by the commentators and leader writers. Most PMs know this, and the wise ones take advantage by introducing their more radical and controversial policies as early as possible. Tony Blair recognised this fact when he lamented his caution in his early days as PM. It is easy to forget that both John Major and Gordon Brown enjoyed glowing headlines in their early months as PM. But then, to use that Westminster cliché, attributed to Harold Macmillan, there occur '...events, dear boy, events'.

How much the honeymoon period permeates the news and feature pages varies. It may be reasonable to assume that the greater the hopes of an incoming leader, the greater the downfall. This syndrome certainly stands up if one examines the experiences of Tony Blair and Barack Obama. It is a very unwise PM or President who believes all the praise or all the criticism.

At the other end of the spectrum, once one person or one party has been in power for a long time, they can expect more negative media coverage. Partly, this is disillusionment about promises not fulfilled or a lack of new ideas. But there is also the boredom factor and, perhaps, some optimism that 'the other lot' might do better.

Aspiring political journalists need to be aware that politicians of all parties often think most of the media is against them and their party most of the time. Some will even have blacklists of journalists they regard as 'enemies'. Politicians also see political bias or even conspiracies in much of the media coverage and believe that journalists have 'their own agenda'. Some do, of course, but it is hard to convince politicians that what turns on most political journalists is a good story, wherever it comes from.

Another way the public pulse is taken between general elections is through local and by-elections. Party leaders will keep an eye on the results of the myriad local council by-elections every week to try to discern a trend. More significant are the elections held every May for various bodies; such as local authorities, devolved bodies or the European Parliament. All are seen as a litmus test on how a Prime Minister is doing.

Political journalists used to be able to expect regular by-elections, perhaps six or seven a year, because an MP had died or been appointed to some grandiose post, such as an EU Commissioner or secretary-general of NATO. These three- or four-week campaigns attract considerable media interest and provide a good opportunity to leave Westminster to dig into some part of the country. Annoyingly, MPs just do not die so regularly these days. This may be seen as a tribute to the NHS or the lower average age of MPs. But the result is that there are now fewer by-elections each year. This may change if more serving MPs are sent to jail for fiddling their expenses or other illegal activities.

The Cabinet

While a PM can look or even feel like quite a solitary figure, he will of course have a close circle of colleagues and friends. There is the Cabinet: the twenty-three or twenty-four most senior ministers who head up the government departments. The relationships, influence and atmosphere of Cabinet meetings will be carefully monitored. The appointments, sackings and reshuffles of a Cabinet always provoke intensive media speculation and coverage. A media favourite is to gauge the body language of the politicians going in and out of the famous black door during a reshuffle. 'What do you think he's got? Home Office? Defence? Or the sack?'

The Cabinet is bound by a concept called collective responsibility to support all Cabinet decisions. If they cannot do so, they are expected to resign. Such events are massive media events and usually seriously threaten the Prime Minister's own position. Geoffrey Howe's resignation from Thatcher's Cabinet and Robin Cook's resignation from Tony Blair's Cabinet are two classic examples.

Weekly Cabinet meetings are meant, of course, to be strictly private affairs with only the PM's spokesman giving a few agreed details to journalists afterwards. Cabinet ministers and their special advisers are not supposed to give their own private briefings, but luckily many of them do, especially to those journalists they know well. While most may be loyal to the PM and their party, they may want to put the best possible gloss on some decision or action, or undermine a colleague. While working for John Major, we would be amazed at the stories which appeared after Cabinets, quoting 'a senior ministerial source' and describing some aspect of the meeting. Most bore little resemblance to the actual discussions and, at times, it seemed that every minister had left with a different perception of the decisions made.

In addition to the Cabinet ministers, there are a couple of others who regularly attend the weekly Cabinet meetings, such as the Chief Whip and party Chairman.

Much of the discussions on future policies and actions go on in Cabinet committees. Political hacks will keep an eye on who is chairing the more important ones, as they are a sign of someone's seniority and the level of trust they enjoy. It is a little different with the coalition government, as which party chairs which committees had to be negotiated more formally.

PMs will have a smaller group of ministers and key aides who are his or her most trusted colleagues and can be expected to be totally loyal to the incumbent. Making contacts with members of this group is important, even though they tend to be depressingly discreet. Sometimes they may bad mouth other colleagues, as happened in the rivalry between the Blair and Brown camps. They will then deny all knowledge if and when these comments are reflected in your stories.

The small group of the closest aides and friends tends to be described as the 'kitchen cabinet' – as in, those who sit around the kitchen table with the PM. It is always worthwhile finding who is in or out of it.

Deputy Prime Minister

There is no formal description of the role and responsibilities of a deputy PM and many PMs have done without one. The reasons why a PM decides to appoint one varies. David Cameron has Nick Clegg because it was part of the coalition agreement. Margaret Thatcher had Viscount 'Willie' Whitelaw, who was one of the few politicians who would tell her the truth in all circumstances and was a useful conduit with other parts of the Conservative Party. John Major appointed Michael Heseltine as his deputy; Tony Blair had John Prescott. Gordon Brown had, quite amazingly, Peter Mandelson – although he did not have the formal title. An obvious attribute in the choice of deputy Prime Minister is that none are secretly angling for their boss's job. Normally they can bring qualities and connections that the PM may not have. But the right chemistry is essential. Much has been written about the relationship between Cameron and Clegg. That's because, if the relationship had not worked, then the coalition government wouldn't have either.

Top civil servants

Sir Humphrey in *Yes Prime Minister* was Jim Hacker's Cabinet Secretary. A good idea of what this role entails can still be gleaned from watching a couple of episodes. The Cabinet Secretary is the most senior civil servant, that is, they are not elected or affiliated to any party and may even serve PMs from different parties. Sir Gus O'Donnell, for example, held posts with successive governments over many years: he was John Major's press secretary; Cabinet Secretary in Tony Blair and Gordon Brown's governments; had a key role in navigating the passage to the coalition government; and then stayed on to serve David Cameron.

At the top of each government department is a Permanent Secretary. As the title implies, they are not party political or elected but civil or public servants charged with running the departments and implementing the government's policies.

Sadly most of these mandarins, as they are sometimes called, never ever see the point of talking to journalists and would probably, if given the opportunity, seriously curtail the freedom of the press.

I had been mildly suspicious about these people who effectively run the country and seemed to live such nicely ordered and well-remunerated lives. Not for them the grimy business of politics. But, at the most senior levels, I later found them an astonishingly impressive bunch. Abilities of officials lower down the scale were far more mixed.

Other ministers

Government departments will usually have around five or six ministers. In order of priority they are usually: the Secretary of State, who is the Cabinet minister; a couple of ministers of state, otherwise referred to as a middle-ranking minister, with specific responsibilities or portfolios; and some Parliamentary Under Secretaries of State (sometimes referred to rather rudely as PUSs), who are junior ministers.

Most of these will spend time and energy in developing a good, working relationship with journalists and will be expected to promote and explain their policies, actions and decisions via the media. Some are much keener on this part of their job than others. And some are much better at it than others, which is proven by a quick study of various ministers being interviewed on television. Please do not ignore those ministers who rarely appear on TV, usually for good reasons, or who keep a relatively low profile. They are often the ones who can give you the best stories and may be flattered that you have bothered to approach them.

(For one of the best descriptions of life as a junior minister, it is worth reading Chris Mullin's *A View from the Foothills.*)

The whips

Whips come in two forms: human and inhuman. A whip is a member of either House who is appointed by their party leader to maximise the votes, implement its policies, maintain discipline among its members and fight other parties every inch of the way. MPs see becoming a whip as an important step on the ministerial ladder.

The position of Chief Whip is highly influential and will be an MP who is totally trusted by the party leader. His job is primarily to 'deliver' the required number of votes for their party. The leader will look to the Chief Whip to tell him of signs of unrest among backbenchers, comment on the behaviour and performance of ministers, recommend the names of MPs for promotion or demotion, and spot any signs of trouble. Most Chief Whips are particularly wary of talking to journalists, rarely if ever give interviews, and relish the mystique which surrounds their operations. They tend to sit silently and often forbiddingly on the frontbench at the end furthest away from the Speaker.

They can be expected to hold files containing personal information about the behaviour or activities of members, although they would never admit it. If there are rumours of a potential 'scandal', the Chief Whip will be one of the first people to advise the party leader on what course of action to take. Few such scandals which break in the media come as a total surprise to the Chief Whip.

More than any other place in Westminster, the whips system is modelled on a traditional boys only club or public school. Journalists love to write about the bullying and arm-twisting tactics conducted by whips to coerce their MPs into obeying the party line.

When Conservative MPs rebelled over the Maastricht Treaty during John Major's premiership, I spotted some specks of blood in the members' lobby right outside the door to the Whips' Office. A perfect way for me to illustrate the pressure being applied by the whips. Just up to deadline, someone rang to tell me that the blood came from the paw of a spaniel, one of the dogs used by security to check for bombs around the place. One occasion when I decided to forget about this call and send my story off unchanged.

Political journalists need to know whips and, in particular, learn if they are responsible for particular pieces of legislation or regions of the country. However, remember that there is one thing which drives them in all circumstances: loyalty to their party.

They will always put the best possible gloss on their party's status and activities. They live in terror of being quoted in person

– and almost never speak in the chamber. And they may try to draw out of you the names and activities of 'troublemakers', that is any of their MPs or peers who may question their party's policies. They are likely to pass on any comments you make about their colleagues. While it may be unfair to say that whips will lie to you, accept they may often not tell you the truth. Gyles Brandreth, formerly the Conservative MP for the City of Chester and a well-known broadcaster, upset some in his own party when he revealed the realities of life as a government whip in his book *Breaking the Code*.

Each vote or division usually takes about ten minutes. Bells ring in various parts of Parliament, offices and even a couple of local restaurants and pubs to alert members (it is similar for peers). Nowadays members are also alerted via mobile phones and BlackBerrys. They then have eight minutes to rush to the division lobby and be counted through by their whips.

Whips also act as 'tellers': it is usually the whips of opposing parties who, in pairs, march up the centre of the chamber and declare the result of each vote. For example: 'The Ayes to the right 242; the Nos to the left, 240. The Ayes have it.' A useful tip when up to deadline is to see who, on entering the chamber after a controversial vote, is the Teller on the left if one was sitting in the Speaker's Chair. If you know that Teller is, for instance, a Labour whip, it means that Labour has won the vote even before the result is formally announced. This itself will produce a lively reaction from MPs in different parties who would also understand the implication.

The written whip

A whip is also the instruction given to all MPs and peers of each party on how to vote on that coming week's business in the chamber. There is a line system which can be summarised as:

> **A three line whip**: three thick black lines under a particular vote, such as '7pm Second Reading, Education Bill'. This is an order that the MP or peer must vote for his or her party. No excuses accepted. There have been occasions, much loved

by the media, when seriously ill MPs have been brought to Parliament by ambulance to vote.

A two line whip: two thick black lines. This, again, requires the MP or peer to vote as ordered, unless they can convince their whip that they have an excellent excuse for being absent.

A one line whip: one thick black line. A request to attend.

MPs of different parties may 'pair' so that both can be absent for non-essential votes; this cancels out each other's votes. This is particularly useful when MPs want to attend constituency events, dinners, are on an overseas trip or, perhaps, have a significant personal or family event. Although such pairings are informal, and not controlled by the rules of the House, MPs must have the agreement of their whips. Clearly the paired MPs must trust each other. Strong and unlikely friendships are often formed from such arrangements, one of which, now part of Westminster folklore, the pairing of the left-wing Labour MP Diane Abbott with the Conservative MP Jonathan Aitken, who became her son's godfather.

MPs are meant to keep these whips (the written kind) totally secret. But political journalists usually have good enough contacts to find out if a three line whip has been imposed on any particular business. This becomes important in two specific circumstances: if any MPs are known to be unhappy with the issue to be voted on and may be absent or even rebel; or when the whip is applied to a vote on a social issue, such as stem cell research or abortion, which some MPs regard as an issue of conscience rather than strictly party political.

Parliamentary private secretaries (PPSs)

The title is confusing because they are MPs who act as unpaid aides to ministers. Please do not confuse them with civil servants or officials. If appointed a PPS, an MP has made it onto the first rung of the ministerial ladder. Often referred to as ministerial 'bag-carriers', they tend to be MPs ambitious for ministerial office, supporting and advising their ministers in the hope of early promotion.

PPSs can act as an important link between ministers and the backbenches, liaising with MPs, spotting signs of unrest or rebellion. The position of the Prime Minister's PPS can be particularly influential and is usually a fairly senior MP without great personal ambitions.

They are very useful contacts for journalists, although they are likely to be loyal and, like the whips, eager to put the best gloss on their party's activities. But they often know what is going on behind the scenes and can give you useful information about what is being planned.

Payroll vote

All the posts above – from PM down to PPSs – together make up the payroll vote. This description is regarded as important because all those on it are expected to vote for, support and promote the government's policies in all circumstances. Journalists will be watching for signs of unrest within the payroll vote about controversial policies as, for instance, the war on Iraq and, in the autumn of 2010, increased student tuition fees. Generally the payroll vote makes up around a third of the MPs on the government benches, although the picture is more confused under the coalition government.

Opposition parties

Facing the government benches are MPs in the opposition parties. The Leader of the Opposition is usually the leader of the party which comes second in a general election. It is a formally recognised role, with the Leader of the Opposition having a salary, a suite of offices and a staff.

Their team will mirror the government's: there is a shadow Cabinet and shadow ministers with specific portfolios. The other parties will also have frontbench spokesmen and women.

The Speaker

Positioned in the middle – that is, not on either the government or opposition benches – is the Speaker, seated on a kind of throne.

Speakers are MPs who relinquish their political partisanship when elected, by the other MPs, to the Speaker's Chair. One of their main roles is to 'chair' the Commons, calling different MPs to speak, keeping order and admonishing those who break the rules. These rules are largely contained in a sort of parliamentary bible called *Erskine May* which, with help from the clerks, guide the Speaker's decisions.

A good Speaker will take great care to protect the interest of backbenchers so that they can question and scrutinise the government and its policies. Until quite recently, Speakers were not generally controversial figures. But the last two, Michael Martin and John Bercow, have changed this – to the joy of journalists.

Although they are not easily accessible to journalists, those based at Westminster may find themselves invited on occasion to the Speaker's House, at the eastern end of Parliament. It is certainly worth accepting, if only to see the amazing décor and peculiar Speaker's Bed.

Key players in the Lords

The composition in the Lords is similar to the Commons. There are frontbenches, but with far fewer ministers, shadow ministers and frontbench spokesmen. In addition to the government and opposition party benches, there are the crossbenches where independent, unwhipped peers sit.

Until relatively recently, there was no formal position of Speaker, instead the Lord Chancellor would 'chair' key debates. In any case, the peers were expected to exercise self-discipline. That has changed to some extent with the influx of former Labour MPs onto the red benches. But there is now Lord Speaker (please note that it is 'Lord' not 'Lords'). To be even more confusing, the first incumbent is actually a woman, Baroness Hayman.

9: The committee corridor

Sheila Gunn

Images come to mind. Some horrible, even tragic; many salutary; a few just plain ridiculous.

It is hard to forget aggressive questioning of the late weapons inspector, Dr David Kelly, by the Commons Foreign Affairs Committee, about speculation that the case for the war in Iraq had been 'sexed up'. He had to give evidence again the next day, 16 July 2003, to the Commons Intelligence & Security Committee. The day after, he was found dead. Compare that with the clever, slick performance by Blair's spin doctor Alastair Campbell on the same issue. And remember the four heads of our leading banks apologising, more or less, for their roles in the financial crisis, which led to the government's bail out?

There is no doubt that Parliament's committee corridors are some of the most fertile territory for journalists and especially for specialist reporters. Enquiries, investigations, hearings and evidence by committees made up of MPs or peers from different parties look into everything under the sun. How often have you seen headlines such as: 'Influential cross-party committee condemns the government's...' or 'Ministers accused of ... by all-party parliamentary committee...'? They are also some of the most accessible events, as you do not need any kind of pass to attend the hearings or to access the evidence.

The web of select committees in both Houses are a key mechanism for scrutinising and questioning government policy and their influence has grown in recent years. For some politicians it provides an alternative career to the ministerial ladder.

For journalists, one of their attractions is the scope for providing a series of stories. These include the announcement of an enquiry into a specific subject ('MPs launch enquiry into scandal of...'), oral hearings and written submissions ('Teachers warn ministers that recent reforms are damaging...') and the final report ('MPs demand change to...').

Even more satisfying is to find, as one often can, gems within the written submissions which few journalists bother to trawl through. Or, better still, to be leaked information about the final report before it is formally published.

The Commons select committee system

While the concept of select committees dates back to the Tudor and Stuart parliaments, the key features of the present system can be traced to Margaret Thatcher's first parliament in 1979. Norman (now Lord) St John-Stevas, the then Leader of the House, introduced the current system of a select committee to shadow the work of each government department, otherwise referred to as departmental select committees. These fourteen new committees started work in 1980.

More recently other committees have been added to the system, most notably the Commons Intelligence & Security Committee, the Environmental Audit Committee and the Standards and Privileges Committee.

Their membership of around fourteen backbench MPs reflects the political make-up of the House of Commons; that is in the current arliament, with a small Conservative majority. While Conservative MPs hold the most chairs, there is a fair sprinkling of chairmen from the other parties.

Here's a fairly typical sample of one day's select committee hearings:

November 3, 2010, witnesses giving evidence on:
Work & Pensions: Proposed changes in housing benefit
Education: Role and performance of Ofsted
Treasury: Comprehensive Spending Review
Defence: Operations in Afghanistan

Environment, Food & Rural Affairs: Future flood and water management legislation

As well as the oral evidence sessions, interested bodies put in written submissions. Both can be accessed through the pages for each select committee on the parliament website. Most sessions are televised, with snippets often used in news stories or features and whole sessions available via the parliament channel.

The usual oral session will last around an hour and a half. Witnesses may make a short opening statement before facing questions from the MPs. While most committees will attempt to organise the questioning beforehand, the MPs have considerable scope to pursue various lines of enquiry. For witnesses in senior posts outside politics, the experience can be uncomfortable, if not downright humiliating. The very word 'witness' makes them feel like they are in a courtroom, being questioned by a roomful of inquisitors, while journalists seated behind them are breathing down their necks.

To gain a sense of the atmosphere, it is worth searching out the coverage of the 'grilling' by the Commons Treasury Committee of four bank executives in February 2009. The three-hour 'showdown' – as it was previewed by the media – focused on their role in the events leading up to the government's bail out of their banks. It still makes great viewing on YouTube – not least because of Sir Fred 'the Shred' Goodwin, former CEO of RBS, apologising with as much humility as he could muster, which was not very much. You need a strong stomach to sit through replays of Dr David Kelly however, questioned at length by MPs about his work in trying to track down weapons of mass destruction in Iraq.

Chairs of the select committees also serve on the Liaison Committee, which monitors the work of the system. An excellent innovation by the Blair government is the requirement for the Prime Minister to appear before the Liaison Committee twice a year. These interrogations inevitably generate extensive media interest and are often regarded as a more effective mechanism for forcing a PM to justify his actions than PMQs.

Powers of select committees

While hearings provide journalists with plenty of material, remember that the committees' reports have no parliamentary or legal force. They cannot overturn government policy or force a minister to make changes. Their strength is in the cross-party nature of the committees and the publicity they generate. You expect MPs in one party to attack those in another party. That is the everyday knockabout of politics.

Involving MPs from different parties, the select committees carry out in-depth examinations of the impact of a particular policy. They decide what to investigate; they agree who and how to question witnesses. Then they come to conclusions and make recommendations, irrespective of which party they represent. More recently, they have demonstrated an enthusiasm for announcing enquiries into issues making the headlines.

The committees have the power to 'send for persons, papers and records' – and to insist that any British citizen appears before them. But here's a health warning: the government can resist a committee's request for 'sensitive' documents.

If it becomes known that certain witnesses have refused to appear, that becomes a very respectable story in its own right. Such reluctant witnesses should be reminded of the press coverage when the late media mogul Robert Maxwell's sons appeared grudgingly before a select committee enquiring into the loss of the Maxwell pensions – and then refused to answer questions. If they had at least made a stab at answering, there would have been far less negative publicity. The televised session of them sitting like a couple of stuffed ducks would be hilarious if one could forget the many employees who were deprived of a decent retirement.

While the cross-party nature of these committees is their key virtue, it also imposes a debilitating effect: to reach unanimous agreement, the reports and recommendations are often dampened down. They have also been emasculated by a lack of resources and the influence of the whips.

Apart from the Public Accounts Committee, the select committees are serviced by a clerk with an assistant and, occasionally, a special adviser brought in to help with specific enquiries. They now have the services of a media officer to handle press enquiries and, in addition, the chairs are entitled to a payment, in addition to their MPs' pay. But in comparison, for instance, to US-style committees, the committees are lean, under-resourced operations.

During Blair's first government, the role of the whips in influencing the membership and, in particular, the chairs of the committees made headlines. A recent and welcome reform is that the MPs themselves have the right to approve membership. Hopefully this will lead to chairs acting more independently of the government and without running the risk of being blocked for offending the whips.

Where are they?

Geographically, many of the committee meetings are held in the long corridor (hence its name) which stretches most of the length of the first floor of the main Parliament building overlooking the Thames. A few are held on the floor above or in Portcullis House, the parliamentary building which sits above Westminster tube station.

For any journalist interested in covering politics, or a specialism with a political element, it is well worth attending some of the hearings. All you have to do is look up the meetings on the parliament website. If a room number is listed, it is in the main Parliament building accessed through the security entrance (give yourself plenty of time) via St Stephen's gate. If it has a name, such as the Thatcher or Wilson Room, it is in Portcullis House, which is far quicker to access as there will not be the usual tourists or visitors.

Committee reports

Reports are finalised in private sessions and most chairs go to great lengths to produce unanimous reports – those backed by all the MPs on the committee. This may lead to some recommendations being watered down which, if journalists find out, can be a good story in itself. Occasionally there will be a majority report, in which some committee MPs refuse to agree all the recommendations. The votes on any recommendations which are not agreed by all the committee's MPs are set out in the final report and, again, generate media interest.

Press releases and sometimes press conferences, together with interviews of committee members, often accompany publication of the reports. These reports are technically made to the House of Commons and sometimes lead to debates. After the first flush of publication, the aftermath is something of a disappointment. But MPs, journalists and others frequently use the reports in pursuing campaigns or arguments. Remember that all the deliberations and reports of these committees are covered by parliamentary privilege and so can be used without any threat of legal action: a real treasury of information, quotes and potential contacts.

Government departments are expected to produce a response to the reports within a couple of months. These tend to be bland documents which focus on highlighting positive recommendations, as in '...welcome the comments...' while skating over the negative ones. However it is an unwise department which totally ignores a committee's findings.

Another aspect of the system which attracts publicity is when a committee goes abroad to study something that is said to be useful to its enquiry. In journalese these are referred to as 'all-expenses paid fact-finding visits' – or merely freebies, junkets or worse. A fact-finding visit to the Caribbean to study drugs policy may justify such cynicism. But judge each visit on its merits. It would be rather sad if committees could not study important policy issues outside the Palace of Westminster. You can, of course, always ask to join them.

Embargoes, leaking and trailing

While the committee chairs and members will usually be keen to attract media coverage for their reports, the issue of leaking or trailing reports beforehand is more controversial. Journalists can ask the media officers to be added to the email list to receive the latest news from specific committees. Most reports are made available to political journalists and those who have registered their interest under embargo.

It is not good or clever journalism to break this 'not for publication before 00.00 hours on such and such a date' embargo and it can damage your reputation. You could also expect formal complaints to be made to your editor or producer.

Leaking or trailing reports is a very different issue. Developing good contacts with committee MPs is an excellent move. Strictly off the record, some may quietly tip you off about some interesting recommendations in a forthcoming report. But please take care. The MP may be using you because he or she wants that recommendation included and it may not have been formally agreed. Remember that the MP, wishing to avoid public chastisement, is likely to deny that they are the source of any leaks, which can put you in an uncomfortable position. You can cover yourself by wording your story very carefully. There is a world of difference between writing 'the influential ... committee will severely criticise the government...' And 'MPs of the influential...committee have questioned the government's policy and are expected to criticise...'

Trailing the findings of a forthcoming report has become a common journalistic tactic. If you have carefully followed an enquiry, listened to how the lines of questioning developed and know the views of the chair, you should be able to make a reasonable guess at the recommendations. While many committee MPs will not tell you these in advance of publication, if they are good contacts, they may be willing to confirm – often with no more than a nod – whether you are on the right lines.

Public spending watchdogs

'Defence project goes £2 billion over budget, is twelve years late – and doesn't fly...' A mild exaggeration perhaps, but not much of one. This could be a fairly typical intro for a report from the two main public spending watchdogs, the National Audit Office and the Commons Public Accounts Committee.

The NAO and PAC are two of the most important ways that government spending is scrutinised and so provide a constant source of good stories. The NAO, headed by the Comptroller and Auditor General (C&AG), audits all central government spending. In other words, they can legally walk into any government department or agency and look into their books.

It publishes reports, both on how government departments are spending your money and on specific projects or programmes, such as child tax credits, new schools or the latest defence equipment. Two areas where the NAO has not traditionally had access, but which are now under discussion, are the accounts of the BBC and the Royal Family.

These days NAO reports are clearly written, but do not obviously guide journalists to the best possible headline. All are accompanied by a press release which usually highlights the most interesting or controversial issues. But great stories can still be found buried deep within the reports, especially for journalists with some knowledge of the specific subject.

Apart from their value for news stories, they are a fantastic source of verified facts, figures and comments on issues which make excellent features or investigations. Aides in the opposition parties, if they have any sense, make good use of them. Data and quotes from the NAO are authoritative and 'independent of government'. And they are, of course, covered by parliamentary privilege. So there is no problem with lawyers.

The reports go to the Commons Public Accounts Committee, the oldest and unarguably the most important select committee. This cross-party group of around fifteen MPs will study them and then, usually, call the relevant senior civil servant before them for questioning. It is something that these officials will rarely relish, especially as they prefer to operate behind closed doors rather than in front of the TV cameras. Just imagine the reaction of Sir Humphrey (that is the Cabinet Secretary of *Yes Prime Minister* fame, rather than the former No. 10 cat of the same name) to an 'invitation' to appear before the PAC.

The committee will then make a report with recommendations to the House of Commons itself. While the department or officials concerned are not forced to obey them, they know it would be unwise to ignore them. The chair of the PAC is traditionally an opposition party MP, although all the committee's MPs tend to see the role as non-party political and an important job in its own right. Sadly for journalists it is one select committee which rarely leaks.

This model of public scrutiny by the NAO and PAC is copied and envied around the world as an example of accountability and a deterrent to corruption. A key reason why the UK has one of the least corrupt civil services in the world (some would argue that it has *the* least corrupt) is the knowledge that the NAO is constantly watching and monitoring them. And, to my knowledge, there has never been a case of anyone bribing an NAO official.

House of Lords' select committees

While the Upper House does not have the same system of committees shadowing government departments, it does have expert committees which can be particularly useful – though rarely for political journalists. The main ones deal with EU issues or science and technology. They receive little media coverage in the mainstream UK media, except from specialist journalists. But occasionally you can extract genuine scoops from either the hearings or the reports of these committees.

One such was an investigation by one of the EU sub-committees many years ago into how EU overseas aid was spent – or, in most cases, misspent. A real horror story – and a particularly satisfying splash in *The Times*. Even more so because it came from a group of non-party political peers using facts rather than emotions – and with no ambition to hit the headlines. The system has, apparently, been improved since then. But maybe not?

10: Reporting the House of Lords

Amanda Brown

Political reporters mostly regard the House of Lords as a story desert, a place where 'nothing ever happens'. It is certainly quieter than the Commons, but that isn't all bad.

The journalist who likes to get away from the media pack trawling the corridors of power in the Commons knows the House of Lords can provide a pleasant and worthwhile diversion. During fifteen years working for the Press Association at Westminster, I may have seen the membership of the Lords change, but its role in making the government of the day think again has, on occasion, produced some excellent copy. It also has more than its fair share of well-known names and characters to brighten political coverage.

The main role of the Lords is as a revising chamber, examining bills line-by-line and sending them back to the Commons if the peers believe that the government of the day needs to think again.

In the early months of the coalition government, membership rose to some 770 peers. This was partly because Tony Blair and Gordon Brown had greatly increased the number of Labour peers during their premierships and then David Cameron and Nick Clegg packed in more peers of their parties to even up the odds. Most are life peers, entitled to sit in the Lords during their lifetime. There are also ninety-two hereditary peers; these inherited their titles or, put another way, gained their seats through accident of birth. These ninety-two remained in the House as a result of a deal done between Tony Blair and the then Conservative leader of the Lords, Viscount Cranborne (now the Marquis of Salisbury). Hundreds of other hereditaries were kicked out. Oddly most of these ninety-two are, in fact, the only 'elected' members of the Upper House – as they are elected by their peers.

Reform? What reform?

What to do about the Lords? This is a question which has troubled successive governments over the past century. Looked at objectively, the Upper House is the most extraordinary place. You bump into plenty of former Cabinet ministers, captains of industry, university vice chancellors, Bishops and the odd Earl. You may hobnob with former trade union leaders, MPs ejected from the Commons by the electorate or those who seem unemployable in any capacity.

You could not make it up. And the one issue on which all political parties agree is that no one would design a second chamber on the lines of the current House of Lords if starting from scratch.

So why does it survive? Mainly because politicians cannot agree on what to put in its place. The current consensus is that there needs to be a bicameral system, that is, two Houses, and that the second one needs to be a largely or wholly elected chamber, likely to be called a Senate. But no one has yet adequately answered the question: then why should a Senate give way to the Commons if both are elected? The other justification for the present system is that, oddly – in a very British way – the current House of Lords works rather well.

The view from the red benches

In describing the work of MPs elsewhere it is clear that they need to balance the demands from their party whips and their constituents, while never totally losing sight of the next general election. The peers do not have the same pressures and can examine government policies and legislation in quite a different way, with a view to the longer term. In addition, for many years, no party has enjoyed an overall majority in the Upper House. This means that a government, even a coalition one, cannot guarantee always winning votes.

Unlike the Commons, the Lords has an influential tranche of peers who do not 'take the whip' from any party. These independent peers are called the crossbenchers and, in practice, stretch across the whole political spectrum. Hence any party which attracts the majority of crossbenchers to its cause is likely to win in the division lobbies.

Reporting the Lords

In recent years the atmosphere has become more informal. But the Lords can still be a daunting prospect to the reporter sent to cover proceedings for the first time.

Getting on first name terms with a peer in the hope that he or she will leak a juicy piece of gossip or unveil secrets about ministerial goings on demands a certain level of skill. Most reporters have earned their spurs on regional or national papers before they join this senior cabal of Westminster hacks, in other words it helps to have the confidence that comes with age and experience.

An apprenticeship spent sitting through dreary council meetings on the local paper turns out to be a surprisingly good grounding for the House of Lords reporter. You instinctively know that much of the daily business will be of little or no interest to you and therefore can safely be ignored. Occasionally you strike gold and a story pops up from nowhere that is guaranteed to put a smile on the face of your news editor.

What does the House of Lords do?

The main role of the Lords is to scrutinise and revise legislation, i.e. proposed changes in the law. So the most likely stories come from the Lords challenging or defeating the government of the day by amending Bills. Unlike the Commons, where attempts to amend Bills is limited by a guillotine, or time limit, the peers take their time to debate and examine Bills.

Governments frequently face such defeats and are made to 'think again'. For instance, in the last few years, the Upper House has protected jury trial, defended habeas corpus and rejected compulsory ID cards. History very often finds that governments would do well to have listened to the Lords. It is worth remembering that it was the Lords who queried whether Margaret Thatcher's poll tax would work fairly in practice.

Sometimes these long, drawn-out discussions which take place mostly during the committee stage and report stages of Bills, can last long into the night. You need plenty of stamina when the clock approaches midnight and there's a new lead story to be written after a late vote.

But there are limits to the power of the Lords. Finance Bills, which enact most of the Budget's proposals, cannot be amended by the peers. Nor can they delay government legislation for more than a year. In practice, whenever a government is defeated in the Lords, a minister puts out a statement vowing to 'reverse the amendment' once the Bill returns to the House of Commons. But most of the Lords' amendments, unless they affect particularly controversial issues, are accepted by ministers. Few ministers relish a prolonged argument with 'experts' in the Upper House – or a stream of damaging headlines such a confrontation is likely to provoke.

There are almost always some key amendments in every session on which the two Houses take different views. It is near the end of the parliamentary session that the fun starts, as controversial Bills are sent back and forth between the two Houses. This period of 'ping ponging' involves amendments – and amendments to amendments etc – whizzing between the two Houses until at last, usually behind closed doors, some sort of agreement is reached. This wheeling and dealing, who blinks first syndrome can provide plenty of stories.

Without a last minute deal the legislation can be lost. This does not often happen as the Lords is wary of killing off a Bill that has been included in a manifesto or the Queen's Speech. But it has been done. The first Bill to allow shops to trade on Sundays was thrown out by the Lords as was the first War Crimes Bill, to continue the pursuit and prosecution of Nazi war criminals. Both later became law but with some concessions. It is more common for certain clauses or parts of Bills to be deleted or added by the peers.

Contacting a peer

Some reporters may be wary of contacting peers, especially the more famous names. But they are generally very approachable and welcome interest in their speeches and work in the Lords. A good way of making contact is to stand in the main lobby of the House of Lords in the hope that the person you are after, will wander into view, assuming of course that the peer in question is in the building. However, if you are not based at Westminster, most of those who are active members will have their phone numbers and email addresses readily available.

It is normal practice in the members' lobby of the Commons for journalists to try and buttonhole MPs as they go in and out of the chamber. In the House of Lords the rules are slightly different. You will of course need to have a Westminster photo pass after completing a detailed security form, provided through your employer.

Thirty years ago when I first worked there, it was forbidden for a reporter to stand in the lobby. The doorkeepers took a dim view of anyone who appeared to be 'loitering with intent'. This made my life very difficult until I had a word with the then leader of the Lords Christopher Soames. I asked him if anything could be done and a short time later, and with Black Rod's agreement, the rules were relaxed and I was allowed to stand in the lobby.

How did I get to speak to Lord Soames in the first place? During the years of the Thatcher government the leader of the Lords held a weekly briefing on Fridays for lobby journalists. This 'off the record' chat was fuelled by a plentiful supply of alcoholic refreshments and was very popular with thirsty hacks.

The convivial atmosphere meant everyone was soon in a relaxed frame of mind. It was on one of these occasions that I made my move and asked if the strict rules hampering journalists could be changed. Lord Soames agreed that something needed to be done. With its kindly and still courteous ways, 'doorstepping' your contacts in the Lords can be a very pleasant affair.

It certainly beats standing around in the cold for hours on end, like a general reporter, outside a courthouse or in the street waiting for a celebrity to appear with a statement. Of course many peers are instantly recognisable. Ex-prime ministers and former MPs, actors, and anyone who has spent a good deal of their time on TV and in the public eye, can easily be spotted. But there are many others who are not at all well known.The best way for the Lords reporter to track down an elusive peer is to sit in the Lords press box, overlooking the chamber, and ask the Badge Messenger (who will be wearing a white tie and tails) to identify him or her for you. You can then track him or her down on leaving the chamber or leave a note in the lobby.

A particularly enjoyable aspect of the Upper House is its various bars, tea rooms and restaurants. Of all the many watering holes at Westminster, the peers' Guest Bar is one of my favourites. It is here that you can meet peers for a quiet drink and a private conversation, but you need to be invited in by a peer. There is a far more lax attitude in the Lords' staff bar, which gives excellent access to the western end of the terrace overlooking the Thames; certainly one of the best places to relax in London, especially on warm summer evenings.

What makes a story in the House of Lords?

The interesting thing about a peer is usually what he or she did in their previous life. Disclosures made in the chamber are covered by privilege and appear in the Hansard official report, so you are quite safe to report the speech or any written material, such as amendments and written statements, without fear of legal prosecution.

Quite often I would get a story out of a seemingly ordinary debate during the passage of a government Bill. For instance, one ex-Labour Lord Chancellor recalled that when he was in office, he thought his rooms were all bugged so he and the Attorney General always used to drive out to the countryside to have private conversations. Or when a Tory baroness who owned up to smoking dope, and the former Labour Cabinet minister who, during one late night debate, shocked everyone by protesting about his treatment by his own party since leaving office. And a famous judge rambled on at length about the state of his marriage due to his heavy workload. Disclosures like this come out of the blue, but they make good copy.

You also have to watch out for the unexpected. Late one evening when the only peers left in the chamber were half asleep, part of the Pugin ceiling crashed down in a huge cloud of dust on the benches in front of me. An enormous wooden 'boss' landed on the seat normally occupied by the Labour veteran Manny Shinwell.

Westminster security measures have made it more difficult for members of the public to stage protests from the Strangers' gallery. This is where visitors can watch proceedings. But in the past I have witnessed books being thrown and even a group of lesbians abseiling into the chamber from a side gallery.

Occasionally a message will appear on the internal monitors asking if there is 'a doctor in the House?' This usually means someone has been taken ill. But sometimes it signals that there's a death and under the Westminster rules nobody is 'allowed' to die on the parliamentary estate. Taking the body away from the Palace avoids the necessity of holding a special inquest.

I once witnessed an elderly peer making a speech and then literally sitting down and keeling over in his seat. A Bishop sitting on the bench in front of him said a prayer, but nothing could be done. One Labour former Foreign Secretary was found dead in his taxi after arriving at the entrance to the House of Lords. There was a row between the taxi driver and the doorman over who paid the fare but in the end the body was taken to St Thomas' hospital where the peer was pronounced dead. Such incidents are of course important stories and you miss them at your peril.

The state opening of Parliament

Ringside seats in the Lords press gallery are difficult to secure for this great state occasion and you have to apply in advance. A notice announcing the event is usually posted up in the press gallery and each media organisation is allowed one place. Reporters are looking for 'colour' stories on this occasion.

On the day, the contents of the Queen's Speech outlining the government's forthcoming programme will have been released to the lobby in the Commons, at 9.30am under strict embargo. Later on, all the relevant government departments put out press releases and sometimes offer briefings about the measures mentioned.

To cover the event you will need to take your place in the press box at least one hour before Her Majesty arrives in the chamber. If you are late you will not be allowed in. TV screens by the Strangers' gallery allow you to watch the Queen make the carriage journey along The Mall and into the Lords entrance. But the hour-long wait before the speech gives you time to check which Lords and Baronesses have turned up and the Badge Messenger on duty usually has a seating plan to help you.

Peers also have to apply for tickets to attend and they wear their red ermine trimmed robes which are taken out of storage for the occasion. The smell of mothballs is overpowering. It is also a chance for the wives of peers to show off their finery and take their seats in the chamber: this often leads to stories by fashion journalists, especially on the hats.

Before most of the hereditary peers were ejected, the countesses, viscountesses and duchesses used to dazzle with their tiaras and diamond necklaces.

Now there are not so many sparklers, but the beautiful evening gowns are still there aplenty. Watch out too for special guests in the diplomatic galleries. Pauline Prescott always used to cut a dash with her big hats and fancy suits sitting alongside Cherie Blair, and sometimes one of the minor royals turns up unexpectedly. Samantha Cameron's decision not to wear a hat made a story in itself.

It is easy for journalists to be cynical about such ceremonial occasions. But the scene is quite magnificent with the judges in their full wigs and robes and all the ambassadors and diplomats in national costume. Her Majesty of course is the star of the show and the Crown Jewels are truly breathtaking. The Queen enters the chamber on the arm of Prince Philip at 11.30am and everyone stands to attention, sitting down again only once they are on their thrones.

Silence falls on the assembly while Black Rod marches down to the Commons and hammers on the door demanding that MPs follow him back to the Lords to listen to the Gracious Speech. The Prime Minister, Leader of the Opposition and MPs crowd in at the bar of the chamber, right underneath the press box. You can watch them on the TV monitor bracketed to the side of the chamber. The speech is usually delivered in around fifteen minutes and then the royal party leaves the chamber.

Adding colour to the state opening?

Again the answer is to look for the quirky and unusual. The famous guests are ones to watch out for, then the clothes and the reactions to the Queen's announcements. In 1981, Prince Charles attended with Princess Diana. They sat on mini thrones at the side of the Queen. It was the first time for decades that the Prince and Princess of Wales had been with the monarch at the State Opening. Of course it was front page news and a gift to the sketch writers. Poor Diana came in for criticism because she had tied her hair into a French pleat.

She was also looking very pale. The real story came out the very next day when Buckingham Palace announced she was pregnant. Choosing what to write that day was no problem.

When the Queen unveiled Labour's plans to ban fox hunting, a loud groan went round the Lords chamber, similarly when she announced the axing of hereditary peers there were audible gasps from the peers. One year the Lord Chancellor nearly fell over backwards while trying to get down the steps to the throne after handing the Queen the Gracious Speech. After that he was given permission to turn his back on the monarch.

It's just a matter of watching every move from the press gallery and catching the sights and sounds that elude the TV cameras.

Amanda Brown is a former Press Association political correspondent.

11: Reporting Whitehall

Colin Brown

Whitehall – get close and then stand back

There are two principal sources for information in Whitehall – apart from leaky ministers – and it is important to know the difference between them.

First, the SpAds, the ministerial Special Advisers, party political creatures by nature. Then there are the government press officers who remain in office serving their ministers whoever is in power.

During the Blair government, Alastair Campbell came to represent almost everything that was supposed to be bad about Whitehall. He was assumed to be the model for Malcolm Tucker, the bullying paranoid No. 10 madman in *The Thick of It*, the wonderful television series about the SpAds where drama parodied real life. Or was it the other way around?

In fact, the SpAds are the most valuable contacts for political reporters based at Westminster. Take, for example, the briefing in the run up to the coalition government's Comprehensive Spending Review in the autumn of 2010. Whitehall press officers are strictly forbidden to brief on announcements which have yet to be made to Parliament. On the Friday of the week preceding the cuts announcement by George Osborne, the Chancellor, the SpAds were called to a Whitehall briefing to coordinate the advance briefing exercise for the weekend press and broadcasters.

Sunday newspapers had lots of speculation about defence cuts, transport cuts, and benefit cuts, but they were given the details of one clear story, briefed by a SpAd: there would be a crackdown on welfare benefit fraud. As a result, the Sunday newspapers all ran stories which were remarkably similar. *The Mail on Sunday* splashed with the headline: 'Three Strikes And You Are Off Benefits'.

It enabled the Sunday papers to report the cuts story with some confidence, while giving the government a relatively positive start to the week with a move which, though controversial, was likely to be popular, and was in fact a very small part of the cuts narrative.

The SpAds operate like cleaner fish on sharks. They try to avoid the government facing wildly inaccurate speculation. They also try to protect the sharks – the lobby journalists – from looking completely foolish. That symbiotic relationship is wide open to criticism, but it is a fact of Whitehall life. And if it did not exist, somebody would have to invent the SpAds, because they do the 'dirty' work, rather than the Whitehall departmental press officers.

SpAds are employed as civil servants on a short contract, most with salaries of £60–70,000 and they leave office when their ministers resign, get sacked, or lose their jobs after a general election. They usually move with their ministers across Whitehall if the ministers are promoted or demoted, and good ones tend to stay in Whitehall for years. Their main role, as far as ministers are concerned, is to put the best gloss on their policies, which is often taken as a licence to 'spin'. This should not be confused with a licence to leak, though the dividing line is often blurred, as with the 'cuts' briefing above.

Whose side are they on?

They are covered by a code of conduct which is available through the Cabinet Office website. It makes it clear that they have more licence to brief journalists on party political issues than Whitehall departmental press officers. It also contains a warning for special advisers to remember that they are part of a wider government. This is to avoid the danger of a SpAd becoming so close to a minister that he or she will brief against other ministers to protect their own.

It says: 'Special advisers are employed to help ministers on matters where the work of government and the work of the government party overlap and where it would be inappropriate for permanent civil servants to become involved. They are appointed to serve the government as a whole and not just their appointing minister...'

This goes to the heart of the troubles between the rival camps supporting Gordon Brown and Tony Blair in Labour's third term of office. And the fact that the war between the two camps could never be quelled underlines the difficulty of preventing it from happening. Not that journalists as observers should be bothered by that. Indeed, when it happens, and it is more likely to happen in a coalition of opposing parties than even in New Labour, it produces a fund of stories from the SpAds.

According to the code, the duties of the SpAds bizarrely include what it calls 'devilling' for the minister, checking facts and research findings from a party political viewpoint; speech writing and related research, including adding party political content to material prepared by permanent civil servants. Although the SpAds are paid for by the taxpayer, including those who voted for another party, the code specifically allows the SpAds to represent the views of their minister to the media including a party viewpoint, where they have been authorised by the minister to do so.

There was criticism particularly in the Blair era about the burgeoning numbers of special advisers hired to operate inside Whitehall after Labour came to power in 1997. Gordon Brown gave a written answer in 2007 saying there were then sixty-eight special advisers across Whitehall, costing the taxpayer a total of £5.9 million.

The code warns:

> Special advisers should conduct themselves with integrity and honesty. They should not deceive or knowingly mislead Parliament or the public...The highest standards of conduct are expected of special advisers and, specifically, the preparation or dissemination of inappropriate material or personal attacks has no part to play in the job of being a special adviser as it has no part to play in the conduct of public life. Any special adviser ever found to be disseminating inappropriate material will automatically be dismissed by their appointing minister.

A SpAd who gains a reputation for lying is no longer capable of doing the job. But that does not stop them dissembling, when they feel the need to. Journalists coming into Westminster for the first time need to understand that language suddenly takes on a precise meaning. You have to be wary of every little let-out clause, every concealed truth, wrapped up in jargon. SpAds practice the same disingenuous language as their political masters, the ministers. So for example, if a SpAd says 'we have no plans to put up taxes', you should count your change. He is NOT ruling out tax increases.

When your contacts pay off

SpAds may be drawn from the ranks of journalists operating in Westminster and may be counted among a journalist's friends. Alastair Campbell was the political editor of the *Daily Mirror* before being appointed as Tony Blair's Director of Communications at No. 10. He and I had shared many a late night story, gone on foreign trips together and even played in the same Commons football team.

Such long-standing contacts really pay off. When I was the political editor of the *Independent on Sunday,* I was in the Canary Wharf office of the newspaper one dull Friday morning, wondering what on earth I was going to do for a lead story that weekend. Campbell called me at about 10.30am out of the blue:

'You know that interview you asked for with the Prime Minister?' he asked.

I had forgotten a letter I had written the year before asking for the interview but went along with it. 'Yes,' I lied.

'Well, the good news is you've got it. The bad news is that it's in Dublin. And you've got to be there for 1pm. And I don't think I can get you a flight.'

I rightly assumed Alastair had got his Downing Street secretary to check flights to Dublin from Heathrow, forgetting there were flights from London City Airport, a few minutes from Canary Wharf. If there was a flight that morning, I just might do it. In fact, I got to Dublin with thirty minutes to spare. A car was waiting on the tarmac in Dublin and we raced over to a small airport across the outskirts of the city, where the Prime Minister's jet, a small BAe 146 from the Queen's Flight, was waiting.

After Blair stepped on board, we got down to the interview pretty smartly – the flight back was barely an hour and I had to get my story before we landed. I still did not know why I had been summoned until, in the middle of the flight, the Prime Minister got onto the subject of health, and volunteered the fact that he wanted to increase national insurance contributions by 1 per cent in order to fund a huge increase in spending on the National Health Service.

I got off the plane and telephoned the office with a scoop that would not only beat the competition hollow, but would also dominate politics for months to come. I did not stop to think about the wider picture. At a time like that, you do not look the proverbial gift horse in the mouth, but the nagging question was: 'Why is he telling me this?' Followed quickly by 'And why me?'

The answer to the first question I learned later was that Blair wanted to get one over on Brown. He wanted to make sure he got the credit for increasing the spending on the NHS rather than his Chancellor. I assume the answer to the second was that I could be trusted as a result of my long contacts with Campbell. It is possible also they wanted me to report the story straight, as a big announcement about the NHS, rather than for it to backfire and to be turned into a 'tax increase' story.

Used or abused?

The question that this poses is whether I was used. The answer of course is 'yes', but I would say in mitigation, I had an outstanding scoop that all my competitors in the lobby would have dearly loved to get. And in the event I used Campbell just as much as he used me.

As a political journalist, you have to be constantly aware that in Whitehall most information can be like *Alice Through the Looking Glass*: not always what it seems. 'Get close and then step back' is a standard journalistic approach to contacts that works in Whitehall as well as anywhere else. You have to build trust with your contacts. 'Hug them close' if you wish, but you must remember you have to remain objective and step back when it comes to producing the stories that count.

Campbell resigned when he decided that he had 'become the story' during Blair's decline in popularity. The story of 'spin' – media manipulation – from Downing Street had become so all-pervasive in British politics that Campbell's departure was supposed to clear the air in Whitehall.

But the coverage of Labour's SpAds actually got worse after Gordon Brown replaced Blair. Miles of column inches were spent criticising the SpAds in Whitehall after emails from Damian McBride, Brown's key media 'attack dog' in No. 10, suggesting lines of attack on Tory politicians were leaked.

SpAds got a bad name, and for a time became the targets for journalists who were quite prepared to bite the hand that fed them. But the cadre of SpAds remain, even in the Conservative–Lib Dem coalition government.

Ministers became increasingly elusive around the Commons when Labour first came to power. They were under orders by Campbell not to go through the members' lobby where they could be caught by lobby journalists hanging around outside the doors to the chamber where they may let slip some story over which Downing Street would not have control. Downing Street used the SpAds as part of their mechanism for controlling the press and the broadcasters. SpAds became the first point of contact when a lobby journalist wished to speak to a minister, for while you may have a minister's mobile phone number or even a home number, getting them to answer the call is another matter. Many times at weekends, when they are at home, their partner answers and says: 'He's just gone to take the dog for a walk…'

Late night calls are a particular problem. The first editions 'drop' on newsdesks around 10.15pm, and if there is anything that needs following up, the political correspondent has to check it out with the minister. Getting the minister late at night to check out a story may prove impossible. The SpAd can prove invaluable in these circumstances.

Of course, they can give you the 'spin', by attempting to put the best gloss on a negative, story which is usually easy to see. They would be very foolish to lie, and most of them do not. But that does not mean they tell you the whole truth either.

As a result, the SpAds' mobile telephone numbers are as jealously guarded as the ministers' in the contact books of most political correspondents.

Every minister has at least one SpAd and possibly two, one for media relations – that is, talking to the press – and the other to advise on policy. It is rare for the policy specialists to have direct contact with the press. A cynic might presume this is because they may be tempted to tell you the downside of a policy as well as the positive aspects, but there are usually plenty of other people around who will give you a negative response once the story is breaking.

Political spinning

The SpAds are important in the news gathering techniques for a political correspondent because they are licensed to brief the journalists on political aspects of a story. SpAds are not officially authorised to leak stories, particularly about the announcements that should be made first to Parliament. MPs are constantly complaining about the media being informed before the Commons about announcements, and ministers can be called to the House by the Speaker if this happens.

But it is rare for a minister to decide to make a big announcement without some advance briefing to prepare the ground for a new policy, or a shift in direction. The briefing is normally in the most general terms, leaving the journalists to interpret it, but it usually comes from the SpAds or the ministers themselves.

SpAds will remain a necessary part of Whitehall, whoever is in power.

'Civil service' press officers

Information or Whitehall press officers can be just as important, but they are completely different to the SpAds. They are career civil servants, not political 'spinners' and are not authorised to brief from a party political point of view.

Their job, very strictly, is to provide information that is in the public domain.

Political correspondents are Jacks of all trades, and therefore usually not specialists in any one policy area – although some have expertise in, say, health, or defence, or economics. The Whitehall press officers are a vital source of factual information to fill the gaps in the specialist policy knowledge of political reporters. They are specifically not allowed to indulge in political briefing or spinning (though some may try) and should tell a journalist who is asking political questions – such as 'Will the Chancellor agree to this when it goes to Cabinet?' – to speak to the Special Adviser.

They are an invaluable source of information for specialist journalists who may be in daily contact with press officers in busy departments covering their patch. They also handle media 'bids' for ministers, because they have the diaries for their ministers and are authorised to negotiate for media exposure for ministers, for example through on-the-record interviews. They are also likely to travel with ministers, unless they are on party political business, along with the SpAds, to such things as factory or hospital visits. They put out press releases for ministers, rather than SpAds.

Who gives the orders

The code of conduct for SpAd also addresses the potential conflict that can arise when a press officer is ordered to do something by a SpAd. The code says SpAds may 'convey to officials ministers' views and work priorities, including on issues of presentation'.

But the code also forbids some of the excesses you may have seen in *The Thick of It*. Malcolm Tucker is not allowed to bully the press officers under the code of conduct. It says SpAds may not:

> ask civil servants to do anything which is inconsistent with their obligations under the *Civil Service Code*; behave towards permanent civil servants in a way which would be inconsistent with the standards set by the employing department for conduct generally; or suppress or supplant the advice being prepared for ministers by permanent civil servants although they may comment on such advice.

Whitehall departments have large press office teams to handle calls from the regional press and broadcasters, in addition to the national media. Often they are arranged like news rooms with specialists for particular areas of expertise, such as shadowing the Secretary of State and junior ministers, as the health department does, or particular parts of the world as the Foreign Office press office is arranged.

These press offices arrange a rota for duty officers to deal with media enquiries out of hours, although their help is often limited. So whether dealing with SpAds or press officers, it is good, long-standing contacts that make all the difference.

And don't forget the permanent secretaries. These are the great panjandrums, the Sir Humphreys of Whitehall, who run their departments like princes in the days of the Raj and treat most journalists as 'the enemy'. They have a close network of their own, and if you can break into it, you can really find out what is going on in Whitehall. But be warned: it's a rarified air they breathe, and not many are allowed into their circle. Still, the novelty of being invited out to lunch by a simple hack might appeal. Try it. But don't tell your friends.

Note: As career civil servants, press officers are under the Central Office of Information which publishes a directory of the telephone numbers for the press officers of all the main Whitehall departments and all the key public bodies including the Bank of England. It is called The White Book *and is available for a fee from the COI at PO Box 2004, Burgess Hill, West Sussex RH15 8WU or online at www.coi.gov.uk/twb*

Colin Brown has been a lobby journalist for over thirty years. He has worked for The Guardian *and was a founder member of* The Independent, *later becoming political editor of the* Independent on Sunday *and then the* Sunday Telegraph. *His books include* Whitehall – the Street that Shaped a Nation *and* Fighting Talk, *the biography of John Prescott.*

Part III:

Dealing with the political classes

12. Working with honourable members and peers

Sheila Gunn

Life on the backbenches

Much of the time, journalists will be working with parliamentarians to scrutinise what ministers are doing: their decisions, policies, spending and what they say. At other times, the media will be questioning and, hopefully, exposing the less honourable actions of those MPs and peers.

Who are they?

The majority of MPs in any parliament are backbenchers. That is, they are not ministers, frontbench spokesmen for the opposition parties or whips. Little is understood of what these creatures, prowling around the Palace of Westminster looking purposeful, actually do. If they are not in positions of power, how do they exert influence? Do they merely obey their party whips? Certainly, the whips would like this to be true.

Being an MP is one of those rare jobs which requires no qualifications and for which there is no formal job description. The Commons select committee on the Modernisation of the House strived for some years to identify and strengthen the roles of backbenchers, with limited success. It summarised the roles of backbenchers as:

> Supporting their party
> Representing and furthering the interests of their constituencies and individual constituents

Scrutinising and holding the government to account
Initiating, reviewing and amending legislation
Contributing to the development of policy
Most MPs come into the House with experience or particular interest in specific issues, such as the trade unions, armed forces or business.

In a survey of the 2005 intake by the Hansard Society, MPs said they divided their time:

49 per cent on constituency work
14 per cent in the chamber
14 per cent in committees
22 per cent other.

However it is alarming to hear new members quietly admit that they had little idea of what the job entailed when they set out to become parliamentary candidates. One innovation after the 2010 general election, which has won praise from both new and sitting members, was an induction week, with the new MPs given guidance on the different parliamentary processes and how to use them.

But it can be seen that the different roles involve conflicts of interest. What if your party requires you to vote for a policy which will damage your constituency? What if your in-depth knowledge of a subject makes you question your party's policy?

Working with MPs

While MPs may be expected to obey their party whips, they will be encouraged to use the plethora of ways available to press the concerns of their constituents, challenge opponents, and if they are in opposition, scrutinise the government.

These tools involve a system of question times, motions, debates, statements, legislation and committees. In using them, MPs will try to attract the interest of relevant journalists, especially those covering their constituencies.

Ideally – as Chris Moncrieff makes clear in his contributions

– MPs and journalists should develop a symbiotic relationship. That does not mean that journalists should neglect their role of monitoring and scrutinising the MPs themselves. There will be plenty of times when one has developed a good working relationship with an MP, and then reports negatively on that MP's words or actions. Do not expect him or her to always understand your role. Many MPs who were 'exposed' in the expenses scandal were extremely upset at stories by journalists who they had regarded as 'friendly', especially in their local press.

Ways for MPs to make a difference

There are a range of parliamentary mechanisms which MPs can use to fulfil their roles of scrutinising government policy, representing their constituents, influencing or changing the law, promoting policy ideas and campaigning on specific issues.

Oral questions

From Mondays to Thursdays when the Commons is sitting, the first part of business is usually question time. This is traditionally chaired by the Speaker and control of it and the selection of MPs to ask questions is one of his or her main functions.

The best known session is PMQs – Prime Minister's question time, the 30-minutes on a Wednesday when MPs question the PM. It is usually the most high profile part of the parliamentary week with the chamber full to bursting point. The weekly exchanges between the PM and the Leader of the Opposition are minutely scrutinised with the Leader of the Opposition entitled to ask up to six questions. It is open to criticism for the yaboo, gladiatorial atmosphere. But few if any leader of any other country faces such regular and relentless questioning on any subject from his or her opponents.

The Order Paper sets out the questions, although only a limited number are reached within the time allowed. For PMQs, most of the questions are 'open', i.e. not on a specific issue, which allows MPs to ask anything they like. But it is also a good opportunity to raise a constituency or campaign issue.

During the thirty minutes, MPs will pop up and down like a jack-in-a-box, trying to catch the Speaker's eye. He selects some to ask supplementary questions of the PM according to a range of criteria: political balance, so that MPs of different parties, including the smaller ones, have a chance; because he knows that certain MPs have specific constituency issues, such as the proposed closure of a local factory; or he may pick a few with particular expertise, perhaps a former minister or select committee member, on the issue raised.

Although most of these MPs are called 'Honourable Members', some are also 'Right Honourable Members', which means they are members of the Privy Council – an honour conferred on certain senior MPs. The Speaker has traditionally given the Rt Hons some preferential treatment, although the present Speaker, John Bercow, appears to have dropped this practice.

Apart from the knockabout of PMQs, there are regular question times to ministers for each of the government departments. For example, about every six weeks Home Office ministers will come to the chamber where MPs can question them on all issues affecting their responsibility for up to one hour. It is the same with other government departments.

MPs table their questions beforehand, so ministers and their officials have some time to prepare their answers. In practice, an MP should be able to phrase his or her question in such a way as to cover almost any subject. Specialist journalists should be able to extract stories from these sessions. Not many political journalists bother to attend these days, unless a minister or a department are facing particular problems. But good ones will keep an eye on the performance of certain ministers and even backbench MPs to help them gauge how well or otherwise they are doing.

Each department will send a couple of press officers to sit in the press gallery to answer journalists' questions during and after these sessions. Or, if you are watching on TV, you can ring up the press office for explanations, comment or interview requests.

In addition to the rotation of questions to ministers from particular government departments, there is business question time. This slot occurs every Thursday when the Leader of the House reads out the 'forthcoming business', which is the agenda for the Commons in the following week. MPs, particularly from opposition parties, use this opportunity to argue why the business should be changed to allow debate on other specific issues. While this may not sound very interesting, it is a chance for MPs to challenge and criticise the government of the day on various policies and actions.

Written answers

Most of the questions on the Order Paper, which sets out the day's business in the House, will not be reached during these sessions. But the department will issue a written answer to it later in the day. These will appear on the table outside the press gallery and also in Hansard. In addition, MPs will table written questions to try to draw out information from ministers.

Thousands of these questions and answers come out every session and good contacts may tip you off on 'interesting' ones, although a certain diligence is needed in scanning through them. This is worthwhile as they are the source of many reasonable stories, provide good ideas for news features and interviews and throw up the odd gem. Colin Brown, who was then on *The Independent,* and I, totally independently, once discovered mention of some highly dubious export licences for Iraq in Appendix G of a long written answer. I vaguely remember a ministerial press officer trying to argue that, perhaps, the mortar launching equipment was destined for pigeon shooting.

One of the problems of question time is that questions have to be tabled days or weeks beforehand. In recent years an innovation has been introduced to allow for MPs to ask 'topical questions' for a short time at the end of the usual question time. This helps both MPs and journalists as it allows relevant ministers to be quizzed about issues in the news.

Urgent questions, formerly called private notice questions (the acronym PNQs was often confused with PMQs), are an important opportunity for MPs to question a minister about an issue seriously affecting their constituency. An MP must apply to the Speaker's Office with a request to ask the relevant question that day. It is up to the Speaker to decide whether to grant it, but he will also inform the relevant Minister who would have to respond to it. As it takes time from the scheduled business, many MPs are not successful. But MPs who do succeed, for instance if there is sudden and extensive flooding in their constituency, generally attract a great deal of media coverage as this may be the first time a minister has been forced to explain what actions are being taken. Parliament's main website carries an excellent factsheet on the different forms of questions.

Early Day Motions (EDMs)

Another growth industry is EDMs. They provide MPs with an opportunity to put on record their views or support for a particular issue and gain support from colleagues. In other words, they are a form of petition. Although they call for an early debate on the issue, in practice this does not happen. But they are important for journalists for various reasons. Firstly, they provide stories which may start something like '…MP today condemned the government's decision to…' or '…MP demanded urgent action on…' MPs themselves also use them for publicity, especially in their local media.

The issues involved can, quite literally, be anything. It is well worthwhile checking the EDM database on the parliament website to gain a flavour of their variety. They could be about the success of Shipston-on-Stour football team, the rising cost of underwear, job losses at the Whittington hospital, human rights in Rwanda, domestic abuse services in Bassetlaw or responsible dog ownership. All are of interest to journalists somewhere in the world.

An MP will table an EDM and hawk it around colleagues, asking them to add their signatures to it. Please be a little wary. Whereas both MPs and journalists find them useful, do not be fooled into thinking they make much of an impact with the government.

They are also seen as a litmus test of how unhappy or happy MPs feel about a specific issue. If, for instance, a large number of MPs sign one questioning their own party's policy on an issue, this is an indication – and a story – about the depth of dissent. For instance the number and names on an EDM expressing concern about the then threatened invasion of Iraq in 2003 revealed the strength of opposition and where it was coming from. Indeed, they put an MP's views on the record which, of course, may one day come back to haunt them.

Debates

Backbench MPs have plenty of opportunity to ask questions and make comments during various forms of debate. Some are of quite a general nature, such as debates on the Queen's Speech, when a day's business may be devoted to debating education and health services. Political journalists take little notice of these contributions unless they scent a potential revolt or perhaps something a little quirky. But it is not a good idea to ignore them totally. If, for instance, you were writing about student fees, you could look up who said what during a debate and contact a relevant MP. After mentioning his or her contribution you can ask some questions. Most MPs are quite pathetically impressed that anyone, apart from family members, has heard a word they say, and so they are very likely to help.

Adjournment and Westminster Hall debates

There are two types of debate which can provide useful material, particularly for specialist and local journalists. These are adjournment debates and their newer siblings, Westminster Hall debates.

The last thirty minutes of each day's sitting of the Commons is devoted to an adjournment debate. A backbench MP will stand up, make points and ask questions on a particular issue. A minister, usually a fairly junior one, will then stand up and argue for the government's policy, answering the key points. After precisely thirty minutes, the person in the chair (usually one of the deputy Speakers) will call 'order, order' and the House is adjourned, that is, finished for the day.

No one can pretend this is the most exciting spectacle in politics. The chamber will be virtually empty apart from the MP and minister concerned, a couple of whips and maybe one or two MPs with an interest in the subject under discussion. Nor are the subjects likely to set the pulse of a political journalist racing. Forthcoming adjournment debates, fairly typical of the genre, cover unscrupulous lenders, pre- and post-16 benefit entitlements for the disabled, educational maintenance allowances in Walsall North, and the future of careers advice services.

But there will be journalists, either specialists or perhaps those working on features on the issues concerned, for whom they will provide useful material and contacts. Perhaps not on that day, but it is certainly worth doing a trawl of Hansard to see which MPs have raised these issues and what a minister has said in reply. And the minister must reply. As former minister Chris Mullin's excellent book *A View from the Foothills* stresses, most of these replies are drafted in some sort of civil service gobbledygook by a junior official. However, since it enunciates the government's official position, the words can be thrown back at a minister at a future point during an interview. By trawling such parliamentary business, it is also possible to identify which MPs have a particular interest in certain subjects. This is very useful when looking for MPs to be interviewed.

Another problem with adjournment debates is their timing. While they take up the last half an hour of business, there is no certainty when they will start. Often one might predict that the MP will stand up at 9.30pm only to find that other business has overrun, adding another hour or three to that day's proceedings. Nevertheless, Hansard does an excellent job of turning out the words spoken in the chamber as quickly as possible if you have missed the debate via the specialist TV sources.

Westminster Hall debates are another form of adjournment debate introduced under the Blair government and modelled on the Australian system for extending the rights of backbenchers to debate and question ministers on specific issues. These debates usually take place on Tuesdays, Wednesdays and Thursdays and are chaired by a deputy Speaker or approved Chairman.

Confusingly, they are not held in Westminster Hall, but in the Grand Committee Room, which is accessed up a staircase off the ancient Hall. For journalists, they are easily accessible, particularly as the Hall is near the entry point after passing through the main security entrance. Nor, like adjournment debates, are they crowded events. But it would be still unwise to ignore them, either as a source for immediate stories on specific issues or for material for interviews or features.

Some are limited to thirty minutes, but most last for one and a half hours in which various MPs interested in a subject can make points and ask questions of the middle-ranking or junior minister. Subjects on a fairly typical day's agenda, which give a flavour of the scope and diversity of the debates, could be community cohesion, affordable rural housing, York's application for World Heritage status, prisoner transfer agreement with Libya, and regeneration in Tottenham.

MPs and their aides use their speeches and responses to generate media coverage, particularly in their constituencies.

Statements

A couple of times a week when parliament is in session there will be statements. Nearly all are given by ministers who willingly or unwillingly come to the chamber to report on some policy, issue or event. There is often little warning that a statement will be 'taken' but they usually but not always occur after question time. In many cases ministers will ask to make a statement, but they may be forced to come to the House because of a sudden or dramatic event. When the PM has attended an important international event or EU summit, he will usually make a statement on the results on his return.

After the PM or minister has made a statement, the Leader of the Opposition or shadow minister will respond. Then other MPs have the chance to question the minister concerned. The time taken depends on the importance of the statement and the strength of the reaction to it, but typically they will take around forty-five minutes. These are another opportunity for backbench MPs to catch the eye of the Speaker or deputy Speaker to make their points or ask questions.

Personal statements

These statements usually follow the resignation or sacking of a senior minister and, in these circumstances can be some of the most dramatic events in Parliament. Those that are part of history include statements of resignation made by Geoffrey Howe in Margaret Thatcher's premiership, Norman Lamont when John Major was Prime Minister, David Blunkett and Robin Cook during Tony Blair's premiership.

The convention is that they are heard in almost total silence and there is no formal reaction to them. For these reasons alone, there is a dramatic almost theatrical atmosphere in the House.

Private Member's Bills

Backbench MPs can help influence government Bills through taking part in the debates, tabling amendments and asking questions through the Bill's passage. But when a government has a workable overall majority, the scope for changing key principles of such legislation is very limited.

However any MP or peer can introduce a Bill of their own. These Private Member's Bills (PMBs) are public bills, like government Bills, and go through much the same procedures in both Houses. It is easy to dismiss these Bills as irrelevant and having little impact because few – usually two or three – become law in any one year, although seven succeeded in the 2009/10 session. For both individual MPs and for journalists, this would be a mistake. They can be used as part of a campaign to persuade the government of the day to change the law; they can highlight an MP's specific concerns and experience; or they may introduce a small but worthwhile change in the law. Sometimes ministers will see what support or opposition a PMB is attracting before deciding whether or not to 'adopt' it or introducing their own government Bill.

The parliament website has an interesting factsheet on the success of PMBs which goes back to 1949 when a Bill was passed banning the docking of horses' tails. In the 2009/10 session, for example, Bills to regulate sun beds and to designate an annual Anti-Slavery Day both made it onto the statute book.

In 1967 the then Liberal MP David Steel succeeded with his Bill to liberalise the abortion laws, which has made him a target for anti-abortionists ever since. And the long, drawn-out campaign in Parliament on banning fox hunting started as a PMB.

Strange as it may seem now, but in her first few months as MP, Margaret Thatcher introduced a Bill to force councils to open their meetings to the press and public. At the time, some Labour-controlled councils in big cities had banned journalists from committee meetings. Her Bill did not succeed, although it led to a change in the law later. It gave her a platform and a profile almost unheard of for a new MP, winning her support from newspaper editors and proprietors and helped her develop friendships with senior figures, such as Keith Joseph, who became so influential in her career.

MPs are free to 'present' a PMB at almost any time. Apart from occasionally provoking some media interest, they usually sink without trace. MPs can introduce a Bill via the Ten Minute Rule Bill or Motion. This takes place around twice a week and involves the MP making a speech of up to ten minutes, calling for a certain change in the law. Again, the Bill goes no further, but they can, more often than not, generate stories. They are most likely to be an issue of particular concern in their constituency or as part of a campaign.

The ones most likely to become law are introduced via the Ballot procedure when interested MPs enter their names in a sort of raffle and those who come top are given time on a Friday to introduce and campaign for their Bills. It only takes objections from a single MP to effectively kill off such Bills, but the chamber is usually fairly empty and many MPs do not want to be seen to object to quite innocent and worthwhile causes.

If a PMB makes it through the Commons, like other Public Bills, they must navigate the similar passage through the Lords. The MP has to find a friendly peer to take over his Bill. Conversely, some peers introduce their own Bills. If one makes it through the Lords, which has a more relaxed system, the peer needs to find an MP to promote it in the Commons. The obstacles are daunting, yet MPs often say that they found it one of their most satisfying experiences in Parliament. It could also have brought them to the attention of their own party leaders and whips who may mark them down as 'someone to watch', hopefully for good reasons.

All-party groups

For a journalist wanting to identify MPs and peers interested in a specific subject, all-party groups are useful. There are two types: subject based – ranging alphabetically from Abuse Investigations to Zoos and country by country – from Afghanistan to Zimbabwe. They vary in size from two or three parliamentarians to a couple of dozen.

These groups do not do anything highly significant, except arrange some meetings, briefings or receptions. A register of them all is accessible on the parliamentary website.

Working with peers

To describe the House of Lords as egalitarian may not be accurate. But oddly, once there, the difference in backgrounds between the peers is virtually irrelevant and they are far more approachable than generally perceived. If you forget to call a knighted MP 'Sir', they are likely to pick you up on it. Yet a peer will more often introduce themselves as 'John Smith' rather than 'Lord Smith' and ignore any difficulties in grappling with the different forms of address. But, to be on the safe side, just call the men 'Lords' and the women 'Ladies' and you should be safe.

If you are writing a specific feature, it is always worth checking whether it has been debated or investigated in the Lords, as you could find some valuable material.

The Upper House does not have the same ministerial questions system; adjournment or Westminster Hall debates, or EDMs. Instead sittings start with four questions on any subject under the sun. Statements made in the Commons are usually repeated in the Lords, usually a little later – and are certainly worth accessing if certain peers are known to be outspoken or controversial. It spends most of its time revising legislation, interspersed with debates.

Conclusions

For journalists, all the above 'tools' are useful, for all contain potential stories, all can help identify and build up contacts, all are useful for identifying the views and specific interests of MPs and peers. In addition all are covered by parliamentary privilege, meaning that a journalist can repeat any of the spoken or written words without fear of prosecution.

One of the most satisfying aspects of journalism is the scope for running a campaign to try to change a policy or a law. The above could also provide valuable material and contacts to help you.

13: Reporting the less honourable members

Andrew Pierce

It was the eminent American journalist I. F. Stone who defined the terms of reference for any aspiring political journalist. He said: 'All governments are run by liars and no one should believe a word they say.'

Forgive me for introducing Tony Blair into this chapter after such a sweeping and damning generalisation about politicians. But it is undeniable that Tony Blair entered 10 Downing Street in May 1997 buoyed by a huge wave of public goodwill after his landslide election victory over John Major. But ten years later when he left, his reputation was in tatters having been accused of one of the gravest lies of all: his reasons for taking his country into war with Iraq in 2003.

Having started at Westminster in 1988 in the press gallery reporting debates for *The Times*, I can recall the young and highly ambitious Tony Blair. He bounced about like Tigger always with one eye locked on the press gallery. He was always destined for great things. But I can equally remember realising very soon after he became Prime Minister that Blair's relationship with the truth was, to put it mildly, flexible. And it came about in the time honoured way that journalists have secured their best scoops – through their contacts. It's often a discreet telephone call to or from the mole. Maybe a quiet word in your ear in a Commons corridor or, more likely these days, in Portcullis House – the busiest, most public, but most gossip laden building in the entire Westminster estate.

Of course, let's not forget a drink or seven in one of the many bars around the Palace of Westminster. Remember to make several exits to the WC to jot down your notes before the alcoholic haze takes over completely.

The devil is in the detail

If you are covering town hall and county councils, force yourself to read every single council document. The stories are often buried in the detail. Do not be deterred by the deliberately obtuse language. The press officers – they never existed when I started on local papers – are a good source. But the officers and councillors, who are always riven by personal ambition, are the ones to target. Try a charm offensive. Lunch. Breakfast. A drink. Telephone them all the time not just when you are desperate for a page lead or splash. Politicians love to be made to feel important even if they are not.

If you are at Westminster go through those written answers which are spewed out every day. And the questions. Don't be deceived by appearances. And always, always read Hansard. It's a treasure trove of stories.

When Blair became PM in May 1997 he did so with strong backing from a public who were tired of the sleazy Tories who had been in power too long. My eyes were opened to Blair on the front page of the *Sunday Telegraph*, which reported in August 1997 that the government had mysteriously excluded Formula One racing from the ban on cigarette sponsorship – after a donation had been made to the Labour Party by the racing chief Bernie Ecclestone. Little Bernie, the big man of racing, had been a visitor at 10 Downing Street, unrelated of course to the donation.

The *Sunday Telegraph* had no idea how big the donation was but it set hares running. By good fortune I was on duty that Sunday for my then newspaper *The Times*. I telephoned my best snouts in the trough of knowledge. I got lucky. One was pretty close to the whole sorry saga. I wrote on the next day's front page of *The Times* that the donation from Ecclestone was £1.75 million while others suggested it might be a six figure sum. The figure was brutally dismissed as fanciful and fictitious at No. 10 briefings by the PM's official spokesman even though it was a Labour Party matter and therefore should have been handled only by party apparatchiks. But the blurring between civil service and party political matters by the end of Blair's reign meant that no one even bothered to point out the separation that had been faithfully observed by the previous Tory administration. In the end, under pressure, Downing Street was forced to admit by the end of the day that the donation was £1 million. It was a lie.

I returned to my contact who was able to fill in the blanks. The next day when everyone else was saying Ecclestone paid £1 million I wrote that a further £1 million was in the post – so the total sum was £2 million. Far from exaggerating the figure, I had in fact underestimated it. Blair, our telegenic new Prime Minister, knew the details but permitted denials and obfuscation in his name to try to conceal them. It confirmed my view that Mr I. F. Stone had a point.

Less honourable tactics

It was the thriller writer Michael Dobbs, in his best-seller *House of Cards*, who so brilliantly lifted the lid on some of the amoral and manipulative schemings by MPs. Dobbs was a deputy chairman of the Conservative Party under Margaret Thatcher in the 1980s. From that period he created the fictional Conservative Chief Whip Francis Urquhart, the entire concept coming from the initials F.U. It followed his route to the top of his governing party with the odd murder thrown in.

Ironically, when Dodds first proposed a work of fiction based on his experiences at Westminster the publishers suggested his script was too far-fetched! Yet while Urquhart was a parody there is no doubt that all political journalists should be armed with a cynic's view when it comes to the outpourings of politicians. A famous trick is of course to examine what an MP says in Westminster and what they do or say in their constituency. It's a variation on the saying: 'Do what I say, not what I do.'

Take Sadiq Khan, the shadow Justice Secretary who ran Ed Miliband's successful campaign to be Labour leader. In 2008 he dutifully and loyally voted for Labour Party policy in favour of post office closures in a Commons division at 7pm – just one hour later he was in his south London constituency speaking against them. Hansard is online within hours these days so he did not get away with the ruse. It would have looked appalling in his constituency but it's hardly a resigning matter. MPs have always tried to please two masters – their party whips who decide their promotion prospects and their constituents who decide whether to issue them with a P45.

Following the money

During the 2005 general election I wrote a front page splash in *The Times* which asserted that the Tories had taken multi-million pound loans from rich benefactors, often with an interest rate barely above the base rate and therefore not obtainable in the market place which they profess to love. This meant the benefactors could avoid the disclosure rules on all donations above £5,000.

The information was buried in the Tory accounts which showed the number of outstanding loans had soared by millions. The stories are always mired in the detail. The Budgets always unravel when financial hacks go through the Red Book, line by forensic line, and find the hidden tax rises and spending cuts. It's painstaking but fruitful. The Tories' accounts looked healthy but there was no explanation for the number of loans that were outstanding.

Tory HQ said it was commercially sensitive and to clear off. But it wasn't commercially sensitive; it was politically sensitive. Not all Tories approved of the way business was being conducted. And all political secrets leak. Even though I had clearly stumbled over a new system of political funding not a word of criticism came from Labour or the Lib Dems.

The following year I discovered why, when the *Sunday Times* exposed that a series of Labour peerages had been blocked. This was because of objections to some of the businessmen who had also made a series of secret loans, which had not been declared to the authorities, to circumvent the same rules on transparency the Tories had exploited.

The Lib Dems had done the same. Hence the radio silence when the Tories were in the dock. The 'Cash for Honours' row inflicted huge damage on Blair's personal standing and integrity as he made clear in his memoirs, *A Journey*.

Yet ironically, Labour had swept into power being whiter than white. It was an easy boast to make. Just before the 1997 general election John Major's Conservatives – who were well past their sell-by-date after eighteen years in power – were on the rack over sleaze.

The boss of Harrods, Mohamed Al Fayed, had made a series of allegations that he had paid Tory MPs, albeit nonentities, cash in brown envelopes in return for them asking parliamentary questions in clear breach of the rules. (Please note that it is details such as the 'brown' envelopes which can make such a difference to a story.)

A number had been called to give evidence *in camera* to Sir Gordon Downey, the then parliamentary commissioner for standards. The report was sealed and was not due to be published until after the 1997 general election. Only a handful of people were aware of what evidence had been submitted to the committee.

I approached everyone who I thought might know. I got lucky. It meant we could print a splash headline: 'Top Tory admits he took £25,000 from Fayed.' His name was Tim Smith, the then MP for leafy Beaconsfield, a former minister, who was standing for election even though he knew this astonishing revelation would come out after the election when he was safely re-elected. He had not declared the money in the Commons register of financial interests and he had already been reselected to fight his seat at the general election. He was shaken by the outrage but seemed safe. Or was he.

I telephoned every councillor and member of the local Tory association that I could find. Within twenty-four hours there was a full scale revolt among the good burghers of Beaconsfield Tories. Smith announced he would stand down at the election. I'd had a hunch, acted on it, and stirred up as much unrest as I could, and he was out.

Flipping, duckhouses and bath plugs

It was to be another decade, and at the butt end of another long-serving government, this time a Labour one, that political journalism reached its apogee with the extraordinary revelations in the *Daily* and *Sunday Telegraph* over MPs' expenses.

Some MPs and peers faced criminal prosecutions. Many more were forced to stand down. Michael Martin became the first Speaker in more than three centuries to face the ignominy of being forced to resign or face a vote of no confidence.

Their downfall came from hundreds of compelling broadsheet pages, resulting in wide-reaching political implications and reform, a global talking point, and a victory in the fight to make British politicians more accountable.

The newspaper bought the CD disc with hundreds of thousands of entries of MPs' expenses dating back to 2005. But it was not simply a case of transcribing the details. A team of hacks worked night and day in what we called 'the bunker' poring over pages of typed and handwritten pages. It was investigative journalism which uncovered the scandal of MPs 'flipping' addresses to avoid capital gains tax.

If the *Telegraph* had not obtained the un-redacted expenses accounts from an insider, we might never have found out for instance, that the Luton MP Margaret Moran charged the taxpayer more than £20,000 for dry rot removal for her second home – in Southampton some 100 miles away from her constituency. Or so many other examples involving bath plugs, duck houses, dodgy videos and the status among our politicians of the John Lewis department store.

Now there is the great weapon for political journalists: the Freedom of Information Act which MPs passed into law but then tried to stop it applying to their own expenses. For all the frontpage stories they provoked, the case for journalism by FoI is still to be made. Cost and time pressures in newsrooms suggest FoI fishing expeditions are likely to reduce.

But there are indications that the campaigners will take up where journalists leave off. Lord Falconer, the former Lord Chancellor, said that 'government did not introduce Freedom of Information in order to do something for journalism' but there is no doubt it has helped batter down doors which otherwise would be slammed shut in our face. A particular problem with it is the time taken for replies to requests. For instance in 2005, a Liberal Democrat peer, Lord Avebury, asked for details of the frequency of telephone calls between Tony Blair and Rupert Murdoch in the run-up to the Iraq war. After more than two years' delay and an initial refusal to accept the ruling of the information commissioner, the Cabinet Office published the information the day after Blair stepped down as Prime Minister.

Other sources of information

Two areas that provide rich pickings for journalists are the register of MPs' interests which is updated almost by the day, and the ministerial code of conduct. David Blunkett had to resign from Blair's Cabinet for a second time because an astute hack read the small print of the code which showed that after he had left office the first time he had taken a lucrative directorship without declaring it to the right authorities. Rules are there for ministers past and present. Have a copy in your briefcase along with the Press Complaints Commission's code of conduct.

When not to go for the jugular

There are times when it is easy to feel sorry for a politician. Who could not feel sympathy for Peter Brooke when he was a Conservative Northern Ireland Secretary? He caused controversy when he unknowingly appeared on an Irish TV show on the same day of an IRA bombing. He sang the song 'Oh, My Darling Clementine'. There was an outcry but he weathered the storm because most journalists knew Brooke was a fundamentally decent man.

Equally in the early 1980s Willie Whitelaw offered to resign as Home Secretary after an intruder Michael Fagan inexplicably scaled the walls of Buckingham Palace and got into the Queen's bedroom. The resignation, rightly, was not accepted by Mrs Thatcher. However, if Her Majesty had wanted him out it would have been a different matter. I have little time for Peter Mandelson but he was effectively bundled out of office by Tony Blair's spin doctor Alastair Campbell – too much power for an unelected official. He was later cleared by an independent investigation but was not given his job back by Blair. It was not fair. That Mandelson had managed to antagonise many political journalists and had few friends on Labour's benches did not help. A lesson, perhaps, for others to remember.

Sex v. money

Traditionally, it was sex which dogged the Tories and money which brought down Labour – the truism that Tories already had the cash and did not need to line their pockets any further.

However under John Major and Tony Blair, a series of politicians lost their ministerial seats for scandals involving both sex and money. Case studies worthy of 'googling' include those involving David Mellor, the first Culture Secretary, who just survived revelations of an extra-marital affair but was sacked by his friend, John Major, within months. And the ups and downs in the political life of Jeffrey Archer. From the last parliament, the stings which exposed the financial ambitions of former Labour Cabinet ministers Geoffrey Hoon, Stephen Byers and Patricia Hewitt will tell you a great deal about the mindset of a modern politician.

Nothing personal

After more than two decades at Westminster I have seen many different styles of reporter. Soon after I arrived in the lobby in 1995 for *The Times*, the then ITV political correspondent Jackie Ashley wrote a piece in praise of mavericks. They were the hacks who ignored the spin doctors who, in turn, ignored them. I was anointed as one of those mavericks along with the legendary David Hencke of *The Guardian* who broke the cash-for-questions scandal which did so much damage to John Major's government.

Then there are the giants like Trevor Kavanagh of *The Sun* who break policy scoops with alarming and monotonous regularity. Big beasts like Kavanagh are genuinely feared by ministers who often ring him to find out what is going on.

Ministers know that Westminster is awash with rumour and intrigue often about them and that the hacks are usually plugged in about who is up and who is down. Exchange titbits. You will be rewarded. Ring them and tell them what you've heard. Take everything you hear with a pinch of salt, but don't ignore it.

When the Lib Dem MP Mark Oaten was exposed for paying a rent boy for sex, I was tipped off that Mark was having an affair with a senior Westminster journalist – a male one at that. I attacked the story with gusto and managed to unearth the name of the apparent lover: Andrew Pierce. As I'd met Oaten only once – in the presence of his far more attractive wife – I can assure you that this was one rumour I never pursued in the pages of my newspaper.

Andrew Pierce is consultant editor at the Daily Mail *and a regular broadcaster on TV and radio, including a weekly Sunday morning slot on LBC. After nearly twenty years on* The Times, *he was appointed assistant editor of the* Daily Telegraph, *becoming the newspaper's public face during the MPs' expenses saga.*

14: Policing Parliament

Sheila Gunn

'[It takes] many good deeds to build a reputation and only one bad one to lose it' Benjamin Franklin

When the former Labour MP David Chaytor was sent to prison for fiddling his expenses, the wonderful Matthew Parris – himself a former MP – said some members were 'pigs' and a few more were 'saints'. In between were a lot of sheep, he added. As so often, he is spot on. Most MPs go into public life for honourable reasons, to 'make a difference'. A few display porcine qualities from an early stage, others develop them as they progress along the political road. And there is a percentage who deserve some form of canonisation, although even they can come unstuck through naivete or by assuming that others in politics are equally saintly.

Parliament has always jealously guarded its rights to police itself. Members of either House did not regard themselves subjected to the same laws and regulations as other mortals. They could be expected to behave honourably.

To the great joy and continued employment of journalists, many MPs and peers have been shown to be less than honourable. A few years ago, political journalists could rarely look forward to seeing politicians arrested, dragged before the courts and sent to jail. There had of course been the cases of Jeffrey Archer and Jonathan Aitken, but their prison sentences came long after they had left Westminster. Then we have been treated to the sight of former Cabinet ministers, Stephen Byers, Geoff Hoon and Patricia Hewitt, caught on camera trying to 'sell' themselves and their services in a newspaper sting.

Various abuses have gradually led to a plethora of formal systems to monitor, police and punish our politicians. There are also some informal ways, some more ethical than others.

Register of financial interests

Rt Hon James Arbuthnot received a tie (value £5) for giving a speech. Sample entry from the register.

Over the years, the requirements for MPs to register all their sources of income has been ratcheted up. The system shifted from MPs declaring in a vague way 'property assets', to registering an invitation to a free night at the opera – or the gift of a tie. Back in the 1970s and even the 1980s detailed disclosures were regarded as unnecessary as MPs were expected to be honour bound to make decisions for the good of the country, rather than for any kind of pecuniary interest. Now MPs are terrified at being castigated for not declaring the merest favour.

Gone are the days when Conservative whips would find it hard to drag in all their MPs during Royal Ascot week where they were being entertained by various companies and lobbying organisations. (Labour whips would plan 'ambushes' to catch out the Thatcher and Major governments before the Tory MPs strutted back to the House, still dressed in top hat and tails.) Many may regard this change as a jolly good thing too. But it is at least arguable whether keeping them at Westminster checking petty forms for ties or flowers is better for the governance of the country.

Something else that has changed is the assumption that being an MP is a full-time job and outside earnings are somehow frowned upon. If anyone could prove that the present members of the Commons are better qualified and more dedicated than the previous generations, then this might be true.

The register and accompanying code of conduct, available through the parliament website, is worth accessing whether for keeping a check on entries from local MPs or identifying new trends. But nowadays MPs are so careful to register everything and anything – and aware of bad headlines if they do not – that it is a lot less exciting than in the past. It may be justified to report that a certain MP has been paid a lot of money for making speeches. But it is worth at least considering whether this is preferable to having no MPs for whom anyone would pay good money to listen to?

Occasionally one scents a whiff of a scandal concerning a particular MP's outside interests. This may come from good, investigative journalism – and the journalists themselves will probably try to convince their editors or producers this is so. It is more likely to come from that MP's enemies quietly suggesting that you check on someone's outside activities.

Good fun can also be had at odd or quirky entries, enabling an enterprising journalist with a light touch to compose an enjoyable colour piece.

In an era concerned with the environment, travelling arrangements can provide good sport. Again, the system has swung from the ridiculous to the absurd. Under the old system the mileage rate was based on engine size, hence it was in the interests of MPs to own gas-guzzling cars. Under the latest system it is all meant to be economy class travel. So you have the ludicrous sight of MPs travelling to Brussels in economy while MEPs on the same train are smirking in business. Nor can MPs rely on turning left on boarding a plane – even when the airline has upgraded them to business class free of charge.

It's all in the family

I employ my wife, Jane Smith, as a caseworker: an example of a typical MP's entry in the Register.

A quick scrutiny of part two of the register will disclose that a significant number of MPs employ family members in their offices. This is still controversial.

Has this system been abused by some to raise the average income of an MP's family? Yes. Do most family members provide invaluable support for MPs? Also, yes. Given the odd working hours and, for most MPs, a two-centre lifestyle (half the week at Westminster, half in the constituency) it is a way for families to stay together. The choice for most MPs' spouses and children is either to remain in the constituency, splitting the family for half the week, or for them to divide their time between the two bases. And then what does the spouse do for those days at Westminster? And, as not many MPs are saints, is it a good idea to leave them to sleep alone for three or four nights a week in the febrile environment of Westminster?

Arrangements made by the former Tory MP Derek Conway provoked the 'scandal' of MPs employing members of their family. He employed his two sons Henry and Freddie as researchers and, at least in the case of Freddie, little could be found to justify his salary. This shone a spotlight into the murky world of MPs' staffing arrangements. Although many regard the Conway 'scandal' as an example of investigative journalism it actually emerged from a complaint by the Labour MP John Mann.

Journalists based at Westminster had long accepted that MPs employed spouses and their grown-up children. They understood why and it was not generally considered an issue. However we had all heard rumours of the odd abuse, such as a wife employed as a secretary who was seen around Westminster only on ceremonial occasions. There was even talk of a couple of MPs who put down their ex-wives as secretaries as a way of paying them maintenance. But then the system was largely kept secret, with journalists having limited rights to demand to see details until the Freedom of Information Act started to intrude into the lives of MPs.

As part of the tightening up of regulations, there is a register for the staff of MPs in which they must declare any outside earnings. Sadly, this rarely makes exciting reading. However there are occasional stories about those, other than family members, working at Westminster. A recent case was that of a blonde, statuesque Russian student working for the Lib Dem MP Mike Hancock. After a six-month M15 investigation she was arrested and served with a deportation order, although it should be noted that she denied working as a spy. Such stories are what we all dream of!

The journalists' register

Yes, if you are lucky enough to make it into the lobby, you too will have to register your own outside earnings. Not thrilling reading perhaps, but a good example for aspiring journalists of how to add to your income by contributing to specialist publications or commentating on TV and radio.

The House of Lords' register

How many journalists have scanned this register? Probably very few. But if you want an indication of who owns large swathes of UK plc – and some other parts of the world – it is worthy of inspection: a social history in its own right. The shareholdings of Lord Sainsbury of Turville alone take up more than two computer screens (who would have thought that those moreish goat's cheese and spinach flans could be so profitable?). The land and property holdings of peers are staggering, as are the number of directorships. But so also are the positions on charities and not-for-profit organisations. In typical Lords' style, it is all rather understated.

The Lords has lagged behind the Commons in requiring members to register and declare their outside interests. This is partly because peers are there *because* of their outside interests and receive no salary for themselves or their staff. (The exception is frontbench spokesmen who receive an allowance called Cranborne money.)

For many years they have been required to declare their interests when speaking in the House. But when I started covering the Lords for *The Times* there were often occasions when they did not. I was told 'but everyone knows he speaks for ... organisation'. Quite how 'everyone', including myself, was meant to know this was never explained. The lawyers will prevent me from giving details, but there was an occasion when a peer advocated amendments which would have benefited a drugs company to the tune of millions of pounds. Sadly, not only was he extremely litigious, but he was quietly and successfully encouraged behind the scenes to shut up. Not a productive journalistic experience, but speaks volumes about the way the place was run.

Gradually, the Lords has aped the Commons in requiring peers to register their interests and to be far more forthcoming in declaring whether someone is paying them to put down amendments or speak for a specific cause. Yet lobbyists know that, if they want a Bill changed, the best chance is to do it in the House of Lords, mainly because no recent government has enjoyed an overall majority. But there is a world of difference between making a good case to a peer about an issue and actually paying him or her to support it.

If you sense or have a tip-off that a certain peer is being paid to table amendments or press a case, then you are on the scent of a half-decent story. Perhaps that peer has never before shown any knowledge or interest in that issue? Then why is he doing it now? Does he have a decent income? Is he a former MP? All questions worth asking.

Parliamentary commissioner for standards

Who can forget Tory sleaze? There was a time in the 1990s when it seemed that every Conservative MP was either raking in sackfuls of illicit payments or had been caught with someone who was not their wife. This is, of course, the popular perception and, more importantly, probably helped – together with the personal lives of members of the Royal Family – to keep at least half a dozen media outlets in business.

Early incidents led to John Major asking Lord Nolan to set up a new Committee for Standards in Public Life, now the Committee for Standards and Privileges. Nolan published the seven principles in public life by which to judge MPs' behaviour: selflessness; integrity; objectivity; accountability; openness; honesty; leadership. Easy enough for the saintly, but quite hard to achieve for most politicians, given their conflicting pressures.

As this did nothing to stem the stream of damaging stories, Major ordered a formal code of conduct for MPs and appointed in 1995 the first ever Parliamentary Commissioner for Standards, Sir Gordon Downey, to police it and to personally oversee tighter rules for registering financial interests. Sir Gordon's tenure is generally regarded as necessary and successful. This was not always the case with his successors.

The Commissioner looks into complaints about MPs for breaches of the code of conduct or discrepancies on the register. But, as will be obvious, once there is a hint of dishonourable behaviour, journalists will follow every twist and turn in the saga.

Commons Select Committee on Standards & Privileges

The Commissioner makes his report to the Commons Committee on Standards and Privileges – a cross-party committee of backbench MPs. A lingering problem is the time taken between filing a complaint and the Commissioner's report – and the subsequent report by the Committee. For reasons which no one has ever adequately explained, it can be many months.

This is a problem for journalists as they must keep reminding their audience of the original allegations; it is even more of an issue for the MP concerned, whose reputation is effectively wrecked from the moment the original complaint is made. Whoever said everyone is innocent until proven guilty was clearly not in politics – or journalism. Much of the committee's deliberations are in private sessions and its members depressingly reluctant to divulge the gist to journalists.

To absorb something of the flavour of its work, access the committee's report in December 2010 on the former MPs Sir John Butterfill, Stephen Byers, Richard Caborn, Patricia Hewitt, Geoff Hoon and Adam Ingram.

The committee ultimately makes a report and recommendations to the full House. The subsequent debate, usually brief, tends to be a cringe-making event for politicians but satisfying material for journalists.

Suspensions and apologies

Do the erring MPs end up locked in the cells beneath the chamber (and they do exist)? Are they fined? Arrested? Well, not really. They are usually forced to apologise to the House and, if really naughty, suspended from the chamber for a certain number of days. These sanctions may sound feeble and, compared to the penalties for those in other walks of life, they are, but they do make these MPs virtually unemployable.

If MPs are suspended from the House for a certain amount of time, they usually lose their salaries for that period. Much worse is that they attract the attention of two audiences: their party colleagues and their constituencies.

Withdrawal of the whip

The reputation of any party can be damaged by the actions of each and every one of its members. No party wants epitaphs such as 'disgraced' attached to any of its advocates. The damage is that much more if a journalist can write descriptions such as: 'a close confidant of the party leader' or 'had been talked of as a potential Cabinet minister'.

A key sanction against an erring MP is the withdrawal of the whip, meaning that the MP will no longer be regarded as a member of that party, although he keeps his seat in the Commons as an independent MP. These rows add to the gaiety of Parliament.

Withdrawing the whip is like sending someone to Coventry, that is, they are excluded from the 'club'. In a party political system, they are suddenly outside, no longer receiving the written whip every week, no longer considered for certain positions in the gift of their party leaders, no longer invited to drinks, meals and receptions with colleagues. They can try to defect to other parties. But few want to take on damaged goods.

Another, more honourable circumstance when the whip may be withdrawn is when an MP publicly – hopefully through the offices of a journalist – rebels against a party policy as a 'matter of conscience'.

However if a significant number of MPs rebel, then the Chief Whip and party leader will have to consider whether or not punishing them will result in even worse headlines and grant the rebels 'martyr' status. Some MPs manage to rebel more gracefully than others. Among the Labour MPs who refused to support Tony Blair's decision on the war in Iraq, Clare Short picked the wrong time and manner to leave office, while John Denham's resignation was a textbook case in how to do it with logic and style.

In more extreme circumstances, even more enjoyable for journalists, MPs defect to another party. Labour MP Shaun Woodward and Labour peer, Lord Howarth of Newport, both started out as Conservative MPs before 'crossing the floor', with Woodward going on to serve in Blair and Brown's Cabinets.

Defections have been out of fashion for a few years, although they crop up in local councils. But given the stresses and strains on the coalition government, journalists may hope they become a more regular feature at Westminster.

Deselection

MPs who rebel or step out of line must face one of the most formidable body of people in politics: their local party. These activists love their party and, to a lesser extent, their MPs. National party officials are quick to exploit their loyalty by urging them to apply pressure to 'obey' their party whips or, if it is too late, punish their MPs.

The key sanction is deselection: when the national party, in consultation with the constituency party, informs the errant MP that they will not be selected as the local party's candidate at the next general election. As we have a party political system with little room for independents, this effectively parachutes the MP into the political wilderness. However this tactic can blow up in the face of the national party if the MP still enjoys strong support from local activists. Party members often have no love for party HQ into which much of the money they raise disappears. Sometimes the local party robustly sides with their MP; more often it is split. Both are wonderful scenarios for journalists.

As Andrew Pierce makes clear, in these circumstances an astute journalist will start ringing up local activists to gauge the level of support for their MP. Calling local councillors, whether on parish, borough or county councils, in the same party is often profitable. Especially as some are likely to think they would make better MPs and are disappointed not to have been selected.

Criminal offences

The knock on the door in the night, the scurrying through the media scrum into the magistrates' court, the clunk of the prison door. Not something one associated with the minutiae of MPs' expenses and allowances until recently.

MPs and peers clearly hoped that the magic words 'parliamentary privilege' exempted them from such humiliations. It is quite easy to see why. So much of the frisson of our Parliament revolves around odd little conventions and a mystique which makes it immune from the rules which govern most of us, for instance, health and safety regulations.

An elderly hereditary peer once told me how his ancestor had been accused of killing one of his servants. As a peer of the realm, he was entitled to be tried by 'by his peers'. He was found guilty and sentenced to death. As a peer, he exercised his right to be hanged with a silken rope rather than the usual rough hewn hemp.

Thankfully we no longer have the death penalty. Sadly, until recently, there had been few criminals serving in Parliament. It is hard, but not impossible, to become excited by the odd speeding or drink and driving offence. If a serving MP is sentenced to jail for more than a year, they are automatically disqualified from Parliament. This does not tend to happen because pressure is put on the said MP by their own party to stand down voluntarily.

Resignations

If there is a shadow hanging over an MP, the usual course of action is for him to tell his local party that he will be standing down at the next election. This means another candidate can be adopted and campaign in the hope of winning the seat at the next general election. Yet the question you may want to ask is: 'Why don't you just go!' The answer is that MPs cannot resign, as any other employee can do, during a parliament.

But MPs do leave. Either because they are appointed to an influential post elsewhere, in the UN, EU, NATO or some other acronym, or in disgrace, as did Labour MPs Phil Woolas and Eric Illsley.

The mechanism is the same in both circumstances. They must apply for what is commonly referred to as the Chiltern Hundreds. It involves the MP applying to the Chancellor of the Exchequer for appointment either as a steward or bailiff of the Chiltern Hundreds or steward of the manor of Northstead. These are 'offices of profit under the Crown' which leads to automatic disqualification from holding office as an MP. Just one of those quirks of the system which journalists need to remember. Some had to make a quick check on the rules when the Sinn Fein MP Gerry Adams decided to resign – and then it was not quite so simple. Adams had always refused to take his seat because it would require swearing an oath to the Queen. So he would not have welcomed the idea of taking an office of profit under the Crown in order to stand down.

The system is far simpler in the Lords where peers can either just stop turning up, as many do, or more formally take leave of absence. But no system currently exists to strip them of their peerages, even if (and when, in the case of Jeffrey Archer) they are sent to jail.

Death

Death may be considered the final sanction and rarely comes at a convenient time. And the present contingent of MPs and peers are a lot less prone to dying than previous incumbents. Without sounding too cynical, this trend is mildly irritating for journalists. MPs tend to be younger; the average age is fifty, with the average age of the peers being sixty-five.

The House of Lords could be considered the perfect format for old age: it is kept slightly warmer than the Commons, the brains of its inmates are kept stimulated and they still feel of some use. There have been numerous peers who are as sharp as ever in their eighties and nineties.

MPs cannot resign, but nor are parliamentarians allowed to die at Westminster either. Yes, to you or me, sometimes it appears that all life has left their bodies but, because of a complicated coroner's procedure at Parliament, they are all said to have died on arrival at hospital, usually St Thomas's across the Thames.

Independent Parliamentary Standards Authority

Those who hoped that the whole MPs' expenses saga would end with the election of the coalition government in 2010 have been disappointed. Following the relentless spate of stories involving bath plugs, duck houses, moats and dodgy videos, control of approving expenses for MPs was handed to the IPSA. It seems to have escaped the attention of most that actually running this authority seems to cost more than the original expenses claimed. In early 2011, tensions are still running high between many individual MPs and the IPSA. In the longer term, a more sensible arrangement will be introduced.

As has been well recorded, the lax expenses system crept in from the late 1990s because MPs and, in particular, the governments were frightened of raising MPs' salaries. It is, at the time of writing, £65,738 a year. In addition MPs can claim a range of allowances, ranging from a maximum of £103,812 a year for staffing their offices, down to a 20p a mile bicycle allowance. Since most MPs now post all their expenses on their website, they veer towards claiming only modest amounts.

The Prime Minister can take a salary (they do not always take the full amount) of another £132,923 a year; and Cabinet ministers another £79,754.

Journalists have derived tremendous enjoyment from the whole expenses saga. The reputation of Parliament sank to sewer level. Matthew Parris's 'pigs' are rightly being vilified, imprisoned or kicked out of Parliament. But at the current salary, I fear that many excellent, decent people will not be able to afford to stand for Parliament or too many less qualified people may take their places.

In the meantime, journalists should keep an eye on the progress of the IPSA and the declarations made by individual MPs. The saga is not yet over.

Nor have the peers been immune from the expenses debacle. While they do not receive a salary, a far more generous system of claiming for overnight stays, subsistence and travelling has evolved over the past ten years. Many assume that all peers are cushioned by comfortable incomes and pensions. This is no longer the case. This is no excuse for the way the infection so prevalent in the Commons has affected some peers, with claims for overnight stays which did not happen and illusory travel expenses. Most are now aware that the media is keeping a closer eye.

15: Demystifying political reporting

Sheila Gunn

'Senior ministerial sources tell me...'
'According to a senior party aide...'
'It is understood that the Prime Minister is set to announce...'

Any scrutiny of the daily drip feed of political news will throw up such references. Very easy to dismiss until you are a political journalist. Then you realise that, unless you earn the confidence of your contacts to talk 'off the record', you will miss out on most of the political intelligence your colleagues are picking up.

Some journalists and politicians certainly play the 'off the record' game too enthusiastically. Whenever possible, identify your sources and include direct quotes. If this is not possible, there are a plethora of rules – official and unofficial – which govern how one reports politics.

A cardinal rule applies to quoting the political classes: ask yourself 'why is this person telling me this?' Look at the conversation from the point of view of you, the journalist, but also of the informant or politician concerned. What do they want out of it? What do they expect you to do with this information?

Other, more recent, factors affect this relationship. Today's politicians are warned by party officials 'never to say anything to a journalist that you do not want to see on the front page of *The Sun*'. Luckily, many forget this. But recent stings, whether it is journalists posing as constituents or as PR consultants, put politicians even more on their guard. Politicians have become extremely wary about what they say, what they assign to emails, texts, blogs and, certainly, old-fashioned letters.

The infamous email from the press officer Jo Moore on 9/11 – 'a good day to bury bad news' – frightened the life out of all emailers around Westminster. An even stricter rule, to never put something in an email you did not want to see published widely, followed exchanges made public in 2009 between Damian McBride, one of Gordon Brown's closest aides, and the Labour blogger Derek Draper about setting up a website to air scurrilous allegations concerning leading Conservatives. Add to that the success of Wikileaks and you can understand why the political classes have become so defensive.

All these incidents make relations between these politicians and Westminster-accredited journalists ultra-sensitive. In all democracies over the ages there has been a way for politicians to talk to certain journalists on a confidential basis. In itself, this is not a bad thing. The key question is: how do the journalists react to the information they are given?

An understanding of the different freedoms and restraints is essential for political journalists.

Parliamentary privilege

Please take advantage of your right to report all words and documents which can properly be described as 'parliamentary'. If these are words, either oral or written, uttered in an official parliamentary event or publication, such as the chamber or a committee, then neither the MP nor peer – or you and your media outlet – can be sued for slander. There are grey areas. And in all cases where there is doubt, you should have your copy or interview 'legalled' to protect yourself and your employer.

Nowadays journalists – and politicians for that matter – do not take enough advantage of this protection to disclose abuses, corruption and scandals. A parliamentary committee in 1999 recommended changes to the rules and David Cameron is committed to introducing a Parliamentary Privileges Bill. But by January 2011, none had been published.

Parliamentary privilege is currently made up of two parts:

1. The privilege of freedom of speech, dating back to Article 9 of the 1689 Bill of Rights, stating: 'that the freedom of speech and debates or proceedings in Parliament ought not to be impeached or questioned in any court or place out of Parliament'
2. The right of Parliament to exercise control over its own affairs.

This privilege has withstood a challenge to the European Convention of Human Rights when an MP made allegations about the behaviour of a constituent who appealed to the European Court of Human Rights.

Recently there have been attempts – luckily, unsuccessful – to interpret the second part as applying to MPs' and peers' expenses and allowances.

However, there are a few essential conditions to remember:

- The accusations must come from official parliamentary business. Repeating allegations made to you by MPs, for instance, in a corridor, via email or over a drink – even if the MP says they are 'on the record' – will not be covered. What you can do is suggest to the MP and peer that they table a question, adjournment debate, Early Day Motion – in fact use any parliamentary device. This would then be protected by parliamentary privilege – but only the words in the document. This tactic may not be considered entirely ethical. But most parliamentarians are appallingly ignorant of the devices they can use to expose wrongdoing.
- If the allegations are in writing, the relevant material has to be a parliamentary paper, such as a speech in the chamber, a written answer, select committee report or EDM.
- The allegations must come from the MP or peer and not from an aide, adviser or official.

A case study on the limitations of this privilege is the Zircon saga. In the mid-1980s, the journalist Duncan Campbell was commissioned to contribute to a series by the BBC called the *Secret Society.* Campbell gathered information about a spy satellite project, Zircon, which had not been given to the National Audit Office (see the chapter on committees for more information). When the BBC backed off from including details, Campbell wrote an article for the *New Statesman* bypassing an injunction. There followed a long, drawn-out row involving the then Attorney General Sir Michael Havers, the opposition MP Robin Cook, who wanted to screen the video of the BBC's (unshown) documentary in the Commons, and the Speaker. The eventual ruling was that screening the video in Parliament was *not* protected by parliamentary privilege.

More recently, there have been instances of lawyers for MPs arguing that parliamentary privilege meant their clients were exempt from arrest. The Speaker reminded MPs in 2008 that, according to the parliamentary bible *Erskine May*, Parliament was not a 'haven from the criminal law'.

More obvious grey areas are press conferences, speeches and briefings outside of Parliament. In other words, if a politician said something slanderous in one of these environments and you repeated them, you could be sued. This is a decision for the lawyers to make. Perhaps it is no surprise that MPs are currently wary about taking advantage of the protection of parliamentary privilege to name and shame individuals and companies.

It is obvious that, if you are investigating a case of serious injustice, suspected corruption or maladministration, parliamentary privilege can be an extremely effective weapon. But quite how it applies today needs more clarity and further challenges to this essential principle.

Embargoes

Thump. A report of 500 pages lands on your desk and you have to do two things: tell your newsdesk/producer within fifteen minutes what it is 'worth' in journalistic terms – such as, early page lead or a report plus an analysis by a specialist reporter and produce your story within two or three hours, complete with reaction.

You will do it of course. Developing a technique for 'gutting' reports is invaluable. With practice, you will soon be able to 'smell' the importance – in media coverage terms – of such reports. (As Chris Moncrieff points out, the knack is to flick first to the recommendations and then ask your good political contacts for comment.)

As this is not ideal for either journalists or politicians, it is common practice for such reports to be given to accredited or relevant journalists a day or two in advance under embargo. This is a strict stipulation that no story should be published or broadcast before a certain time. Journalists have time to read the report and write up their stories in readiness for pressing the button at the earliest time stated on the embargo. You should put a warning on your copy stating the embargo time.

The wording on the press release and usually stamped across the report's cover is along the lines of:

NOT FOR PUBLICATION BEFORE 01.00 hours, WEDNESDAY, FEBRUARY 22, 2011

Documents most often made available under embargo include reports from Commons select committees, the National Audit Office and government departments. Please do not break the embargo. It damages your reputation but also discourages the organisation from releasing early copies to *all* journalists. Not clever.

But this is not the whole story. Journalists are not meant to discuss the report, its findings or recommendations with others before the embargoed time. However, given the time pressures, it has become common practice for journalists to ask – very quietly – for reaction. If, for instance, a broadcast journalist wants to arrange an interview to get reaction to the report, he or she may give indications to the potential interviewee so that he/she can prepare to respond. They should not give specific details in advance, but arrange to talk further once the embargo time is reached. But sometimes difficult judgements have to be made.

If the report's authors discovered that a journalist had given an opponent information about its contents, they have every right to make a formal complaint. Editors and producers, while putting pressure on their journalists to produce the first and best coverage, tend to have a serious sense of humour failure about such complaints.

Check against delivery

A similar system is the release of speeches under embargo with an extra stipulation: 'To be checked against delivery'. These are usually speeches by senior politicians well away from Westminster. Are they checked against delivery? No, not often. The idea is to give a speech to journalists in the hope of coverage. But it is often not entirely suitable for the actual audience.

This sounds like some sort of deceit. If so, it is a fairly harmless one, but perhaps one which adds to the cynicism surrounding politicians. As a political journalist, you want a story. The press release with the speech will often provide you with one – if only a few lines in a running story. And it is the politician's words on the record. The audience wants to hear the politician, but is unlikely to want to listen to a 30-minute speech on the entrails of education policy after a three-course dinner. These events are often on a Friday evening when everyone is quite 'relaxed'.

What about identifying a guest to feedback to you what a controversial politician actually says? Especially their ad libs, jokes, replies to questions. I learnt while doing a stint on *The Times* Diary that it is often the small sentences uttered almost as an afterthought that make the best story. Here are two personal – and inglorious – experiences of this syndrome.

As a NCTJ journalism student in Cardiff, I was sent to report a speech from the then Labour Cabinet minister, George Brown, at the local chamber of commerce. Finding the place was hard enough (luckily I always give myself an extra fifteen minutes on any journey). The room was smoky, smelly, quite horrible and my presence was not welcomed. With a sigh of relief, I was given a copy of his speech. Phew, this is easy, I thought. GB came in late and not walking in a straight line. He told a few jokes, most of which would be totally unrepeatable nowadays but were actually quite funny. He drank brown stuff from his tumbler and replied to a few questions in the same vein. I summoned up the courage to ask him about his prepared speech on the way out. He smiled: 'Oh yes, those are my words. You can use what you like,' pinched my bottom and left. Everyone seemed happy.

This is the system. Whether they are uttered or not, you are entitled to use both the speech given to you and the words actually said.

Fast forward a couple of decades to the 1997 general election campaign and I am working for the then Prime Minister John Major. We'd managed to reach agreement on his speech to a rally in Scotland, with his strongest ever warning about Labour's threat to the break-up of the United Kingdom. I briefed the journalists on the gist of it, giving them a few direct quotes. Both Jon Sopel for the BBC and Tom Bradby for ITV included them in their early evening news programmes. Other journalists filed their stories, with an eye on the deadlines for early editions. *The Independent,* which went to bed earlier than its rivals, carried the story on the front page of its first edition. I was not unhappy.

Major then took the stage and, ignoring the lectern where the agreed speech had been placed, spoke off the cuff for fifty minutes. The journalist in you will understand why the press corps was, at this point, contemplating how to string me up. 'But he hasn't said a word of it!' was the general sentiment, with some expletives attached. Oh dear. I told them to treat the words in the unspoken speech as 'his words', that is a statement. Knowing that their newsdesks and producers might be unamused, I suggested putting them on to me to explain in person. As many of them pointed out, Tony Blair's team would never have allowed such a lack of discipline from their leader. I am quite happy for history to judge that one, although my comments to my then boss should remain unrepeatable.

On and off the record

Judging when you can quote politicians and aides directly, and when you have to camouflage their identity may seem confusing. Try, wherever possible, to include as many direct quotes as well as some paraphrased sentences in your stories. A story based entirely on non-attributed quotes is unsatisfactory. Not only do you risk losing the trust of your audience, but your employers are not likely to be impressed if you are incapable of finding one person to back up your story on the record. Very rarely do the circumstances justify it.

Politicians may say to you: 'What are you going to quote me as saying?' If you have a good note or recording of the conversation, you do not have to regurgitate it for approval. This can lead to a negotiation with the politician who is likely to try to water down the comments. If a politician bullies you, do not be afraid to stand your ground. But there are few hard and fast rules: it depends on the issue, the politician and the weight of the story.

Basic rules should help you. Assume that you can quote anything said:

- In the chambers of Commons and Lords
- In open sessions of parliamentary committees
- In ministerial and party-political press conferences
- During live and pre-record interviews
- In written parliamentary material, such as Hansard, committee minutes and reports.

Take care to avoid quoting sections of sentences out of context. Some politicians also believe that they have the right to delete something they say in a pre-recorded or taped interview. No, they do not. But it is up to you to decide – depending on the story or issue involved – how you report it. If someone has made an obvious slip of the tongue – and we all do it – you may want to consider whether the words are important enough to land the politician in it.

Assume that you have to establish what you can and cannot quote:

- In briefings
- In the Commons and peers' lobbies, corridors, watering places
- On the fringes of events outside Parliament
- At ministerial lunches or drinks

- During receptions or parties in government offices
- At party conferences.

Try to establish the basis of any conversation from the word go. Many politicians will automatically assume that such exchanges are off the record.

Between ourselves...

'Don't quote me but...', 'Take my fingerprints off this one, but...', 'Look, I'd never say anything against him but...'

There are excellent and terrible reasons why journalists cannot identify all the sources of their stories. More disputes break out between journalists and the political classes over the former's rights to report the latter, or to identify the source of their stories, than in any other area of political reporting.

An example commonly cited is that of the early morning comments made by Andrew Gilligan on BBC Radio 4's *Today* programme alleging that No. 10 'sexed up' one of the dossiers pressing the case for war on Iraq.

Certain principles are worth remembering at all levels, from parish councils to Westminster. If politicians or their spokespeople do not stipulate from the word go that a conversation is off the record, a journalist has the right to assume that it is not. There are few things more irritating than your political contacts giving you splendid stories in graphic detail and then commenting: 'But of course I never told you any of this!' This happens all too often.

In theory, you have every right to challenge them – and it is certainly worth doing so at times or, at least, to negotiate the right to use some quotes. The decision you take will depend largely on the circumstances. If your contact has talked too freely through inexperience or a genuine misunderstanding, you may want to be sympathetic. But remember that your rivals may not exercise such understanding and could end up with the stronger story. Even more challenging is deciding how to use quotes from valued political contacts who you are reluctant to antagonise. Again, it helps to reach an early understanding about anything you can quote and how it is attributed. It is also worth remembering who pays you!

Whatever the circumstances, politicians have an unpleasant habit of strongly denying what they have told you once their words are made public. If the interview is face-to-face, it helps to keep – and to be seen to keep – a good note of their words. Tape recorders are usually used by both sides. If you cannot use them, one of the advantages of a good shorthand note is that others are unlikely to be able to understand what you are writing. Do not underestimate the advantage this gives you.

If you have an email, save it. If over the phone, tape sensitive conversations. Remember that politicians also tape record their telephone conversations and, if talking to a minister in his or her office, assume that a civil servant is listening in and making a note.

Chatham House rules

Those involved in public life, especially senior politicians, diplomats and officials, are prone to telling journalists that they are free to attend and report such-and-such event or speech – but it must be understood that it is 'under Chatham House rules of course'.

The facts: Chatham House is the home of the Royal Institute for International Affairs. There is only one rule, devised in 1927 and refined in 1992. It is: 'When a meeting, or part thereof, is held under the Chatham House rule, participants are free to use the information received, but neither the identity nor the affiliation of the speaker(s), nor that of any other participant, may be revealed.' Hence it is comparable to 'non-attributable sources'.

It originated to guarantee anonymity to those speaking at Chatham House. The argument goes that this allows a freer and more constructive discussion on international relations. Certainly senior civil servants and diplomats have used it to put forward views which they would not usually dare to express outside their own offices.

Quite sweetly, you will meet those who start all manner of meetings with the words 'of course this is all on Chatham House rules…' They expect journalists to interpret this as a block on putting a name to the speaker but referring obliquely to a 'senior diplomat' or 'former ambassador'. But if the story is significant enough, the identity of the speaker tends to come out somewhere, sometime. One development fired an Exocet through this comfort blanket: the identity of the speakers being made public via new technology, such as tweets. For this reason, at meetings with more than one known journalist, seasoned politicians and officials are likely to live by the dictum that your words may well become public one day.

In spite of this wariness of being quoted, it is surprising how many off the record conversations are conducted between journalists and politicians day after day.

Take my fingerprints off this but...

There is nothing new about political propaganda, although techniques for media management and manipulation have become ever more sophisticated.

As a general rule, broadcast and news agency journalists are under greater pressure to stand up their stories with on-the-record or attributed quotes than newspaper journalists. Oddly, editors and news editors of down-market newspapers may be more insistent that their journalists can genuinely stand up their stories than those on the heavier papers.

As other contributors make clear, the magic ingredient in being a successful political journalist is to develop judgement. Distinguishing between what's a challenge, a problem, a disaster or a crisis. This is particularly so in reporting information received off the record.

Scenario 1: An MP quietly hints 'strictly off the record' that he is 'seriously worried' about decisions being taken by their own party leader. How do you report it? Well, that depends on various factors: Is he planning to go on the record later? Is he reflecting a wider group? Is it on a single issue or a wider feeling of disillusionment? Is he an ex-minister, someone who has not been put forward for greater office and feels resentful? Can he point to others who feel the same?

Scenario 2: A small group of MPs are prepared to express dissatisfaction with a party policy but do not want their names published yet. What connects them? What support do they have on the other benches? How widespread is concern on this issue? How do they plan to make their unhappiness known (apart from via you)? Are they actually prepared to rebel, defy the whips?

Scenario 3: A middle-ranking minister – and a good contact – has privately expressed fears about a Bill. What is her standing? Is she alone? Is she being spoken of as likely to be promoted/demoted by the leadership? How far will she go? Resign? Speak out publicly? Defect?

The balance between reporting such non-attributable stories or waiting until you can find further verification officially is a fine one. It is poor practice to build a story on one unsubstantiated quote, not least as the person concerned is almost bound to deny they were the source. The difference between those who become well-established and respected journalists and those who do not is very often a willingness to make those extra calls to back up a story. But if political journalists ignored all the information they receive off the record, our media would be poorer for it – and so would the readers, listeners and viewers.

Gossips and rumours

Some years ago, a political aide told me he had carried out an experiment. He started a mildly mischievous rumour about an opponent and then waited to see how long it would be before it was repeated back to him as an authoritative statement. It was a matter of hours. Beware of the danger of being swept up in the feeding frenzy of confusing totally unsubstantiated rumours as a story. You need to base it on something more tangible.

Gossiping is part of political life wherever you operate. It ranges from the harmless to the vicious – to the potentially ruinous to individuals involved. Hopefully, for instance, the days when a politician's sexuality was considered an important story are long gone. But perhaps not. In fact if I believed all the speculation I'd heard, it would seem that most senior politicians are bisexual.

Also take care of reacting to rumours that 'a big story is going to break about...' Certainly it would be an excellent idea to make a few calls to see if there is any substance to it. But if you report such a speculative story without any collaboration, you are opening up your employer – and possibly yourself – to a law suit. And this can happen if you report a story from another media outlet. If in doubt, ask the lawyers to look it over. Lawyers retained by newspapers and broadcasters – as opposed to any other lawyers – generally strive to help you find a way through the legal obstacles.

16: Dealing with spin doctors, PRs and press officers

Nicholas Jones

More often than not political correspondents are spoilt for choice when reporting government announcements or the launch of new policies. White papers, parliamentary statements and background notes spew out from Whitehall departments and party headquarters at an alarming rate. The challenge for journalists is to assess and interpret what is on offer: will a government decision lead to higher taxes or a hike in charges? Are jobs at risk? Is established party policy being turned on its head?

These are the sort of questions which official briefings frequently fail to clarify and which journalists can struggle to find the answers to without the help of trusted sources. Tighter deadlines and increased competition help to explain why the news media has become ever more dependent on the guidance of political spin doctors, government information officers and the burgeoning band of public relations executives who represent commerce, industry, sports and entertainment.

Occasionally the media has control of the agenda. When reporters are firmly in the driving seat, able to dictate the latest twists and turns of a story, it can be the government of the day or a large corporation which is on the ropes. But the day-to-day experience of most journalists is that they have to contend with ever-stricter controls over the flow of information to the public from the state and big business. The balance of power has tipped firmly in favour of the political propagandist and the world of corporate public relations. Therefore the reporter of today has to understand how the media can be manipulated and that requires coming to terms with the influence which spin doctors can wield.

The government news machine

When a Whitehall department or a government agency is keen to promote a new policy, or has an announcement to make, there is rarely any shortage of data; access to briefings and interviews is usually readily available. In the hope of being able to influence the news agenda and prepare the public for the decisions which have been taken and which are about to be announced, ministerial statements and speeches are regularly trailed in advance, often on an exclusive basis. So insidious has been the process of politicisation that information officers employed by the state tend increasingly to be under the control of spin doctors belonging to the party in power. Each week's schedule of government announcements is carefully timed for maximum publicity and therefore the greatest political impact.

But when the tables are turned, and governments or big business are on the defensive, even run-of-the-mill enquiries about 'Who said what, where and when?' can be stonewalled. At such moments, when basic facts and figures are in such short supply, journalists face a testing moment in their relationship with the traders of information. All sorts of dodges can be deployed to avoid giving a straight answer or to throw a journalist off the scent, although the golden rule for professional public relations officers is that they must not mislead reporters or tell an untruth. Spin doctors invariably put the interests of their party first and their guidance has to be seen in that light. But political propagandists, like all other information officers, can rapidly lose credibility once they gain a reputation for deceiving the media.

Intense competition between print, broadcasting and now online journalism holds the key to understanding the shift in the balance of power between the media and the public relations industry. As the overall level of output has expanded so has the rivalry between competing news outlets. The pressure on journalists to secure exclusive stories, interviews and photographs has become intense.

How PR infiltrated politics

Among the first to exploit the growing vulnerability of journalists were public relations consultants representing business interests in the City of London. Techniques they perfected have increasingly become the norm whenever attempts are made to manipulate news coverage of politics, sport and entertainment. Brian Basham, himself a former business correspondent, switched to public relations and established a reputation as one of the hidden persuaders in the key merger and takeover battles of the early 1980s. He subsequently gave advice to Peter Mandelson after his appointment as Labour's communications director in 1985. He found that financial journalists were so desperate for scoops and tip-offs about hostile bids and share flotations that they were eager to cooperate with public relations consultants in the hope of beating their rivals. Basham told me he came to the conclusion that political correspondents were under comparable pressure to deliver exclusive insider stories about the goings on in Whitehall and Westminster:

> I was the one who coached Mandelson. I had to explain to him that news and information had become a currency, which could in effect be traded with journalists in return for sympathetic treatment... Someone in authority in a public organisation, political party or business who had control over the flow of information could easily pick out a young journalist, hand over exclusive stories and turn that reporter into a star ... that is what Peter Mandelson learned from me ... and it was the political correspondents who were ultimately delivered into the hands of the political spin doctors.

The so-called 'spin machine'

Once Tony Blair's press secretary Alastair Campbell was installed as the Downing Street director of communications in 1997 he effectively re-wrote the rule book so that the Whitehall publicity machine could raise 'its game' and 'grab the agenda'.

Previous restraints were specifically relaxed to allow civil service information officers to brief journalists on future announcements, in an attempt to ensure that the government could get its message across in a 24/7 news environment and whenever possible was 'ahead of the game'.

Trailing the contents of ministerial statements became so institutionalised that it is now regarded as accepted practice in Whitehall; the main proposals in a Budget or financial statement tend to be publicised in advance because governments are fearful of upsetting financial markets. But the constant pressure to manipulate the media has resulted in day-to-day control over the flow of confidential data to their trusted news outlets being exercised increasingly by the politically appointed special advisers who act as ministerial spin doctors. Civil servants have less authority in determining what is being said on behalf of ministers and their departments and a lack of political neutrality is being blamed for declining levels of trust in the credibility of government information and statistics.

However much the journalists of tomorrow might think they will be able to resist the blandishments of party propagandists, the reality of reporting politics is that the Mandelsons and Campbells of this world – and their successors – have become very adept at influencing the news agenda. In my opinion spin doctors and their ilk will continue to exercise a malign influence over political reportage given the highly politicised nature of the national press and its dominant role in providing a platform for political news and views.

Political bias at the top

Newspaper owners and editors are extremely fickle when dispensing political patronage and their shifting loyalties cannot be ignored by correspondents and reporters. Whereas the *Daily Mirror* has been a consistent supporter of the Labour Party, *The Sun* has revelled in the political promiscuity of its proprietor Rupert Murdoch. It backed Tony Blair in the 1997 general election and then reverted to the Conservatives in 2010, the year when both *The Guardian* and *The Observer* decided to endorse the Liberal Democrats. The Fleet Street tradition of advising readers how to vote is as strong as ever and party strategists are greatly encouraged whenever a national newspaper switches its allegiance.

In spite of repeated protestations about the impartiality of their reporting, most political stories in national daily and Sunday papers tend to be slanted, at least to some degree, to reflect an in-house editorial line. The partisan nature of this coverage is easily exploited by canny spin doctors with the offer of exclusive interviews, articles and access designed to appeal to a particular newspaper's agenda. Woe betides the reporter or sub-editor who fails to take account of this inbuilt bias. Some stories get headline treatment, others are played down and quite a few are ignored altogether if the editor thinks they would help publicise an opposing argument or look like promoting a rival political cause.

Radio and television correspondents are not immune from the pressures which spin doctors can exert. Broadcasters depend on a rapid access to news and information; they need facts and figures instantly and also immediate background briefings. Unless radio and television newsrooms maintain a good working relationship with the communications staff in government departments or at party headquarters, there is a danger they can get pushed to the back of the queue when questions need answering or interviews are required in a hurry.

As with the printed media, information traders do whatever they can to keep the upper hand and one power spin doctors take delight in is selecting which broadcaster should get preferential treatment and be given the all-important advance warning about the timing of a meeting or an announcement. Intelligence which might seem innocuous to the public but is vital to the forward planning of news bulletins and programmes. Radio and television newsrooms are as addicted as newspapers to claiming 'exclusives'. Whenever a newsreader says the 'BBC has learned...' or credits a political correspondent with this 'exclusive report...' it is highly likely that the hidden hand of a propagandist has played a part.

Developing useful contacts

Political journalists have to decide for themselves what sort of relationship they want to develop with party press officers and the communications staff of government departments. Contact can easily be maintained on a pleasant, matter of fact basis which allows respect and then a degree of trust to develop. Neither side seeks to take advantage of the other, sensing that this might jeopardise an effective way of doing day-to-day business.

Sometimes the journalist takes the initiative, perhaps suggesting lunch or a drink, in the hope a friendship might flourish and open the door to more informed off-the-record guidance and then perhaps to exclusive tip-offs and access. Alternatively a spin doctor might identify a promising potential conduit for promoting the party line or for planting stories to damage a political opponent. Broadcasters have to be meticulous in respecting confidences because unless they can be relied upon to honour embargoes they might miss out on critical advance briefings by Downing Street. Political editors for the leading channels are often briefed on an operational basis and might well be told, for example, about the Prime Minister's future movements, perhaps a visit to the Palace or a trip abroad, advance warning which gives time for camera crews to be deployed and sound recordists to take up position.

Downing Street briefings

Collective briefings given by Downing Street press officers on behalf of the Prime Minister are a regular fixture in a political reporter's life at Westminster. Guidance is also given in the lobby room in the House of Commons, at party headquarters or perhaps at the back of a conference after an important speech. Briefing correspondents en masse requires a deft touch and what causes the greatest angst for the No. 10 communications chief or for a party spin doctor is a non-stop barrage of hostile questions from journalists hunting in a pack. If the lobby is in pursuit of a potentially damaging story, whoever is briefing might have no alternative but to engage in diversionary tactics.

In my thirty years as a BBC correspondent I was frequently chided for stepping out of line by persisting with an 'unhelpful' line of questioning during Downing Street briefings. The best defensive tactic is to identify, ridicule and hopefully isolate a potential troublemaker. Margaret Thatcher's formidable press secretary

Bernard Ingham never had any difficulty putting me in my place and I am sure his routines would be just as effective today.

In March 1988, following the seizure of BBC footage of two soldiers being dragged from their car at an IRA funeral, I asked if Ingham would remind the lobby of the full extent of government legal action against journalists. He paused for effect and then said coldly it was time that BBC reporters like myself decided whether we were 'part of society or apart from society'.

When at a subsequent briefing I tried repeatedly to ask about the government's classification procedure for secret documents, he displayed his aptitude for isolating maverick questioners. As I patiently rephrased my enquiry Ingham put on a show of mock surprise. At an appropriate moment he looked solemnly at the assembled journalists, saying: 'This laddie thinks he's got an exclusive.' There were cackles all round. Having diverted attention he moved swiftly to the next question.

A decade later, Alastair Campbell deployed precisely the same techniques on Tony Blair's behalf but with none of Ingham's finesse. My reports for BBC Radio on a threatened fire fighters' strike in the run-up to the 1997 general election prompted a tirade of abuse as reporters gathered for a Labour Party news conference. Campbell let rip the moment he saw me: 'So that's the story then, a trade union dispute ... I just love the way you guys in the BBC decide what the issue is ... John Major only has to fart to get on the news. If Tony Blair does something positive you don't report it.'

My fascination with the black arts of media manipulation was used against me whenever Campbell had the opportunity. During one Downing Street briefing he noticed that I was still busily taking notes about what he thought was some arcane point and he interrupted his remarks to point out, to the amusement of the assembled lobby, that 'Nick Jones is the only correspondent still taking notes, obviously having an orgasm on spin over there in the corner.'

Speeding up the spin machine

Peter Mandelson's put-downs were in a class of their own and every political reporter who has dealt with him over the years probably has a tale to tell. His rebukes were often delivered in a follow-up phone call or a handwritten note. I knew how much he distrusted my work and in the years he was Labour's director of communications he made numerous complaints to BBC managers and editors about my radio and television reports. During one encounter he pointed out, with only the merest hint of menace in his voice, that I should realise he was having lunch next day with John Birt, then the BBC's deputy director general.

When I wrote an article for *The Guardian* in 1993 about signs that Mandelson was shifting his attentions from Gordon Brown to Tony Blair I was subjected to a torrent of abuse: 'I feel such hurt... You have abused trust and friendship, all because you want to make yourself a media star... You have woven one or two facts and embroidered them into a rich tapestry... I hope I never have any contact with you ever again.'

The lesson of my experience is that political journalists need to develop a thick skin. Spin doctors use bluster and abuse to help fend off awkward questions and fire a warning shot over the bows of a recalcitrant correspondent. The golden rule is never to take the bait. If correspondents start answering back or lose their temper, a crafty spin doctor will think nothing of going over the head of a reporter direct to an editor or producer – and the resulting aggravation tends to be a needless distraction.

Labour's reputation for attempting to bully and intimidate the media was constantly exploited by their opponents and once he was elected party leader in 2005 David Cameron promised that a future Conservative administration would turn its back on the spin of the Blair–Brown years. In the event the inconclusive result of the 2010 general election, and the formation of the first peacetime coalition since the 1930s, threw up a far greater challenge for Cameron and the Liberal Democrats' leader Nick Clegg.

They each took with them into office key members of their campaign teams and they then faced the unprecedented task of trying to amalgamate two hitherto hostile teams of highly partisan propagandists. Among the party apparatchiks working in Westminster and Whitehall, spin doctors tend to be the most tribal and welding them together into one harmonious group required a transformation in the traditional mindset of political public relations.

One of Cameron's first tasks was to give a pep talk to the sixty-six special advisers appointed by the two parties; they all became temporary civil servants alongside the Conservatives' chief spin doctor Andy Coulson, who was installed as the new Downing Street director of communications, and the Liberal Democrats' former communications chief Jonny Oates.

If any member of the coalition's newly appointed cadre of ministerial advisers was caught preparing or disseminating 'inappropriate material or personal attacks' he or she would 'automatically be dismissed' by their appointing minister. Cameron said he wanted no repeat of the anonymous and negative briefings which became so corrosive under Blair and Brown and he reminded them in no uncertain terms of the need to refrain from using the news media to attack each other or their partners in the coalition.

The importance of timing

Unless struck by misfortune, an incoming government can expect a lengthy honeymoon with the news media because a freshly elected administration can set the agenda with a constant flow of announcements. Journalists clamour for information on policy decisions and there could be no better time for a spin doctor eager to find a newspaper, radio or television programme prepared to trail the contents of a forthcoming ministerial statement. But the longer a party is in power the harder it gets for political propagandists and the greater the likelihood of a fractious relationship between journalist and spin doctor.

Nicholas Jones was a BBC political correspondent for thirty years. His books include Strikes and the Media *(1986),* Soundbites and Spin Doctors *(1995),* Sultans of Spin *(1999) and* Campaign 2010: The Making of the Prime Minister.

17: It's the economy stupid!

Professor Steve Schifferes

These days political journalists need some understanding of public spending, budget deficits and the economy to be able to do their job effectively. This is a big change from before, when such specialist knowledge was usually the preserve of economics correspondents – although the two specialist types of reporters have always competed, especially in relation to big set-piece events, such as Budgets. And nowadays it is not just domestic but also international economic policy that is required reading for political correspondents, with the global spread of the economic crisis and the impact of trouble elsewhere on the UK economy.

With the 2011 government facing the largest deficit in peacetime UK economic history – a consequence of the biggest financial and economic crisis since the Great Depression of the 1930s – the problems of the economy, of the banking sector and of public spending are likely to dominate political debate for years, if not decades, to come.

But in order to understand the debate we must first understand where responsibility lies.

The main players

The two most important figures shaping government economic policy are the Chancellor of the Exchequer (in charge of the Treasury) and the Prime Minister (who is also, as engraved on the door of No. 10, the First Lord of the Treasury).

When they agree, the course of government usually runs

smoothly, but unfortunately – or fortunately for journalists – they often fall out, with both political and economic consequences that go beyond their personal struggle.

Relations between PMs and their Chancellors

Tensions between Chancellors of the Exchequer and Prime Ministers have always been the stuff of political reporting. It reached its apogee in the titanic battles between Gordon Brown and Tony Blair for the soul of New Labour, particularly from 2001 to 2007. In spite of Tony Blair's agreement to leave domestic economic policy to Mr Brown, the two repeatedly clashed on taxes and spending, and reform of public sector services, such as health and education. Mr Brown's predilection for more redistributionist policies led to 'redistribution by stealth' through such measures as the Education Maintenance Allowance and the tax credit system (now being partly dismantled by the coalition government.) Meanwhile Tony Blair's frustrated attempts to introduce more market discipline in health and education are now the driving force behind many of the changes in health, education and local government being introduced by the new government. The paralysis at the heart of New Labour after 2001 was an important reason why spending increases were not matched by tax rises (except for a one-off increase in National Insurance payroll taxes) during the years of prosperity.

Of course there is nothing new in such battles. Mrs Thatcher famously sacked two Chancellors for not being 'one of us' only to appoint a third (John Major), who shortly thereafter replaced her as Prime Minister. Harold Wilson, in his first term in office, tried to get round his Chancellors (Jim Callaghan and Roy Jenkins) by appointing an 'economic czar' (George Brown at the Department of Economic Affairs), which led to division in decision making – and then delayed the inevitable devaluation of the pound in 1969. Harold Macmillan, however, suffered little political damage when he sacked his Chancellor (Lord Thorneycroft) in 'a little local difficulty' for being too right wing.

Mrs Thatcher was not unique in employing an economic adviser to keep her Chancellor at bay, even if Sir Alan Walters became rather too much of the focus in her battle with Nigel Lawson over exchange rates and shadowing the nascent euro.

Labour Chancellor Gordon Brown's advisers, notably Ed Balls, became powerful figures in the Treasury, often controlling who would be granted an audience with Mr Brown. It was a sign of Mr Brown's growing weakness as Prime Minister when it emerged he had been unable to carry out his plan to appoint Mr Balls to Chancellor in a Cabinet reshuffle. (Mr Brown had fallen out, in an even more damaging conflict with his Chancellor and former ally, Alistair Darling, over whether the UK was entering a recession, and whether spending cuts would be necessary.) And the signs are that the tensions could continue for Labour even in opposition, with the Leader of the Opposition Ed Miliband (who also worked for Mr Brown) belatedly appointing his old rival, Mr Balls, as shadow Chancellor.

If the conflict between Chancellor and Prime Minister dominated the last Labour government, things are different so far in the early stages of the coalition government. PM David Cameron has generally deferred to his campaign manager and Chancellor George Osborne in matters of economic policy as they remain the best of friends.

A more interesting relationship in the current government is between the Chancellor and his chief lieutenant, the Chief Secretary to the Treasury (who also sits in Cabinet). It is the chief secretary who is responsible for controlling public spending, a role which frequently puts him in conflict with other government departments and in the public spotlight as the architect of cuts.

Under the coalition government, this role has been filled by a Liberal Democrat and, after the abrupt resignation of David Laws, is currently held by Danny Alexander, one of the chief architects of the Liberal Democrat–Conservative coalition deal. It remains to be seen whether this decision has allowed the Conservatives to 'dodge the bullet' of responsibility for the big spending cuts, putting the Liberal Democrats (who also control sensitive portfolios such as higher education) in the spotlight, and taking the political flak. Political journalists would do well to keep a close eye on the way the relationships between these key individuals develop.

The third man

There is, however, another key player in the economic policy making – the governor of the Bank of England. He has become increasingly important since 1997, when the Labour government granted the Bank of England's Monetary Policy Committee 'operational independence' to set interest rates.

Governor Mervyn King was an active player in the debates over what to do during the financial crisis. He displayed astute political survival instincts when Labour politicians tried to blame him for the crisis (they had to settle on blaming the financial regulator, the Financial Services Authority, and the deputy governor instead). It was Mervyn King's testimony before the House of Commons Treasury Committee in September 2007 that turned the tables, and this body – which provides parliamentary oversight for Treasury functions – has also become more important, particularly under its former Labour chairman, John McFall (now Lord McFall).

The IFS

For all journalists covering public spending and budgets, one independent organisation looms above all others in importance: the Institute for Fiscal Studies, which provides impartial analysis of budget and spending decisions in a timely fashion (normally holding a press conference the day after the Budget).

There are other independent economists and forecasters who provide commentary, from both think tanks, academia and private sector organisations like banks and consultancies, but none can match the speed or firepower of the IFS.

The set pieces – Budgets, autumn statements, and spending reviews

For political journalists, much of the coverage of taxes and spending decisions by governments comes as set pieces – in particular the annual Budget when the Chancellor announces his tax and spending decisions for the financial year (thus it usually occurs in March just before the financial year ends on the first Monday in April).

The coalition government threw out many of the other budgetary innovations introduced by Labour, most notably the 'pre-Budget report', which normally took place in November and was in effect a mini-Budget, where both spending and tax decisions were signalled in advance of the actual Budget.

Instead, we now have a scaled-down 'autumn statement', required under legislation so that the Chancellor can update his economic and public spending forecast, but so far containing few substantive policy announcements. In the past, Conservative administrations had used the autumn statement each year to announce their spending decisions, while taxes were announced in the Budget.

The coalition also replaced Labour's two-year spending review, which looked forward to future government spending plans, with a one-off Comprehensive Spending Review in October 2010, which was intended to set departmental spending plans for the next five years until the planned election in 2015.

For the future, then, government policy for both taxes and spending will be set in the Budget. And therefore it is the Budget where the key decisions are made as to how the burden of reducing the budget deficit is to fall between increasing taxes or cutting spending.

Reporting the Budget: the Red Book

In the Budget the Chancellor will produce an economic forecast for the next two years, and a projection of how public spending will be affected by his proposed tax and spending changes. This is usually the most closely watched portion of his speech, especially as in recent years all governments have adopted targets to restrain themselves from excessive spending.

The Budget is followed by a few days of debate followed by a series of votes on resolutions which approve the key proposals in principle. But most of the announcements become law through the Finance Bill. This crucial piece of legislation goes through the same stages as other Public Bills with one difference: the House of Lords debates the Bill's proposals but has no power to amend or revise them. This is in recognition that the key decisions on taxes should remain with the democratically elected House of Commons. This was established after a battle between the radical Liberal Lloyd

Budget Terms

AME: annually managed expenditure, the spending the government cannot directly control, but estimates on an annual basis, such as benefit payments
DEL: departmental expenditure limits, the spending the government plans on a multi-year basis for specific departments like defence, health and education
Capital spending: the spending on bricks and mortar buildings, roads, schools and hospitals
Current spending: spending on year-by-year government services such as teachers' salaries, purchase of supplies, and transfer payments (e.g. pensions)
Revenues: all receipts received by governments, including taxes and charges
Constant prices (or real prices): prices adjusted for the effect of inflation
Cash prices (or current prices): prices not adjusted for inflation
Budget deficit: the difference between spending and tax receipts each year
Government debt: the total outstanding borrowing by the government made up of all the accumulated deficits over the years
Cyclically adjusted budget deficit (or structural deficit): the part of the budget deficit that is not dependent on the swings of the economic cycle (i.e. will not go away when economic growth resumes)
Spending envelope: the overall amount of DEL spending the government is planning for a particular year, as set out in the Budget
Fiscal year: the government's year runs from April to April, when most tax changes come into force

George and the House of Lords over his 1909 'People's Budget', which raised taxes on the rich.

Details of the Budget are set out in the Red Book, a large tome which gives full details of the economic and spending forecasts and is pored over by experts for several days after the Budget announcement in the House of Commons. It is to the Red Book that one must turn for the accurate information about the real effects of the Budget on the economy: where it is taking money out or putting it back in; and the scale of the changes in public spending.

Following the Budget, there are usually further details of

spending plans that are announced by individual departments. These are usually spaced over several days to give maximum publicity to any new programmes that are to be put into place. As with Budget announcements, journalists need to be careful that these are not re-announcements of policies which have already been proposed before, perhaps with some more detailed costings.

Pleasing the markets: the Budget rules

It should be noted that in its Budget, the government normally has two very different audiences in mind – the financial markets, who need to be reassured that the government is being tough on the public finances, in order to encourage them to continue to buy government bonds to finance the deficit; and the general public, who need to be reassured that the economy will recover soon, bringing the prospect of lower unemployment and higher wages, and who are more interested in the detail of public spending.

The financial markets matter because, in order to function, all governments need to finance or refinance their borrowing by going out into the market and asking individuals or financial institutions to lend them money. These loans are fixed-term bonds issued by the government at a certain interest rate and maturity (i.e. between one and ten years). If financial markets lose confidence in the government's ability to manage their finances, they will refuse to buy government bonds, forcing the government to raise interest rates on them to make them more attractive. This, in turn, increases the cost of government borrowing and can become a vicious spiral.

As a result of the spiralling budget deficit and growing government debt, when the coalition government came to power the amount of debt interest they were paying each year had doubled to around £44 billion per year, and was expected to double again to just under £80 billion by the end of their term in office – a sum equal to 12 per cent of all government spending, greater than the size of the education budget.

The financial markets lost confidence in the UK's ability to manage its deficit when Labour's self-imposed budget rules collapsed in the crisis.

But what rules do govern the budget deficit?

The UK government, unlike those countries in the eurozone, is not obliged to adhere to the Maastricht Treaty limit of a deficit of 3 per cent of GDP, but has created its own self-imposed spending rules to reassure the markets. Under Labour's now abandoned 'golden rule', the current budget deficit (that is, excluding capital spending on such things as schools, roads and hospitals) should 'average' zero over the 'economic cycle as a whole' – a policy that was difficult to implement as the definition of the economic cycle was often adjusted retrospectively.

The current government has a less complicated rule – to reduce the 'cyclically adjusted budget deficit' to zero within the life of the parliament (i.e. in five years). This does leave some wriggle room over the definition of 'cyclically adjusted' (i.e., excluding the effects of the recession – which begs the question of whether UK output can ever be expected to return to 'normal' levels; if not the cuts can be less). But it is undoubtedly a tougher standard that is driving the large (25 per cent) spending cuts now sweeping across most UK government departments – and it is this target which is being closely watched by financial markets.

The government has also established a new body, the Office of Budget Responsibility, to determine whether the government is likely to meet its fiscal targets. It makes estimates, released at the time of the Budget and Autumn statement, on how the UK economy is doing, and whether the government is meeting its targets for reducing the budget deficit. It is intended to be independent of the Treasury in order to increase the credibility of government forecasts, and is run by a former head of the IFS, and its estimates will be closely watched by journalists.

Taxes v. spending

It should be noted that from the point of view of markets, it is equally possible to balance the budget by increasing taxes as well as by lowering spending.

But for both political and economic reasons, the coalition government has favoured spending cuts rather than tax rises as its preferred means of cutting the deficit – although the government has introduced one big new tax increase, raising VAT from 17.5 per cent to 20 per cent. But 80 per cent of the reductions in the budget deficit are to come from reduced spending, and only 20 per cent from higher taxes, many of which had already been introduced by Labour.

In contrast, Labour in power was planning on 66 per cent of the reductions coming from spending cuts, and 33 per cent from tax rises – and now in opposition some in Labour suggest that the balance should be 60–40.

Spending cuts are often preferred by financial markets – because they are seen as less easily reversed by future governments and are seen as less likely to 'crowd out' private enterprise and private initiatives, which may be essential to promoting economic growth, especially as the government's role is diminishing.

The leading economic think tank, the OECD, has produced studies which suggest that spending cuts are more effective in stabilising budgets over the long term. There is the counter-argument that in terms of fairness, public spending cuts are more likely to fall on the poor, while tax increases, especially on income, hit the rich. The coalition, however, under the influence of its Liberal Democrat partners, has been trying to stress the progressive nature of its tax increases, which have involved some increases in capital gains taxes that hit the rich, and a staged increase in the personal allowance designed to take more people out of the tax system at the bottom end of the income distribution. But as 30 per cent of the population is too poor to pay any taxes, this is hardly full-bloodied redistribution.

Spending decisions in the Budget

On spending, the Budget lays down what is called the 'spending envelope', laying down global targets for both current spending (on things like teacher salaries) and capital projects (like roads and bridges). These are known as 'Department Expenditure Limits' (DELs). But nearly half of government spending is not directly under the control of departments, most notably items such as benefit claims (which depend on the number of people claiming) and the debt interest on the national debt (which depends on interest rates).

So the government also publishes an estimate of 'annually managed expenditure' (AME) which together with department spending makes up total managed spending.

One trick often played by governments, which the keen journalist should look out for, is to present spending figures in cash terms rather than adjusting for inflation – something that is contrary to good practice but has been increasingly used by the current government to reduce the apparent size of spending cuts. It is also important for journalists to check whether projections for future spending and revenue are presented in real (constant) or nominal (current prices).

Another common tactic is to leak selective details of headline policies that the government would like to generate favourable coverage. It is the most common 'spin', with the Sunday and Monday papers often full of speculative but well-sourced stories ahead of the Budget, which is usually presented on a Tuesday or Wednesday. The opposite approach is usually taken by departments which fear spending cuts, and warnings of the consequences of Treasury demands on individual department spending. In the 2010 spending round, this proved an effective way in which the Defence Secretary, Liam Fox, tried to limit the damage to his department budget – although he still lost HMS *Ark Royal*, his aircraft carrier, and its Harrier jump jets.

The coalition government also eliminated the custom of the previous Labour government to hold a spending review (giving a three-year forward plan for departmental spending) every two years. However Labour did fail to have its normal spending review, due in 2009 before the election, claiming that economic circumstances were so uncertain that it could not specify the level of cuts necessary in three years' time.

In contrast, the coalition has decided to conduct just one spending review to set out a long-term path for public spending cuts until the next election, with many of the cuts front-loaded so that they mainly happen in the next two years (and hopefully are less salient by the next election).

So there are no plans for further spending reviews at the moment, although the details of spending cuts are being spelled out at the departmental level and changes in relation to specific programmes, if not to overall totals, could be made every year.

Public spending is also reported on a monthly basis by the Office for National Statistics, so economists and reporters can monitor the government's record in meeting its targets – although such monthly figures can be subject to big fluctuations, especially around income and corporation tax deadlines.

The politics of spending cuts

In considering how fast to cut overall public spending, the coalition government was mainly concerned with reassuring the global financial markets that the UK was not about to sink into an abyss, like that of Ireland or Greece, where it lost a grip on its public finances. The fact that the Greek crisis occurred during the UK general election in May 2010 added to the urgency of the task for the new government.

However, in implementing the detail of the spending cuts that are unprecedented in their scope and severity (amounting to some 25 per cent of total government spending over four years), political considerations are more important. So 'popular' areas of spending that are believed to have widespread public support, notably health and education, have been relatively protected – with both departments securing a real-term increase in their budgets (in the case of schools, however, of only 0.1 per cent over four years). This was also true in the case of Labour, where these areas saw the fastest increases in spending (with a doubling of spending on the NHS over eight years).

Another tactic to manage the political impact of the spending cuts is to try and make them less visible. This means more severe cuts to capital spending projects, such as the schools building budget. These have a long lead time and their impact are less obvious than cuts to current school budgets which would involve making more teachers redundant. Capital spending by the coalition government is going to fall by 50 per cent, as opposed to the overall cut of 25 per cent, something Labour had also planned to do – and it was also a leading tactic in implementing cuts during the Thatcher years.

Central v. local government spending

Capital spending only amounts to 10 per cent of government spending, down from 20 per cent during the Thatcher years. So the government is also trying to shift the locus of decision-taking to other bodies, notably local government, which is responsible for around £180 billion of government spending.

Spending cuts for local authorities are particularly large, with a 17 per cent cut in the first two years alone. But the government is increasing the 'freedom' of local authorities to manage their budgets any way they like by abolishing many ring-fenced spending categories. Ministers hope that the public will blame the councils, most of whom are not Conservative-controlled, rather than the central government, for the scale of the spending cuts to local services. At the same time they are urging local councils not to cut 'front-line services' but reduce back office bureaucracy by 'efficiency savings' – the perennial chant of all governments who want to avoid hard decisions about spending. Labour also tried to get efficiency savings in central government spending, with decidedly mixed results. Recent research casts doubt on at least half of the claimed £35 billion in efficiency savings they said they had made.

Hidden charges: stealth taxation

Finally, governments can also try to shift the cost of services onto users through higher charges and fees. This strategy is currently being applied in several areas: the government's plan to charge council tenants higher rents, the proposal to raise consumers' energy bills to help fund major investments in green power and new nuclear power generation and the plan to charge university students much higher tuition fees in order to fund higher education.

To work politically, however, this strategy is more effective if the public remain uncertain about the scale of the changes and where responsibility lies. Hence the plan to triple tuition fees to £9,000 per year produced the first major test of political will for the coalition government, and may have seriously damaged the Liberal Democrats (who fought the election on a pledge not to raise tuition fees) for many years to come.

Managing the economy

Ultimately the whole government, and not just the Treasury, bears the responsibility for managing the economy.

The Treasury with its 'fiscal judgement' is responsible for setting some of the key parameters of the economy: how much government money to inject into the economy or how much to take out in order to reduce the deficit.

Unfortunately it is often difficult to understand the current state of the economy accurately. The main figures on the growth of the economy (GDP) are reported only every three months (and look back several months) and can be subject to frequent revision up or down.

The government and many economists try to rely on other indicators which are reported more frequently, such as monthly surveys of business and consumer confidence, unemployment and inflation figures. But these can only give a partial picture of the state of the economy and some, like unemployment, generally lag behind other changes.

The Bank of England

With government spending so constrained by the big deficit, another instrument of economic policy – monetary policy, or interest rates, which is managed by the independent Bank of England – has become increasingly important. The Bank announces its decision on interest rates every month after a two-day meeting of the Monetary Policy Committee that normally finishes on Thursday lunchtime.

As the government deficit has grown, more responsibility for ensuring the economic recovery has fallen into the lap of the Bank, which has maintained interest rates at unprecedented low levels for a very long time after the financial crisis broke. Officially, the Bank's sole objective in setting interest rates is to keep inflation at around the government's target rate of 2 per cent. But informally the Bank under Mr King has increasingly prioritised economic growth. In order to boost the economy further when interest rates were low, shortly after the crisis the Bank introduced a policy of 'quantitative easing' by which it bought government bonds in order to drive interest rates even lower and stimulate the economy.

The jury is still out on whether this policy has achieved its objective. What is clear is that the Bank of England's policy makers are now unsure as to whether they should inject more stimulus to ward off a recession, to keep things as they are, with low interest rates to ensure a recovery, or raise interest rates against the threat of future inflation, which has remained stubbornly high and above government targets despite the economic slowdown. At some point, it is likely that the Bank will have to start raising interest rates, and its skill in doing so will play a critical part in the strength or otherwise of the economic recovery.

During the current crisis, the role of the Bank will need to be closely watched by political journalists. The closeness between the governor and the Chancellor could come under strain if higher rates of inflation force the Bank to start raising interest rates. The current Chancellor has staked a lot on the role low interest rates could play in helping the economy to recover, and in turn has received the endorsement of the Bank governor for his programme of spending cuts.

Sharing the blame

The scale of the economic crisis that hit the UK between 2007 and 2010 fatally undermined Labour's reputation for economic competence and helped make it almost inevitable that the Conservatives would be the overall gainers in the 2010 general election. The state of the economy will play a central role in who can win the next election, so the battleground in the future will be the scale and scope of any economic recovery – although the debate on how effective Labour was in dealing with the crisis will go on. What is sometimes forgotten in the debate about the size of budget deficits is that, without major government intervention, the world financial and economic system could have really faced meltdown, leading to a 1930s-style Great Depression.

Britain was more vulnerable to a slump than most countries for one simple reason – its relatively large and international financial sector compared to the size of its economy. The success of the City had been a constant refrain of both Labour and Conservative governments, and maintaining its competitive advantage by light touch regulation was embraced by New Labour as much as by the Conservatives – not least because, in the good times, the City and its bonuses was providing up to 30 per cent of tax revenues.

There is likely to continue to be a big debate about the future role of the banking sector in the UK, and how tough the new regulatory system – redesigned by the coalition government – should be. But it will not be the UK government alone that shapes banking reform. Both international bodies and the EU are already closely involved, and will constrain the room for manoeuvre for any government.

Looking forwards

Governments often overstate the influence they have on the economy, denying responsibility during bad times – or blaming others – while taking the credit during economic booms. In truth, the UK economy is not big enough to influence the overall development of the world economy, but Britain, as a trading nation, is highly exposed to international economic conditions.

It would be all too characteristic if, at some point, the Chancellor – following the tradition of many Chancellors before him – started to look at the lack of recovery in international conditions as a reason for slow growth in Britain, or blame foreign speculators.

As a result no journalist should don blinkers, reporting on UK-centric economic and financial decisions and results without taking into account the wider situation of the world economy.

Steve Schifferes is Marjorie Deane Professor of Financial Journalism, City University, London, and former economics correspondent, BBC News Online.

18: The birth of a Bill

Sheila Gunn

'Ministers under pressure to reform the law...'
'Pressure group launches campaign...'
'Radical shake-up in ... laws urged by party policy makers'
'Influential think tank demands change...'

Government departments compete every parliamentary session to secure a slot in the timetable to introduce 'their' Bills. It can be a masochistic contest, based on which ministers can bring in the most and heaviest Bills. Who thinks up the ideas for all these planned changes in the law?

There is no longer one simple process, rather a range of conventional routes. But sussing out new policy ideas, reporting on campaigns and pressure groups and spotting potential reforms provide satisfying fare for journalists. While political reporters hunt down these stories, they are even more important for specialist journalists. Sometimes of course the media itself plays a role in persuading a government – and the opposition parties – to change its policy or the law.

Sources for new policies

The most usual parentage of a proposed change in the law is:

- the PM's policy unit
- other government departments' policy units
- party policy units

- political/parliamentary pressure
- think tanks
- pressure or campaign groups.

The gestation process usually, but not always, takes far longer than nine months.

Common features are timing, a growing consensus that 'something must be done' and the continual search by political parties to update and improve the laws for the benefit of its citizens.

Whether raising taxes, restricting immigration or tightening the drink/driving laws, the magic ingredient is timing: what is unacceptable one year may become law with little dispute the next. Sometimes this is due to a change in public attitudes, sometimes through economic circumstances or perhaps through a successful campaign.

The late, great Viscount Whitelaw, Margaret Thatcher's deputy Prime Minister, was known for his short, sharp comments on political events. Thatcher was keen to liberalise the Sunday shopping laws and introduced a Bill to do so. The House of Lords killed it stone dead. When I challenged Whitelaw on this, he reacted with his usual style. Giving me his unnerving look and a strong gin he opined: 'Timing is everything in life. This was not the right time for the Bill. Within the next few years, it will be the right time.' His prediction proved correct and the law was changed in 1994 with little fuss.

The 'something must be done' syndrome can infect the political classes swiftly or creep up very slowly. Journalists can play a part. Ministers, but more especially their senior civil servants, dislike being pushed into changes in the law too quickly. And the House of Lords hates hasty legislation.

The example often cited is the 1991 Dangerous Dogs Act. Following a vicious attack on a child by a dog bred for fighting, the media was suddenly full of stories of similar attacks. This was not because of a sudden and sharp rise in aggressive dogs, just that they had become more newsworthy. Under pressure the then Home Secretary, Kenneth (now Lord) Baker brought in a Bill to ban and destroy certain breeds, such as American pitbulls. This was fast tracked through Parliament. It is not judged to be a good law, although that probably had far more to do with the way it was implemented.

Conversely an issue may roll around Westminster and Whitehall for years before a government agrees to a change of policy. For instance, campaigners had been calling for a ban on smoking in public places for decades. The tipping point came when Tony Blair's government gauged that public attitudes had changed, that there was widespread support in Parliament and bans in other countries had worked well. The subsequent Bill then went through Parliament with surprisingly little opposition.

Reforming local government finance is a quite different issue: policy makers in all parties know that the present system is not perfect. But they remember the poll tax, and its role in Thatcher's downfall. The old rating system was widely considered to be grossly unfair as it did not recognise people's ability to pay. Also many local residents on good incomes paid little towards local services, while some with low incomes faced high annual bills.

Policy makers in No. 10, the Treasury and relevant government departments sat down and devised the community charge (immediately dubbed the poll tax by journalists). A good case study in how not to introduce a new law. Not only did they use Scotland as a guinea pig to try it out first, but they ignored warnings by peers, some MPs and councillors that you cannot suddenly ask great swathes of the country to pay a new tax for the first time without a reasonable transition period. The outcome is history.

The continuous process of examining our laws and pressing for changes may be a key part of a democracy. But once ministers leave office, many accept that too many Acts of Parliament – often with unintended consequences – are passed. It is salutary to consider the Licensing Act brought in by Blair's government with great fanfare, with the intention of introducing a more civilised 'continental-style' drinking regime and combat binge drinking.

The Prime Minister's and government departments' policy units

Some of the best brains in the country have flourished in No. 10, conjuring up new policies and reforms. Penetrating its inner workings is a challenge for a political journalist. Its incumbents are wary of mixing with journalists at all, although political commentators often fare better. Some would say that few of these policy makers mix with 'normal human beings'. They are personally appointed by the PM and owe their loyalty to him personally and his party. Membership of the policy unit of a new PM is always closely monitored by political journalists.

Those developing policies in government departments vary but, apart from the role played by special advisers (explored by Colin Brown) they focus on more modest changes in the laws affecting their responsibilities.

The more radical and forward-thinking ideas are expected to come out of the No. 10 operation. For this reason, it can be resented by ministers and officials if these ideas impact on their work. For instance, during the Blair–Brown years, we now know that No. 10 and No. 11 ran quite separate units, effectively in competition.

With a new government, the emphasis is usually on legislating for key parts of the successful party's election manifesto. In a coalition, of course, manifestos are not worth the paper they are printed on – a fact which seems to come as news to too many journalists.

Pressures then start to build up on the government to bring in other changes in the law. Some may be accepted, most rejected. Two or three years down the road, the PM and his circle will be anxious to show that they still have plenty of proactive, fresh ideas – and are not coasting or merely reacting to events. The focus then switches to looking towards the next general election. The label which sends a chill down the spines of politicians is that they've 'run out of steam'. At the same time the opposition parties will be grabbing the headlines with their 'exciting new policies'. The governing party will want to be seen to be at least as innovative.

Party policy units

All the parties have those dedicated to working up new policies. You should have key players in your contacts book, although most are warned not to talk to journalists.

Much of the governing party's policy making goes on in No. 10, although there will be some work done within the party HQ – especially within the eighteen months before a general election. Then there are the alternative reforms coming out of the main opposition party's HQ. Nor should you neglect the smaller parties, although there is a temptation to focus attention on what may seem to be more outrageous ideas. But it is worth remembering that what may seem outrageous today, may well become mainstream thinking one day.

Once upon a time, the annual party conferences played a key role in policy making. This was wonderful for journalists as they could spend three weeks at various seaside resorts reporting the consequent rows, splits, reference backs, storming out type of activity. Perhaps that is why the parties have largely put a stop to it. Party conferences now play little or no role in dictating their party's policies.

However new policies usually need to go through various internal processes, which tends to throw up some interesting stories. But be warned: their aides often use a political journalist to 'trail' a new policy. That is, they brief a journalist, who then – as it is an exclusive – gives it prominence. 'The ... party is set to announce a new policy...' for instance. If the reaction is good, then they continue to work on it. If hostile, they can always deny that they are planning such a reform.

Political and parliamentary pressure

The tools used by backbench MPs and peers to apply pressure to change the law are outlined elsewhere. Their success depends to a large extent on how successfully they generate support.

Think tanks

Institute for Public Policy Research, Policy Exchange, Fabian Society, Demos, Social Market Foundation, the Adam Smith Institute: just a few of the UK's leading think tanks, which, as the name implies, research and think up new policies. They represent a particular strand of political thinking, such as left-of-centre, free market, right wing. A regular scrutiny of political and national media will throw up references to their reports and work as in 'according to the influential left-of-centre think tank...'

Developing good contacts, monitoring the work of the more influential – or, at least, joining their email networks – is almost certain to pay off. Which ones have most influence depends to a large extent on the political cycle, that is, who is in and out of office. For instance, the IPPR was New Labour's think tank, testing and working up many of the policies for Blair's first government; Policy Exchange did a similar task for David Cameron.

Four features of their work of interest are:

- regular publications with new research, data and proposals for changing the law
- regular events to launch the new publications or host speeches by senior figures
- their involvement in party conference activities
- they are often a training ground for the politicians and party officials of the future.

Most struggle financially and their staff rarely earn much money, which makes them quite grateful for some hospitality. Their events are also useful for making new contacts with politicians and their aides, deepening your knowledge of policy issues and demonstrating your own dedication to your job. Free wine is often on offer. Just remember never to accept that third glass. More than a few have come unstuck that way.

Pressure & campaigning groups

Student loans? Joanna Lumley and the Gurkhas? Third Heathrow runway?

Once known, you are likely to be bombarded with material from those campaigning for a change in the law on all manner of issues from abattoirs to zygotes. Given time restraints, you will often reach for the delete button. But at least stash away some of the contact details, for you never know when they will be timely and useful.

Many MPs and peers become attached to specific campaigns

and will sensibly encourage your support. Try to help. You can learn a lot and also develop a productive working relationship with the parliamentarian concerned. When I was keeping an eye on a complicated Bill to do with copyright law, I was approached by some very senior peers, including the former PM Lord Callaghan. One effect of the Bill was that Great Ormond Street Hospital could soon lose the royalties from J. M. Barrie's works, such as *Peter Pan,* on which it depended. Officials did not want to make an exception for this one hospital, but pressure from the peers together with *The Times* helped persuade them to find a way.

Some journalists become campaigners themselves, though it is wise to discuss this with your colleagues and newsdesk if there is a risk that you are losing your objectivity.

One step further is to persuade your own media outlet to back or even instigate a particular campaign. It can be immensely satisfying – as long as you do not forget that you are a journalist, not a politician. All the contributors to this book have undoubtedly helped to make a difference on occasion to whether a campaign succeeds or not. The issue may be a simple one. When on the then *Surrey Daily Advertiser* I learnt that the local health authority planned to close Cranleigh Hospital because of financial cuts. My editor agreed to run a campaign to raise an agreed sum of money to save it. With tremendous help from local residents we did – and it is still thriving today.

'We propose a change in the law...'

Once a government has decided to change the law, there is generally quite a long process before a Bill is introduced. All these stages generate media coverage.

The usual process is for the relevant government department to publish a Green Paper – outlining its ideas for reform, although the details are still open to consultation. Expect a press conference or launch event, together with a statement in the Commons. This will be followed by a White Paper, a more formal statement of how the government intends to change the law. Again, a launch and statement in the House can be expected.

Political journalists will cover them to some extent, particularly if they are extremely controversial. But the specialist journalists will usually provide most of the coverage. What can cause some friction is the tendency for the political journalist's name or comments to be given most prominence, with the specialist's analysis following on.

19: Changing the law

Chris Moncrieff

The two most important occasions in the parliamentary calendar are Budget Day and the State Opening.

In the past, Budget Day was a nightmare for reporters. There was largely no assistance or advice from the Treasury and journalists had to rely entirely on their shorthand, rushing out of the chamber and immediately dictating copy down the telephone, straight from your notebook.

I used to wake up on Budget Day mornings wondering whether I would still be in a job by 6 o'clock that evening. It was a horrendous process, with no time to check anything with colleagues or rivals.

Some of the language used by Chancellors of the Exchequer is by no means clear. They do not simply say 'ten pence on a bottle of wine', they hedge it round with all kinds of legalistic and financial qualifications, so you take your life in your hands when you precis it down in your copy to '10p on a bottle of wine' – you can't be quite sure that it is as simple as that.

The responsibility for an agency reporter on these occasions is as awesome as the stress involved, since all the evening papers, many of the broadcasters and others always used Press Association copy because it came out so quickly. So, if you made a single mistake, that error could appear in a hundred or more media outlets – a daunting thought. It is a wonder, indeed, that more mistakes were not made.

But in recent years the arrangements have become far more civilised and Budget Day, once the worst day of the parliamentary year, is far less stressful; a miraculous transformation from the bad old days. The Treasury could not be more helpful. A senior official comes into the Press Association room in the press gallery shortly before the Chancellor opens his Budget. He is armed with a copy of the speech which he keeps close to his chest, sits down and listens to the Chancellor on headphones, checking his copy of the script with the actual delivery.

As each foolscap page is completed, he hands it to a reporter who files it straight away, without having had to write a word of shorthand. Sometimes the Treasury even provide us with major Budget announcements boiled down to a handful of words, for instance 'income tax up 2p' which is precisely what news agencies want.

Additionally, once the Chancellor has completed his Budget, a whole mass of documents suddenly appear in the press gallery, including a verbatim text of the speech (invaluable for the morning paper reporters, who are required to sum up the Budget in more depth than the evening papers).

The documents include the now famous Red Book (jokingly described as 'the Unread Book') which contains masses of detail which the Chancellor does not mention in his speech, plus complicated diagrams and graphs. Hence sometimes it is as much as three or four days later before the full impact of the Budget becomes apparent.

The Chancellor's Budget speech is traditionally followed immediately by reaction from the Leader of the Opposition. The shadow Chancellor does not intervene until the following day, when he's made a more considered appraisal of the Chancellor's proposals. Very soon after this the Chancellor will briefly meet lobby correspondents, usually off the record and unattributably, to answer the immediate questions that arise. He will then go on television to make a ministerial broadcast explaining his reasons for what appears in the Budget. The shadow Chancellor is given the opportunity to reply on television the following day.

Leaks, trails and whispers

Until recently, Chancellors used to go into 'purdah' for several weeks before the Budget, remaining silent and tight-lipped to avoid being seduced into accidentally divulging some of its contents before the event. This was largely because prior publication could affect the financial markets. Nowadays, however, Chancellors appear bolder and no longer feel the need to adopt a Trappist silence in the run-up to the Budget.

The Conservative government's last Budget before the party's cataclysmic defeat at the 1997 general election was leaked in advance in its entirety to the *Daily Mirror*. Astonishingly, the paper did not divulge any of its contents and 'sportingly' handed it back to the Treasury, simply boasting that they had got it. The then Chancellor, Kenneth Clarke, hugely embarrassed though he was by this leak, must have been mightily relieved that the *Mirror* did not make use of its spoils.

One thing political reporters should look out for in the weeks before a Budget is the Treasury dropping vague hints about its contents. They have been known to send out signals (all unattributably of course) that it will be a terrible Budget, hitting people very hard indeed. This may not be as innocent as it sounds.

Sometimes the objective is to predict a Budget whose contents are far less severe than the Treasury is making out. This means that people who are bracing themselves for the worst possible outcome, find that the Chancellor's proposals are not so bad after all. Or rather that is what the Treasury hope they will think. As a result, although it might still be a cut and burn Budget, it is greeted with some relief. On top of this, it has become almost habitual in recent years for the Treasury and others actually to divulge some of the contents of the Budget, something unheard of in the past.

I have sat through recent Budgets where the major 'announcements' have all been deliberately leaked in the previous weeks. And although Chancellors try to suggest that their Budget proposals are all 'new' in terms of news items, they are often simply recycled old hat.

It has become a tradition that Chancellors are allowed to deliver their Budgets without any interruptions or interventions while they are speaking, although there have been rare occasions when this tradition is breached. So an intervention by an MP, even a friendly one, is worth reporting. You should also check beforehand what the

Chancellor is drinking while delivering his speech. The Chancellor, on this one occasion, is allowed to sip an alcoholic beverage as he speaks. On no other occasion in the House of Commons chamber is alcohol permitted. Sadly for journalists, most Chancellors now stick to water.

Immediately after the conclusion of the Budget speech and the on-the-spot response by the Opposition leader, I used to hotfoot it down to the members' lobby to get instant reaction to what the Chancellor had been saying from backbenchers and others. Remember, papers will always use what they get first. It is much better for you, or one of your colleagues, to get straight down to the lobby, rather than to telephone an MP and wait for him to ring you back. The MP will probably reply – if he bothers to reply at all – when it is far too late. The golden rule, therefore, is to take the initiative yourself, keep the ball in your court wherever possible, rather than wait for ages for a member to respond.

In years gone by, on Budget Day, and indeed on State Opening Day, Westminster used to resemble Ladies' Day at Royal Ascot. The women MPs would dress in all their finery and many of the male MPs donned morning suits and toppers for the occasion. There was always a 'sidebar' or subsidiary story on the often glittering attire on display. Alas, that has now fallen into desuetude and it is difficult to distinguish Budget Day from any other routine parliamentary day. Even so, it is well worth keeping an eye open for the unusual, because there are still some parliamentarians who like to flaunt their finery at these big parliamentary events.

Pomp and circumstance

The State Opening of Parliament is the most spectacular and brilliant event of the entire parliamentary calendar. It is a day of unrivalled pomp and pageantry which is probably not equalled anywhere else in the world. In basic and blunt terms, the State Opening is the occasion when the Queen arrives at the Palace of Westminster to open each new session, and in doing so announces in deadpan, unemotional terms the government's programme for the coming twelve months.

It is one of the few occasions when you can see the monarch

wearing the Crown and sitting on the throne in the House of Lords. Members of the House of Commons are summoned over to the House of Lords, where the peers are clad in their robes and finery, to hear the Queen deliver the speech, an event which will usually last no more than ten minutes or so. And although it is called the Queen's Speech she will have had no part in writing it. It is prepared by ministers and sets out all – or rather some – of the legislation which the government hope to introduce.

The MPs then troop back to the Commons where the sitting is suspended for a few hours to enable the debate proper on the contents of the Speech to begin in the afternoon. In fact, like the Budget, there is often very little that is 'new' in the speech. Much of the proposed legislation will have been leaked by the relevant departments in the months running up to State Opening, even down to the number of Bills to be introduced.

So one of the tasks of the reporter is to comb the speech to see if, in fact, there is anything new in it, or whether there are any surprising omissions of Bills which had been promulgated earlier.

Copies of the Speech are normally made available to the Press Gallery a few hours before it is delivered (usually around 11am), thus giving reporters the opportunity to prepare a considered, rather than a rushed, piece. But these stories are all strictly embargoed until after the monarch has finished reading it. These copies are invariably accompanied by a large wodge of papers, provided by government departments,setting out useful background information on the measures in the speech.

These will, of course, be touched upon by the political reporter in his initial overall story about the contents of the speech, but the background material would be sent to the specialist correspondents, such as for health and transport, to prepare a more detailed appraisal of the proposed legislation and to get reaction.

The days when *The Times* and the *Daily Telegraph* in particular used to run full pages of a parliamentary debate, in chronological order, with little attempt to put the highlights at the top of the story, are long since gone. Nowadays the tendency even among the 'heavyweight' papers is for shorter, snappier stories. That is why very often only the salient and most interesting snatches of a full day's debate on a particular Bill are likely to see the light of day in print.

What the papers want now, more than anything, are stand-alone snippets, and not a long, rolling report of the day's proceedings, although that kind of report is also available from PA.

How a Bill becomes law

Legislation starts with a first reading, which is merely the nod of a head. The second reading (one of the most important parts of its progress through Parliament) is a debate on the overall content of the Bill, in general rather than detailed terms. Assuming the second reading is passed, the Bill goes into committee; a scaled down body of the parties' representation in the Commons itself. These committees usually sit twice a week, sometimes more, and discuss the Bill line-by-line. Often these committees produce stories, but they are extremely time-consuming, and you may have to sit through hours of legalistic jargon before reaching anything interesting. That is why, with so much else going on in the Commons, you have to think carefully whether you can afford spending so many hours on what can be a fruitless, unproductive occasion. But there is nothing to stop a specialist journalist covering these committees, although it is a good idea to leave a little time to make it through security at the entrance.

One particular advantage of attending these committees is that it enables you to achieve rapport with individual MPs who are physically very close to you. The more MPs you know, and who know you, the more your life in the Commons will be agreeable and fruitful.

If it passes the committee stage, then the Bill returns to the full House of Commons for the report stage where any alterations made in the Committee are reported to the House as a whole. These changes – and any others that need to be made – can be approved or otherwise. After that the Bill may have a third reading, which is normally a brief appraisal of the Bill in its revised form, if it has been changed during its progress through Parliament, but these are not usually influential.

After that, assuming once more that it has successfully passed through all its stages, the Bill will go to the House of Lords where it undergoes similar treatment.

It is assumed that all Bills start in the Commons. This is not right. To even out the workload between the two Houses, in every session a few Bills which may be long and complicated but do evoke sharp political differences will start their progress in the Lords. When all stages are passed, they move to the Commons.

Any amendments made by the Lords to the Bill have to go back to the Commons for approval or otherwise. If the Commons rejects any of these amendments, the Bill returns to the Lords – and there can be ping-ponging, with the Bill going backwards and forwards between the two Houses until agreement is reached. The general rule is that the Commons has the last word, but in practice, many of the amendments made in the Lords are eventually accepted by ministers so long as they do not wreck or greatly change the key policies. The idea is that the Lords does two things: improves the Bill using the expertise of the peers and in a more relaxed atmosphere; and occasionally asks the government to 'think again' on more significant issues.

Ultimately, that is barring political accidents, the Bill receives Royal Assent and becomes an Act of Parliament. What happens then? Do not expect most changes in the law to become immediately obvious. It can take some months – and observant specialist journalists should monitor the new laws as, so often, they have an unintended impact. The courts also have a role in interpreting the laws, especially if there are legal challenges. All of which can provide you with fertile material.

20: Writing a political sketch

Ann Treneman

I am constantly being told that I have the best job in the world. I hear this from editors, politicians, doctors, students, random people I meet on trains and other journalists. When I was asked to try out as sketchwriter of *The Times*, I was told that the queue of people who had expressed interest stretched round the block. But as we sketchwriters say to each other when we hear this comment yet again: they would say that, they don't actually have to do it.

Sometimes, by way of an explanation, I tell this story. Years ago, I was talking to a journalist who had been around the world, covered war and famine, a fabulous writer with a wry sense of the ridiculous and a fine line in description. He said that one day he had been asked to fill in for the sketchwriter who was ill. So he went to the Commons. He watched. Thought up some jokes. Then he began to write it up. But what he wrote didn't work. He tried again. Failure. He went to the loo – and cried. 'I thought, so this is what I've come to, crying in the loo because I have to write a sketch in the next hour and I don't have the first idea how to do it.'

There have been many times that I've thought of that to comfort myself as I've sat at my desk, my screen blank (or, even worse, my mind). Certainly my first week, in the autumn of 2003, was nothing short of terrifying. I may have been a journalist with twenty-five years' experience but this was something else. I sat in the press gallery, with its wooden writing desks and bench seats, overhanging the marvellously ornate Speaker's Chair, observing events below. It was like watching a foreign film. I needed subtitles. What were the honourable members going on about? And, more to the point, who were they? I needed captions. Some days, there was no obvious theme. I needed a plot and I needed it fast. But, most of all, I needed to file 600 words by 6.30pm and IT HAD TO BE FUNNY. No pressure, then.

It's a British thing, sketchwriting. The press and the politicians in most other countries (America and France spring effortlessly to mind) take themselves far too seriously to countenance such a thing. Of course, other countries have humorous comment pieces and feature-ish political pieces but they do not put them together to make a sketch which is, if you wanted a definition, humorous reportage with a dash of spite or fun (or both). For inspiration, read Addison, Samuel Johnson and Dickens (Sketches by Boz). Or there's always Matthew Parris, my predecessor at *The Times*, and the late Frank Johnson of *The Times* and the *Daily Telegraph*, whose learned confections could be as light as an angel's wings.

So what does it take to write a sketch? If you are to do it day in and day out, you need stamina and a super-high boredom threshold or, to put it another way, not find it boring to be bored. It helps to have a talent for description, a streak of cruelty and a love of fun. You need a fascination with politics and the ability, to use the technical term, to cut through the crap. It is not required that you have the skin of a rhino but it helps.

And, before I get to the detail, a word about motivation. Every sketchwriter is different and, to be successful, you must stay true to yourself. While, in general, I approve of vendettas, for me, spite for spite's sake just doesn't work. Indeed, usually I find that strong opinions get in the way, skewing things, bringing the tone too close to serious. Readers hate being lectured. I am not party political and, as governments change, that is also quite helpful. I don't like bullying but, on the other hand, you have to call it as you see it. People ask me why I hate this or that person but I don't hate them at all: I may be disgusted with what they are doing – or saying – but, in general, for me, it's not personal.

The who, what, where, when

I don't want to ruin a good myth, but we do not make it up.

(Actually Samuel Johnson did but he's dead). Personally, I want to see something live and in person as television is a poor substitute, not least because the camera lies and, if you are watching it while it's lying, so will you. On the other hand, Frank Johnson wasn't so bothered ('It's so much more real,' he would say). But we are among the most assiduous attenders of Parliament. Many is the day when, in the Commons press gallery, there are the five regular sketchwriters, one reporter from the Press Association, two Hansard recorders and one of the penguin attendants. That's it. That's democracy in action.

It used to be that we only sketched when Parliament was sitting and all activity centred on the Commons or, less often, the Lords. This remains our main ambit but we may also go off-piste to cover a speech, a press conference or a by-election campaign. Sometimes we travel overseas, though rarely. During an election, we are constantly on the road which is invigorating and makes for some great days out. This is from my favourite sketch when I went campaigning in 2005 with Ann Widdecombe in her version of the Popemobile:

> I envisaged this to be a golf-cart type affair. It would be cute and blue and, crucially, it would have a roof. When I arrived at the blue door that opens into the blue room that is the Maidstone & The Weald Conservative Association, a very strange object was parked outside. It was a Mitsubishi flat-bed truck. The back had been turned into some kind of platform, with a large plywood box that was plastered with 'Vote Widdecombe' signs and festooned with bright blue balloons.
>
> Even then I didn't realise what I was looking at.
>
> 'Doesn't Ann have a Popemobile?' I asked a man holding a bunch of balloons.
>
> 'That's it!' he said. 'I hope you've brought a hat!'
>
> I looked outside. The water was running down the gutters like a small river. I didn't need a hat. I needed a wetsuit. (26 April 2005)

Most days it is obvious what is the most sketchable event. We love PMQs for that reason among others. But sometimes it's a guessing game. You can find out what's happening in Parliament from the website (www.parliament.uk) though last minute statements can pop up unannounced. Or the political parties send out an operational note though they often try to dissuade the sketchwriters from attending. (I wonder why.) Some days the newsdesk knows exactly what it wants, other days it's up to us. Every once in a while there is a frustrating day of miscellany. One day I watched the Education Secretary for two hours, then the Home Secretary for an hour, then the Foreign Secretary before going to the Lords for a debate. I ended up sketching the debate. Well, no one ever said it was always going to be easy.

You may notice that I often use the word 'we' as if the sketchwriters work in a pack. (One of the favourite questions we get is: What's the plural noun for a group of sketchwriters? We often say it is a 'sneer'.) We don't, although we usually know each other's movements. Sometimes newsdesks have different demands and some sketchwriters have obsessions such as when Simon Carr of *The Independent* became enamoured with the public bill committee stage on a European Bill. At least we always knew where to find him.

The how

Every sketchwriter works differently. Some carry a very tiny notebook and make only the scratchiest of notes. I have sat next to Frank Johnson when he wrote down only one or two words, neither of which appeared to have anything to do with what we were watching. Most of us are more attached to traditional journalistic methods. We do not need perfect shorthand but we do take care to get things on the record accurately. I take notes and use an old-fashioned tape recorder the likes of which, I am convinced, is only used these days by me and blind people. Unless I am very strapped for time – i.e. less than an hour to write – I will then listen to the tape and transcribe the bits that seem interesting. I find this particularly useful for accurately recording dialogue, for which I have a penchant. Getting something verbatim is especially effective not only for knowing what was said but gauging the reaction to it.

Gathering information

In general with sketching what you see is what you sketch. You go, you watch, you write. You are painting with words. You are not in the painting. I have only once asked a question at a press conference (Labour press conference at a ludicrous 8am and everyone was grumpy: it happens). Quentin Letts, of the *Daily Mail*, loves asking the most fearlessly pointed question possible but, in general, we are seen and not heard. But, sometimes, outside a committee room, we often find ourselves tantalisingly close to our victim (sorry, subject). Of course, politicians talk to us at their peril but, amazingly, most do. Indeed most seem to think they know us. Certainly I was surprised when Lord Mandelson (for it was he) approached me in the corridor. 'Hello Ann,' he said, eyes languid. I noted that we had never, actually, met. 'Haven't we?' he purred. 'But I feel as if I know you so-o-o well.'

What am I looking for? It is not, at all, what a news reporter is. They want facts, figures, trends, splits. I want to remember what it looks like – exactly. I want description. I write down colours. I will note down the exact order that people are on the frontbench. Hair is huge, obviously, and always worth a notation (indeed Simon Hoggart has made Tory MP Michael Fabricant's wig famous). During the Dave and Nick 'wedding' in the garden at No. 10 in May 2010, I drew a diagram of the terrace, the trees, the path, the wisteria (when I saw that wisteria, I thought of the wisteria that Dave had had trimmed on expenses and had to pay back, feeling ridiculously pleased by that connection).

Body language is vital. During the fierce tuition fees debate, all three Lib Dems on the frontbench were hugging themselves as if they were their own comfort blankets. Gordon Brown often had everything crossed that he could. I want not only the words but how they were said and at what volume. I try and remember all the senses: if there is a smell, I write it down. I went to Battersea Power Station for the Tory manifesto launch in 2010: outside it was a dystopia of concrete and dirt and, in the air, was a rotting smell from nearby rubbish trucks. Inside the launch had an 'urban gritty' construct, outside it was just smelly. These things matter. I want people to feel like they were there.

I want movement and interaction. Nick and Dave flirting in the garden. Gordon Brown almost pathetically thrilled that Barack Obama and he were in the same room. Some of the strongest sketches are the serious ones that record emotion, particularly sadness or tragedy. This is from my sketch of David Cameron's statement on the Bloody Sunday inquiry:

> There were tears in the chamber and, also, fears. But we saw true leadership from David Cameron, who talked of the Saville Report with stark simplicity, abandoning any attempt at sophistication. His words, he told us, were painful to say. For many present, they were obviously painful to hear.
>
> 'I am deeply patriotic,' Mr Cameron began, his suit black, his back ramrod straight. 'I never want to believe anything bad about our country.' Then he said 'But...' and the ranks of MPs grew utterly still, another rare occurrence in the chamber. 'What happened on Bloody Sunday was unjustified and unjustifiable,' said the Prime Minister. 'It was wrong.'
>
> His words could not have been more measured if they had been accompanied by a drum beat. There was a clarity that no one could misinterpret. His apology, when it came, seemed the only thing that he could do. And it, too, rang out like a bell. Everyone's eyes were on him, including those of the Rev. Ian Paisley, up in the gallery, his gravel voice mute for once. (16 June 2010)

Writing the damn thing

When I asked my colleague Simon Hoggart for his top tip on how to be a sketchwriter, he said: 'Be yourself.' Andrew Gimson, from the *Telegraph*, said, 'Remember you cannot always hit a six.' In other words, some days you have to accept that your sketch will not be brilliant. Indeed, some days I view it as a miracle that it exists at all.

After some particularly lively event, a reporter will often say to me: 'That should write itself for you.' If only. Sometimes the ones that should be the easiest are the hardest to write. In general, those big set-piece events such as Budgets and the Queen's Speech are, actually, quite hard to do, not least because everyone has high expectations. I must have covered a dozen 'speeches of his lifetime' and they are never sketches of a lifetime. Often it is the quirky little sketches that you remember, such as this one from Dave's party leader launch:

> Dave is always accused of being from the Notting Hill set. After yesterday I think we can drop the accused bit. Everyone was so smooth it was like being in a room of shiny pebbles. It was as though someone had gone over them all with a giant pumice stone until there were no rough edges at all.
>
> Dave even served us strawberry smoothies. Smoothies at a political launch! Whatever next? Aromatherapy? Truly, the days of being forced to drink instant coffee served in styrofoam cups with teeth marks already embedded in them could be numbered.
>
> I must admit it was all rather soothing. The theme of the party (for that is now how I thought of it) was 'chill'. The room was white and circular. The music was calming with lots of little chimes and bells and what-not. I am only surprised that we were not handed little white towels and lavender eye-pads. I felt the desire to close my eyes and imagine I was somewhere else. (30 September 2005)

At first, it took me a minimum of two hours to write a sketch. Now I can do it in half that time if pushed. I never really know what I'm going to write until I am sitting in front of my computer. If I have thought of something funny earlier, it's often not so funny when I write it down. When I get stuck, I revert to an old trick that I used to do when I was a feature writer, I imagine that I'm telling someone in a pub what it is I want to say. You have to think laterally, follow tangents, see invisible connections. Popular culture – movies, TV, songs – offers a rich canvas. I like comparisons, often with types of animals, though nothing too laboured. Sometimes I don't pick out themes until listening to the tape. I can write the whole sketch only to rip it up and start again. For instance, I had almost finished sketching George Osborne's age of austerity speech at the 2010 Tory Party conference and had just got to the very end when he kept going on about how 'over the horizon' everything was going to be wonderful some day soon. Suddenly I thought of 'over the rainbow' and 'Judy Garland' and the Land of Oz-bourne. I started again. I had finally found a theme.

All sketchwriters like to develop their own characters. I see George Osborne as a scorpion and forever may it be. Gordon Brown *was* a big clunking fist, a bull charging round in search of a china shop. The most interesting thing about Alistair Darling was his eyebrows which, like caterpillars, had lives of their own. I may exaggerate but I don't lie (actually I do sometimes but I always note it afterwards with a comment like: I may not have actually seen that.) In the end, it's faction, not fiction.

A sketch must, like a soufflé, be light and filling at the same time. Get it too light and, like eating too many sweets, reading it makes you feel rather queasy. I do trivia but not too much. I mention clothes rarely. I try not to be too cruel in actual description: I can remember saying that one MP looked like Lurch from the Addams Family and, when reading it the next day, regretting that: there is usually a way of writing without being that horrible. But you have to be honest: if someone is short, they are short. If they are fat, they are fat. If they are pompous, so be it in print. If they have a speech impediment, it must be mentioned but not in a nasty way. In general, the only thing worse for a politician than being written about is not being written about. And for that, I am truly grateful.

Ann Treneman has been the sketchwriter for The Times *since 2003. Previously she was a feature writer for* The Times *and* The Independent. *She is the author of* Annus Horribilis: The Worst Year in British Politics.

21: Reporting opinion polls

Andrew Hawkins

The fun of reporting political polls is two-fold. First is the game played with politicians who pretend to pay no attention, yet the truth is they are terrified of them. Gordon Brown was widely reported to be completely obsessed with polls when he was Prime Minister although he was notably less eager to do anything differently because of them.

Second, some polls – but not all – present incontrovertible evidence of a reality which the politician does not want revealed but, when faced with the numbers, they are powerless to deny. The supreme example of this was in the immediate aftermath of the first 2010 general election campaign leaders' debate on 15 April. Before the party spin rooms had time to influence the post-match analysis, at least two instant polls were published (from ComRes and YouGov) declaring Nick Clegg the winner by a mile.

Polls can, too, present dangers for journalists, and sometimes entire media outlets as well. So the intention of this chapter is to explain some of the processes, players and pitfalls in reporting on – and commissioning – political polls.

A word of clarification first. We do not restrict the term 'political polls' to only those that are market research for political parties or polls commissioned by the media. Political polls are used very extensively by a huge range of organisations that have a point to make. What began with straight PR polling ('eight out of ten cats prefer Whiskas') has now spread right across the political arena. Polls are now used for myriad purposes. It could be to make a company look good with policy makers ('nine out of ten of our low income customers like our energy prices'), to raise the profile of an issue ('nine out of ten people wrongly think their car is low carbon'), or to try to persuade policy makers to support/oppose/ steer clear of a measure ('nine of ten people worry that legalising assisted suicide would lead to vulnerable people being persuaded to die prematurely'). Indeed, it has become pretty much *de rigueur* for any good campaign to show that they have public or stakeholder opinion on their side.

The good, bad and the ugly

So any good political journalist must be able to distinguish between a good and bad poll. They must know what to report and what it's OK to omit, and they must know what to look for if they want to get behind the spin and into the real data.

There are two organisations governing the conduct and publication of opinion polls. The Market Research Society (MRS) is concerned with both these aspects. Its members are individuals involved in the commissioning or conduct of surveys and polls (there is no real distinction between these terms). The significance of the MRS is that it can discipline individuals who break its code of conduct, which is fairly broad and rigid. No pollster wants to be the subject of a successful MRS complaint, yet some campaign issues (fox hunting, pro-life issues and the like) will seldom be the subject of a change in the law without some poor pollster getting caught in the crossfire.

The MRS code is more concerned about probity than the transparency of poll data. By contrast, the British Polling Council (BPC) is concerned solely with enabling readers of polls to make up their minds about polls on the basis of access to detailed information about how the poll was conducted. The BPC has fourteen corporate members including all the main media pollsters – ICM, ComRes, Populus, Ipsos MORI and YouGov.

When it comes to reporting political poll findings, there is little need to worry about MRS membership but it is essential to ensure that the organisation conducting the poll is a BPC member. The importance of this cannot be emphasised enough; the internet has brought immediacy to the poll market and a non-BPC member publishing a political poll will usually be rubbished into oblivion by poll-watchers and pundits. The same does not necessarily apply to non-political polls but, for anything to do with politics, BPC membership is non-negotiable.

Spotting the story

What then does a journalist need to bear in mind when faced with a political poll? First, consider who commissioned it. This sounds obvious – party political polls are usually easy to spot – but any good journalist will be put on alert if organisations such as Marie Stopes publish polls showing that most people believe abortion is 'a woman's right to choose' but omit to ask the public whether they would like the upper limit to be shorter than six months' pregnancy.

With political parties the classic ploy is to talk up their prospects based on 'private polling' which is almost always unpublished. This is the most ridiculous poll-related wheeze going. In an age when polls are published literally daily, it is pretty much impossible for a party or politician to alight on a fresh revelation of their own popularity based on data that will be the same as, or very similar to, polls commissioned by the media.

At the 2004 Conservative Party conference Lord Saatchi made a spectacle of himself when he claimed that Tony Blair's poll position was 'irrecoverable' and that private polling for the Conservatives showed them to be so far ahead of Labour in key constituencies that they were going to oust Blair from No. 10. Needless to say, the substantiating evidence was never produced and – to remind ourselves – Tony Blair romped home the following May with a lead over the Tories of some nine percentage points and a majority of sixty-six seats. Private polling, to the political journalist, should be roundly ignored.

After asking who commissioned a poll, the political journalist should insist on seeing a copy of the questions asked. It is not necessary that questions should always posit neutral statements; after all, we are often trying to elicit a response in the public that may be based on emotion or instinct. But the question should be balanced. That is, if a question tests a range of statements, there should be an even balance of positive and negative ones.

One of the worst culprits of poor poll design is the *Daily Express*. Recent examples of dodgy poll questions from that newspaper include these little classics:

> 'Do you agree? Is Brown appalling?'
> 'Should failed asylum seekers get hand outs from Britain?'
> 'Should pensions go up by 45 per cent?'

By contrast, an example of a perfectly acceptable statement-testing question would be:

> Q. Do you agree or disagree with these statements about David Cameron? (agree/disagree/don't know)
> a. He is in touch with ordinary people (i.e. positive)
> b. He is making a mess of managing the economy (negative)
> c. He is proving to be a statesmanlike leader (positive)
> d. He is penalising the poor to make the rich even more better off (negative).

The key point is that respondents must have an opportunity to express their views freely, they must not be led to particular conclusions, and they must not be influenced by an overwhelming pressure in early questions that results in skewed answers later on. And this attention to the wording of a question really can make a difference. For instance, if respondents are not prompted by party names in a voting intention poll, the Liberal Democrat vote share will be depressed by around two or three percentage points.

Wording matters: how, where and when questions are asked

Also of tremendous importance is the method of fieldwork. Almost nobody conducts political polls face to face any more, although many people erroneously think this is still the routine way of obtaining people's political views. During the 1990s telephone polling became cheaper, faster and more accurate than face-to-face polling.

Notwithstanding the increased acceptance of online polling, telephone still has the best track record at predicting general election results.

Online polling has the advantage over telephone in terms of cost and sometimes speed. But there are sometimes concerns about reaching demographic groups that are notorious for having lower internet penetration, such as the elderly and those in lower income brackets. For some, too, the difficulty of obtaining a random sample leads to criticism of online polling. The objection, they say, is that pollsters are sampling people who have internet access (about 75 per cent of the population), who have opted to join this particular online panel, and who choose to take part in this particular survey. Not everyone shares these objections.

To its credit, online polling is usually preferable when surveying on issues such as health or sexual behaviour, as well as on financial subjects that would otherwise be too sensitive for a telephone interview. Of course, this makes good sense. Telephone polls are usually conducted among a completely random sample of the population. Respondents may be asked if they would be willing to be called back at a later date but they can always say no. By contrast online polls are mostly (but not exclusively) conducted among members of pre-recruited panels, using survey software that links a respondent's answers to their personal details. It ought therefore to be harder, not easier, to ask an online panellist about sensitive subjects.

Then there is the issue of sample size: when is it big enough? For a telephone poll among a nationally representative random sample of the GB population (polls seldom include Northern Ireland), the standard minimum size should be 1,000 people. Online national polls tend to be larger, with 2,000 being fairly routine.

The laws of statistics tell us that, with a representative sample of 1,000 people, a 50 per cent poll finding will be within 3 per cent of 'reality' in nineteen out of twenty polls. This means that we should expect one in twenty to be out of kilter: it does happen and it *should* happen. It can therefore be scary when a poll finding contradicts established wisdom, but that ought not to deter reporting on poll results that appear dramatic – provided that the other basic rules of polling have been followed.

For other sections of society, sample sizes can be less obvious. One particularly striking group where sample sizes vary considerably in terms of their reporting is GP surveys; the BBC has in the past happily reported a poll predicated on a sample size of 200 doctors which gives a margin of error of just under 7 per cent – a margin which would never be tolerated in reporting on a poll among the general public.

For polls of smaller groups, such as among MPs or head teachers, the rule is always that more is better. It is almost always at least as important to ensure that the sample is not just large enough, but that it is also representative enough of the population being tested. If in doubt, google 'margin of error calculator' and plug in the sample size to check that the margin of error is not larger than about 5 per cent. This should be a reasonable rule of thumb for something that is not an exact science.

Finally, when looking at a poll's methodology, a journalist needs to consider the timing of the interviewing. Conducting voting intention polls can be notoriously tricky over Bank Holiday weekends when you tend to sample too many Labour voters. Every press release for a poll should contain information about fieldwork timing so it should be obvious if the interviewing period straddles anything important.

Also on fieldwork timing, it can sometimes be difficult to determine when a poll has exceeded its shelf life. For instance, if a poll is conducted in the first week of January, is it still fresh if published in February? The answer is, it depends. If it is a voting intention poll, definitely not, as it will have been superseded by several others that will be much newer. If it is a poll of public attitudes towards an issue such as nuclear power then, so long as nothing high profile has happened since (or during) the fieldwork to influence people, a delay of a month or even two is usually fine.

In digging into the timing of a poll, also look to see how long it took to conduct. Online and telephone polls should really take no longer than a week or so; if the fieldwork period is longer than this without an obvious reason then be suspicious.

How to write it up

So much for the probity of a poll, how should they be reported?

Media organisations occasionally go through periods of doubt and make pronouncements that they will henceforth not lead stories on poll results. It never lasts – happily for us, good polls can prove simply irresistible as a hook for a story. Nonetheless it is worth taking the trouble to get the story right.

First, a poll story must contain a description of the population sampled. This can simply refer to the fact that it is the public, voters, doctors or whomever. The body of the story need not cite the exact sample size unless it is an unusual audience such as local councillors. If the newspaper reporting the poll also commissioned it, there should be an end note to the story citing fieldwork method, date, weighting, and where readers can download the full tables. The end note should also say that the polling company is a member of the BPC, if that is the case.

How a poll is weighted is important. This concept should not be frightening; it is simply an adjustment to ensure that the actual sample in the poll reflects the composition of the population you are modelling. So, if there are too many women and too few men in the sample, we slightly exaggerate (upweight) the views of men to balance out their representation in the results. All polls of public opinion should be weighted to be representative demographically in terms of age, gender, region and social group (usually expressed as AB, C1, C2, and DE). Political polls are usually weighted to be politically representative as well.

The practical implications of weighting (or more likely not weighting) become obvious at certain times. For example, if reporting on the instant polls after televised political debates, it is important to know whether a poll is weighted to be representative of the general population, or only of the estimated viewing audience. If the latter, then for two of the three leader debates during the 2010 election campaign the audiences were skewed towards older people and Conservative supporters, which partly explained why some instant polls had David Cameron doing better than in other polls.

It is also best practice to name-check the organisation that conducted the poll. This is not merely vanity on the part of the polling company. Newspapers that do polls themselves are never taken seriously beyond their own threshold. The *Daily Express* was mentioned earlier; their in-house 'polls' (often referred to as 'voodoo polls' by the polling industry) require readers to call a premium-rate telephone number to take part. The proof is of course in the pudding: the newspaper's front page splash on 26 November 2010 was that 99 per cent of people wanted Britain to leave the European Union. The fact that the findings were never even mentioned by other journalists speaks for itself. This is particularly important for journalists commissioning their own media outlet's polls. One of the main reasons your employer will part with a hard-fought budget to commission a poll is to get secondary coverage elsewhere – to be making the news themselves. If you report it badly, others will too. Or, worse still, they won't report it at all.

Other ways to feel the public pulse

Political reporters should be aware of the value of other types of research too. The 2010 election saw the advent of worm polling, where a pre-recruited audience operates a handset and gives continuous reaction to each speaker. The responses are aggregated into a continuous graphic or 'worm' and tracked over time. This is extremely difficult for the political reporter to write up; for instance it will not do simply to measure reaction by looking at the area of the graph beneath the 'worm' line. Worm polls are more useful as an indication of how an audience is feeling at any single moment. During the leader debates, we noticed that our worm (for ITV News) often plummeted when leaders talked about the difficult economic decisions to be made, and that they recognised how hard it would be for people to adjust to a tighter spending climate. The truth, it seemed, was difficult to stomach.

Then there are focus groups – the source of ridicule by some, but also the potential source of much rich material for the political reporter. Focus groups typically involve eight to ten people, such as Conservative voters, older people, or working mums, who take part in a guided and moderated discussion. Their purpose is to ask *why* particular views are held, and what would make people change their opinions.

Some can be daunted by the prospect of reporting on a qualitative event such as a focus group. But in the heat of an election campaign, when news that is fresh or exclusive is at a premium, a focus group can offer a wealth of quotes and context that would otherwise be impossible to obtain. Clients of polling companies are seldom brave enough to use the output of focus groups as a PR hook, but it has been done – most memorably by *Liberty* who commissioned ComRes to conduct focus groups among Muslim men to explore attitudes towards the Labour government policy on Control Orders. The article worked well, by explaining the views of a hard-to-reach audience, in a way that a quantitative poll could never have.

In conclusion, polls can provide a fabulous hook for stories and generate genuinely surprising insights. When reporting a third party's poll, the political reporter should principally be looking to see that it was conducted recently, over a short time period, among a sufficiently large number of people, with robust and objective questions, and by a BPC member. If commissioning a poll of one's own, any of the BPC members should be able to advise on how to get all the other elements right.

One final encouragement: most polls published to advocate a policy position will contain data the commissioning client won't want you to report on. The really good reporter will exercise their right under BPC rules to see the full data tables (believe me – it doesn't happen often) and dig around to test the story to destruction. Don't take the press release analysis at face value; question its assumptions and draw your own conclusions.

Andrew Hawkins is founder and chairman of ComRes. A barrister by training, he founded ComRes in 2003 having worked in political consultancies, polling firms and senior in-house communications roles. ComRes provides specialist market and opinion research to major corporations, charities, NGOs and governments. The company is retained pollster to ITV News, The Independent, Independent on Sunday *and the* Sunday Mirror.

22: Politics on TV

Joy Johnson

How free are the broadcasters to cover politics and politicians? Devolution, a multiple channel media, unlimited information on the internet and rolling 24-hour news have all meant that, while restrictions exist, rigidity has increasingly become unsustainable. In practice, we have a partisan press but a regulated broadcast media, with objectives and standards laid down by the BBC Trust and Ofcom. The Royal Charter is the constitutional basis for the BBC. It sets out the public purposes of the BBC, guarantees its independence, and outlines the duties of the Trust and the Executive Board. The current Charter runs until 31 December 2016.

Ofcom licenses all UK commercial television and radio services, and its broadcasting code sets out the rules which television and radio broadcasters must follow. So what may appear to be unnecessary restrictions on how journalists cover politics are actually responsibilities, obligations and above all statutory requirements that must be complied with. There is a public service duty for news to be presented with 'due' impartiality and with 'due' accuracy.

The use of the word 'due' however allows for editorial leeway – interpreting it is key. It is generally taken to mean making editorial judgements based on fairness that takes into account political context and the main political arguments. That sounds perfectly common sense and in tune with public service obligations. Yet it's also quite ambiguous: what does fairness mean? And does abiding by the 'main political arguments' mean arguments outside the prevailing orthodoxy are neglected?

Searching for a way through

For the political journalist there is scope to challenge restrictions. Ric Bailey, the BBC's chief political adviser, is adamant that it is not about the 'maths', but about good editorial judgement. In other words it shouldn't be about a 'ritualistic clock watching' between the three main parties. Critics will argue that this does happen and debate is frequently a 'ping pong' between the two main parties, with the Liberal Democrats – before the coalition government – an afterthought. In an adversarial system that is not surprising. In an era of coalition government however, there will be tensions as to how the broadcasters determine balance, and how the parties 'fight their corner'.

Journalistically the BBC's editorial guidelines, based on its responsibilities and obligations to impartiality, provide the framework. Within this framework Bailey believes that journalists should not be editorially inhibited. Should a journalist have concerns, the mantra is to 'refer upwards'. For BBC political journalists, this is generally to the chief political adviser. For existing and would-be journalists, there are no excuses for not knowing the rules, since all the guidelines are available online.

We should also remember that restrictions are accepted by journalists in order to achieve future objectives, usually to gain access. At times like this, restrictions morph into rules of engagement. While the starting point may be the popular conception of a journalist as a 'seeker of truth' who 'holds the feet of the powerful to the fire', the reality frequently develops in more mundane directions. With the broadcast media's capacity to reach the masses, that initial mutual suspicion between politician and journalist, can give way to mutual benefit.

There is an extensive body of work that provides an academic examination of the media; perhaps the pages of *Power without Responsibility* now in its seventh edition are the most 'well-thumbed'. The book does what it has always done and provides the wherewithal to understand the history, the theory and the politics of the British media.

Its very title captures the essence of any critique of the British press. Power without Responsibility – the prerogative of the harlot throughout the ages – coined by Rudyard Kipling and later used in 1931 by Stanley Baldwin in conversation with the media baron Lord Beaverbrook. Using Rudyard Kipling's quote, Baldwin was no doubt summing up the frustration felt by politicians down the ages.

This chapter will attempt to navigate through the labyrinth of rules, restrictions and codes of conduct, statutory requirements and editorial guidelines.

Covering Parliament

Geoffrey Robertson and Andrew Nicol (writing in *Media Law*) described the rules devised by the Supervising Committee governing the televising of the House of Commons, when cameras were finally allowed in 1989 as: 'Calculated to avoid embarrassment when MPs misbehave.' Whenever there is disorder, the cameras must switch immediately to the Speaker. The public gallery and the press gallery must not be shown. The rules were slightly relaxed by the Committee after the first six months of televising as the House had produced no obvious danger to the democratic process. So there we have it. Rules were 'calculated to avoid embarrassment' – a harsh, yet accurate indictment.

As absurd as it may seem in a mature democracy, TV cameras were only allowed into the chamber twenty years ago, and there was a ferocious debate at the time between MPs from across the political spectrum. The case in favour was based on the inalienable fact that citizens in a modern democracy should be able to watch their elected representatives at work. The case against was that TV cameras would destroy the sanctity of Parliament. To our more jaundiced view of the behaviour of MPs in Parliament, it is not its sanctity that comes to mind. In interviews following the vote, an ardent opponent Roger Gale, Conservative MP for North Thanet, was concerned that the damage was 'controlled'. On the opposition benches, Labour MP for Bassetlaw Joe Ashton wanted to make sure that proceedings weren't 'reduced to entertainment'.

Former executive producer for the coverage of Parliament Dr Suzanne Franks recalls:

> When the Commons finally voted to allow the cameras in (on an experimental basis) the broadcasters were taken by surprise,

> because the proposal had been rejected so many times before – and the Prime Minister herself (Margaret Thatcher) was firmly opposed. They were both shocked and also pathetically grateful. This meant that the broadcasters bent over backwards in the negotiations, anxious to accommodate the politicians and the parliamentary authorities. Hence they agreed (remarkably) both to pay for the privilege and to abide by the restrictions that were imposed in terms of camera positions and limitations on choice of shots.
>
> The broadcasters were aware that this was originally only an experiment and that they had to maintain good behaviour at all times or else the permission would be withdrawn. However the cameras very soon became part of the furniture and the politicians gained confidence. Hence the more onerous shot restrictions were withdrawn within the first few months although the general principles still remain.

Camera shots may have been incrementally relaxed, but how the footage is used is still tightly controlled. They can't be used in light entertainment programmes; if in a magazine programme they have to be clearly delineated as a separate stand-alone item.

With generational change among MPs and officials, Roy Scotton, general manager for Bow Tie TV, the operators contracted by Parliamentary Broadcasting Unit Ltd (Parbul) – the independent company made up of directors from both Houses to provide the TV pictures to broadcasters and Parliament – believes that initial suspicion has given way to trust. Attitudes have changed. Originally cameras inside the chamber were a necessary evil; now they are part and parcel of parliamentary proceedings. The straitjacket of the head and shoulder shot has been loosened; the restrictive, wide shot is now varied. For broadcasters the greatest relaxation in the chamber has come within the last few years. Previously a cut away was only allowed if a member had been mentioned by constituency. This has been reinterpreted. Now if, for example, health economics come up in a debate and there is a health or treasury minister on the opposite front bench, a reaction shot can be used. It must be remembered however that restrictions on editing and how the pictures are used are still rigorously policed. Internal editing must be contemporaneous so a journalist can't take a 'useful' shot from earlier as an edit point.

Nicholas Jones, a former BBC political journalist and author, has long campaigned for greater freedom. In a lecture to the Royal Society of Arts in 2003 he posed an obvious journalistic question: should the remote cameras remain under the absolute control of the parliamentary authorities, or should broadcasters and press photographers have the freedom to choose the pictures which they think are the most newsworthy? Seven years later the iron grip on what is shot and what is transmitted has gradually eased. It is still the case that, at the slightest disruption, the picture switches to the Speaker. That does not mean to say that broadcasters won't try to stretch the boundaries, because they do. For example, when in May 2004 a protestor from Fathers4Justice threw purple flour filled condoms from the public gallery during Prime Minister's Question Time. One of them hit the then Prime Minister Tony Blair, prompting a major security review.

Despite the restrictions and subsequent complaints from parliamentary authorities, the BBC insisted on slow motioning the footage and transmitting it in all its news programmes.

What we didn't see, incidentally, was the government Whip shepherding out his MPs once the sitting was suspended. Ushering out MPs might have been instinctive but, had it been more than dyed purple flour, it wasn't terribly smart.

Ignoring journalistic values and acquiescing to the authorities over the flour throwing incident, particularly when pictures were available, would have meant depriving the public of a legitimate story and the broadcasters simply refused to bow to pressure.

Pursuing journalistic practice and news values outside of Parliament is the norm. Tracking shots and images as underlay for political commentary that gives context to prevailing circumstances is commonplace. Inside Parliament this is simply not allowed. In John Mayor's final years as PM – and with a disappearing majority – the television networks could not show the nine Ulster Unionist MPs sitting with their leader, David Trimble, even though they held the balance of power.

Today with the coalition government we have a similar situation. On the frontbench Liberal Democrats and Conservative ministers sit side by side. This is not repeated on the backbenches. The Liberal Democrats sit apart. Even with the recent relaxations, it is not possible for a broadcast journalist to ask those directing the proceedings to pan from the frontbench to show the various blocks that politically make up the coalition.

Coverage outside the chamber

Dr Franks said that a surprise success story of the broadcasting experiment in 1989 was the televising of select committees:

> This happened almost as an afterthought. The restrictions were less onerous and broadcasters discovered that the committees had a particular drama of their own which made for good TV. Watching ministers or other witnesses being grilled by well-informed MPs very soon became a staple of news and current affairs coverage.

And while they aren't as powerful as their US counterparts in Congress, they have nevertheless acquired significant influence. The Commons Public Accounts Committee is generally regarded as the most powerful, although others make their mark. During the financial crisis, four top bankers from the Royal Bank of Scotland and HBOS giving evidence to the Treasury Select Committee, apologised for their role. An image that made front pages around the world.

Changes are taking place with the governance of broadcasting Parliament. Negotiators who finally broke down the barricades were not going to allow restrictions on images; control of the images and how they are used become a permanent barrier. Nor were they going to allow money to stand in the way; they also agreed to pay for the feed. Now, after twenty years, broadcasters have decided enough is enough and have expressed unhappiness. Only two other legislative bodies around the world charge for coverage regarded as in the public's interest. So the not for profit company, Parliamentary Broadcasting Unit Ltd (Parbul), will cease to exist and Parliament will bear the cost. Broadcasters will still have to pay for the select committees they choose to cover. Given that the recent reforms with members and its chairs elected by their colleagues, instead of being handpicked by the whips, should make them even more newsworthy and therefore a price worth paying.

Camera points are also sited in central lobby – the central meeting place between the Commons and the Lords – in committee corridors and Portcullis House. So political journalists can now do pieces to camera and interviews within Parliament where the action is happening. With an authentic backdrop of the central lobby, viewers can see and feel the buzz after set-piece events. Barriers preventing the electorate from seeing the elected at their place of work are being broken down. That doesn't mean unrestricted freedom. Journalists can't do political stories without reference to Parliament, can't doorstep members and can't chase after politicians who are walking down the corridors.

College Green – that patch of green opposite Westminster which becomes a democratic forum during big political events – still sees plenty of activity. During the coalition talks, all the broadcasters had temporary studios on the green for running commentaries and rolling news in the days before a government was formed. Here, at least in part, the drama could be freely played out with the major (and frequently minor) political players seeking the media spotlight. College Green at such times is turned into a carnival of political activity with marquees providing shelter.

During the Major years, when the Whip had been withdrawn from serial rebels belonging to his own side, one maverick used to call into 4 Millbank, where the main broadcasters have studios, to offer himself for interview. He then moved on a few yards to College Green before crossing the road to the Commons. He wanted to get over his Eurosceptic message as often as possible and believed his time was more usefully spent bending the ear of political journalists than talking in the chamber.

Nicholas Jones in his book *Spin Doctors and Sound Bites* recalls that, during the first Gulf War Paddy Ashdown, then leader of the Liberal Democrats, 'used to march up and down College Green early in the morning looking for television outside broadcasts and present himself to be interviewed… Junior producers would be "bullied" into putting him on air'.

Lib Dems, fighting for their share of airtime, have enjoyed considerable success outside of the humdrum of everyday politics by exploiting their expertise: Paddy Ashdown on strategic defence issues, Menzies Campbell on foreign affairs and Vince Cable on the economy.

But whatever the restrictions, when the story warrants it Parliament demands to be covered. Remember Margaret Thatcher's speech only weeks before she was ousted by her own party: a tour-de-force, even with a mid shot and a backdrop of a row of men's legs. Similarly in the chamber, the late Robin Cook, on resigning as Foreign Secretary, gave a powerful exposition on why he would not be voting with his government on the war in Iraq. And only weeks into the coalition government, David Cameron's speech, accepting the findings of the Saville inquiry into 'Bloody Sunday' summed up, in a calm but persuasive way, his prime ministerial style.

Covering elections

Democracy demands that broadcasters abide by rules and, yes, restrictions. Newspapers are allowed to be partial and to promote a particular political party or politician. Broadcasters are not. Standards are regulated by the BBC's Charter and its producer guidelines contain detailed requirements on impartiality and accuracy. For other broadcasters, the Ofcom Code fulfils that role. During elections the BBC has its own rules in the politics and public policy section of its producers guidelines.

Broadcasters are required to apply due accuracy and due impartiality not only for UK elections but around the world, as well as for referendums. Journalists have to give 'weight' to major political parties defined as Conservative, Labour and Liberal Democrats in the UK; SNP and Plaid Cymru in Scotland and Wales; in Northern Ireland Democratic Unionist Party (DUP), Sinn Fein, SDLP and the Ulster Unionists – although the 2010 election saw the DUP wiping out the Ulster Unionists.

Journalists also have to consider giving appropriate coverage to other parties. A major relaxation to election coverage came with a revised Representation of the Peoples Act 2000. Prior to this, candidates who refused to take part in a constituency/ward report or debate, effectively pulled the plug on a report, depriving the viewers and listeners of the local 'skirmishes' in the election race.

A further hindrance to covering constituency reports has also been removed with the list of all the candidates now merely required to be posted on the web.

With the opinion polls tightening, and the drama of the TV debates and 'Cleggmania' being played out, pollsters and commentators predicted the possibility of a hung parliament, in the run-up to the 2010 general election. A possibility that led to this admission from one former tabloid editor, David Yelland:

> I can say this with some authority (because) in my five years editing *The Sun*, I did not once meet a Lib Dem leader, even though I met Tony Blair, William Hague and Iain Duncan Smith on countless occasions. (Full disclosure: I have since met Nick Clegg.)
>
> I remember in my first year asking if we staffed the Liberal Democrat conference. I was interested because as a student I'd been a founder member of the SDP. I was told we did not. We did not send a single reporter for fear of encouraging them.

While newspapers could take such a stance, broadcasters can not. That's not to say that the Lib Dems received equal time. As Nicholas Jones pointed out:

> Once we were in a pre-election period or the campaign itself, the Liberal Democrat add on clip was pretty well obligatory ... in longer packages there would usually be an introductory thought as well. At Lib Dem manifesto launches etc there would be a substantive story about their plans.
>
> The rough basis during the campaign was to give Labour and Cons 30 to 40 per cent each of each package with the 10 to 20 per cent for Liberal Democrats, plus occasionally nationalists etc, depending on the story.

> The Liberal Democrats did better in studio discussions ... and this was highly prized exposure as the programmes were duty bound to invite a Liberal Democrat along for most discussions. The Liberal Democrats always said that their opinion poll ratings went up at an election time because of the exposure on television and radio...

General election TV debates 2010

The 2010 general election changed all that. The TV debates integrated Nick Clegg – and thus the Lib Dems – into the story; not as an add-on, but in their own right.

Ever since the first American presidential debate between Richard Nixon and his young, good-looking rival, John Kennedy, in 1960, US style debates have been on UK broadcasters' agenda. Politicians had fought them off either because an incumbent did not want to give away any advantage or a challenger was reluctant. Margaret Thatcher in 1979, and Tony Blair in 1997, were wary of risking an opinion poll lead. Broadcasters have also in the past allowed the politicians off the hook by not acting together..

The 2010 election was different. Gordon Brown's premiership had been riven by discord within his own ranks. The worst economic crisis for decades and the expenses scandal meant that Members of Parliament desperately needed to reconnect with the voter. Party leaders understood this.

In spite of Gordon Brown's communications skills having been repeatedly mocked, some of his strategists believed that a debate would allow him to triumph when it came to policy details. David Cameron, with the most to gain, had demanded a debate since the start of his leadership in 2005. Previously this demand would have been rebuffed automatically. But Peter Mandelson, then Business Secretary, started dropping hints to the *London Evening Standard* in July 2009 that a debate could be on the cards:

'I don't think Gordon would have a problem with that,' said Mandelson, Brown's most powerful Cabinet ally. 'While Cameron is good with words, he doesn't have the ideas or policies to back them. I think people would see through the smile. The more the public sees of them, the more they'd realise that Gordon is the man with the substance.'

Ric Bailey, the BBC's chief political adviser, started pulling together broadcasters for discussions to secure a TV debate. In the meantime Sky News announced that it would transmit a live debate and 'empty chair' any leader who refused to take part. John Ryley, Head of Sky News and one of the prime movers behind televising the leaders' debates, said his channel would no longer accept the status quo. Bailey said that while he would certainly not have opened discussion from a position of threatening to empty-chair anyone, he wouldn't have ruled it out completely further down the line.

Bailey too was determined that this time was going to be different. And the way that it was achieved was to strip away any complications. The BBC cast the debates as prime ministerial to emphasise the point that this was about who would be the Prime Minister of the United Kingdom. The SNP read that as a device to exclude them. Sky and ITV branded the debates, 'leaders' debates'. Crucially all the broadcasters agreed a formula of 3x3x3. That is, three broadcasters would host three live debates (ITN, Sky and the BBC) – with the three mainstream parties each having parity – equal time and equal positioning during the debate. Concentrating on the election of the UK Prime Minister made it harder for the SNP and Plaid Cymru, and other parties, to mount a successful legal challenge. Within that formula, the BBC would abide by its requirement to be balanced with subsequent leaders' debates in Scotland, Wales and Northern Ireland.

With the broadcasters agreeing their negotiating position among themselves, discussions then took place with the political parties. While the Conservatives and Lib Dems readily agreed, Gordon Brown wanted to have more debates among Cabinet ministers and for the debates to start earlier than the actual four weeks of the campaign. Ryley believed that anything other than the four-week intensive period of the campaign would undermine their role to focus the voters on the issues at hand.

In the event Channel Four (which wasn't part of the 3x3x3 formula) had a successful debate between prospective Chancellors, and Andrew Neil, anchor of the BBC 2's *The Daily Politics*, chaired ministerial debates. But when it came to the main events, the broadcasters stuck to their original position.

Ryley said that there had been a number of 'sticky points,' but by 21 December 2009 he thought, 'this is going to be a goer'. That day all three parties signed up.

The deal is done

A final agreement was reached. But was it easy? Of course not. It contained a staggering seventy-six points. The main reason why the broadcasters didn't kick up a fuss over this micro-management is because they were undoubtedly relieved at cracking the impasse. Some of the seventy-six points could be regarded as the normal rules of engagement in mounting programmes of this nature, such as selecting an audience that was broadly a demographic and political cross section. While it may seem obvious, it still needed spelling out, so point forty-one determined that the programme would start with all three leaders on set and standing at their podiums. And fifty-one stated that, at the end of the programme, the three leaders would shake hands. Gordon Brown at the end of the first debate ignored that particular rule and left the platform and started shaking hands with the audience, quickly followed by the other two leaders when they saw what he was up to. In the event it didn't do the former Prime Minister much good – the instant tracking poll and the comments in the 'spin room' made Nick Clegg the winner.

Other points in the agreement seemed to mimic the restrictions on parliamentary coverage, with rules that there would be no close cutaways of a single individual audience member while the leaders were speaking unless a leader directly addressed an individual member. Without the normal audience reactions, the debates did not mirror a traditional BBC *Question Time*.

From a political perspective, giving Clegg equal time and equal status, appears to have been a tactical mistake. Certainly the Labour and Tory concessions of parity was a surprise to John Ryley, who put it down to the single-mindedness of Lib Dem negotiators: 'They were driven by one goal – parity of time and stature.'

The debates gave Clegg publicity his predecessors could only have dreamed of. Yet despite the media phenomena of 'Cleggmania', the Lib Dems ultimately lost seats. Perhaps, however, the coverage played a role in elevating him to kingmaker and subsequent coalition partner.

Bigotgate

Political gaffes are meat and drink to the political journalist and, in the 2010 general election, Gordon Brown's gaffe went right up the running order. The encounter with Gillian Duffy during a walkabout in Rochdale seemed on the surface fairly run of the mill. Her conversation with the then Prime Minister was not part of the organised choreography, but she took the opportunity to quiz him on Eastern European immigration. The Prime Minister pointed out that there were reciprocal arrangements – British people left to go to Continental Europe. The exchange ended with Mrs Duffy happily talking about her grandchildren and hopes for them to go to university. Trouble started for Brown in his car on the way to his next engagement. Forgetting that a microphone was still on his lapel, Brown launched into a tirade about what happened, blaming his staff for the encounter and accusing Mrs Duffy of being a 'bigoted woman'.

During an election campaign, it is common practice for the party leaders to wear a microphone. This allows for a smoother walkabout with camera crews being able to keep a distance as politicians engage with members of the public, albeit such access is usually controlled by the politician's aides. The sound tape is pooled, and made available to all broadcasters.

Brown's discomfort was made worse when Jeremy Vine, BBC anchor of Radio 2's phone-in programme, replayed the exchange and TV cameras caught the PM with his head in his hands. So should the tape have been played? At the BBC, when tape recordings are made without the participants' knowledge, transmission editorial staff have at the very least to refer upwards to the controller of editorial policy. Given that the microphone was being used by agreement, the fault was arguably with Brown and his aides for not removing it. In any event Sky had already shown the tape, so the BBC followed suit – it became editorially unacceptable to have suppressed transmission.

Opinion polls

Strict restrictions cover the broadcasting of opinion polls during an election campaign. The Representation of the Peoples Act 2000 introduced a prohibition on the publication of exit polls before the polls close. The ban relates to a statement regarding the way a person has voted. Forecasts of the result, which are based on such information, are also banned. This statute is supplemented by the Ofcom Broadcasting Code, which prohibits discussion and analysis of election or referendum issues after polling stations have opened until they are closed.

Geoffrey Robertson and Andrew Nicol in *Media Law* argue:

> This is an unnecessary restraint on free speech, apparently passed because political spin doctors feared that party supporters would not bother to vote if early exit polls showed that their party was well in the lead. But it is more likely that exit polls would spur the citizens' interest and encourages them to go out and vote...

David Cowling the BBC's editor of political research has a pragmatic response to Robertson and Nicol:

> Whatever the arguments about the legitimacy of banning the publication of exit poll figures before voting finishes, there is a practical problem in doing so. Exit poll figures simply change throughout polling day. In the 2010 election exit poll, the first wave of results suggested a clear Conservative victory, but as the day progressed the figures narrowed until, by 10pm, the broadcast figures showed the Conservatives twenty seats short of a majority. Why would the broadcasters, who pay hundreds of thousands of pounds for an exit poll, want to release incomplete and probably inaccurate figures before the close of poll?

There are other restrictions on the use of opinion polls set out in the BBC's producer guidelines and Ofcom code which highlights restrictions on the reporting and analysis of polls.

But it is worth remembering a key point: under normal circumstances something that is new is news; with voting intention polls it is the opposite. It is the trend that matters. Poll results that defy trends need to be treated with care. Not surprisingly, such a poll is frequently referred to as a 'rogue'.

Conclusion

Covering politics is a privilege. With access to the powerful, political journalists are frequently at the centre of history in the making. At other times it may merely seem a job. Parliament has often been regarded as 'boring', with programme editors complaining of 'empty green benches'. That is an aberration. Circumstances change. Set-piece occasions, such as Prime Minister's Question Time, Budget Day or, as in the 2001 parliament, the debate on the war in Iraq, guarantee attendance in the chamber. The coalition government with its inbuilt tensions should mean that Parliament once again takes on an importance it frequently lacked when governments had large overall majorities.

For broadcasters the coalition government presents challenges on how to maintain balance and impartiality. For the BBC both those responsible for news programmes and those responsible for parliamentary coverage on its dedicated channel, balance will rest on points of view rather than by parties. In other words, if on the government side there is no disharmony, then there will be one interviewee representing Conservative and Liberal Democrat and one from Labour. If there is disagreement, then one of the interviewees would be a dissident Conservative or Liberal Democrat.

As for the TV debates, now that the fifty year stalemate has been broken, it may be assumed that there is a new status quo. Perhaps. Negotiators in the future will always push for their man or woman to have the upper hand. What is certain is that this is a new, fast-changing era of politics with three leaders who have all recently entered Parliament with teams of advisers who have grown up with television. It is hard to imagine that the Labour leader Ed Miliband who, along with Nick Clegg, entered Parliament only in 2005, and David Cameron four years earlier, refusing to take part in a TV debate. Nevertheless as John Ryley predicts: 'They (the leaders) will, I hope, see the benefit of the TV debates, but all politicians are pragmatists when it comes to wanting to win an election. The status quo may change again. If there is a single lesson for the future it is that TV companies need to be adamant they will "empty chair" any leaders who don't show up for the 2015 debates – or whenever the next election takes place.'

There is likely to be little further change in how Parliament will look on our TV screens. With the introduction of BBC's Democracy Live website, able to stream eight feeds live and recorded from select committees, from both chambers and the devolved assemblies, there are likely to be further changes on the embedding of video. Would-be political journalists can now access the same feeds that stream in newsrooms.

Restrictions still exist but our political theatre is often the best stage in town. As we have seen with the TV debates, and the chipping away at the restrictions covering Parliament, broadcasters must keep pushing at the barriers that prevent legitimate journalistic endeavour.

Joy Johnson is a visiting lecturer, teaching politics and journalism at several universities. She is a former political news editor at the BBC and previously worked as a journalist at ITN.

Part V:

Out of Westminster

23: It's election time!

Sheila Gunn

The roads to Westminster

There's a saying in politics that you must start campaigning for the next election the minute the last one is over. This also applies to journalists. As soon as an election result is known, it is worth pondering the impact. How will the new councillors or MPs perform? Will the defeated parties be fielding new candidates at the next election? What will come out of the post-mortems held by the losing parties? Are there splits over their campaign strategies or individual policies?

For most political journalists, your first experience of covering politics will be at a local or regional level. Your first contacts are likely to be the local MP and councillors, together with candidates and local party officials. Whatever party they support, they all display similar characteristics in dealing with journalists:

They believe you are biased against them and may even have 'your own agenda'

They think you have a responsibility to cover all their activities

They will complain if you do not

They will plague you with, mostly, dead boring press releases and terrible photographs of people standing around

They will whinge if these are not published

They will take offence if you write about their internal affairs, such as selecting candidates or differences over campaigns and policies.

A mild exaggeration perhaps, although this perspective is also drawn from my experience as a local party activist, councillor and parliamentary candidate.

Who do you need to know? The elected representatives and the candidates, key people in the local party, such as the chair, and agents. MPs and councillors will be in regular touch with their local media and, hopefully, will want a symbiotic relationship; both have a role to play in a democracy. Tragically, economic pressures on local media means that these relationships are under threat. One result is that elected representatives will use other methods, such as blogs, tweets and leaflets that look like independent newspapers, to communicate directly with local residents.

As Richard Osley illustrates, there is a satisfying job to be done in reporting politics in the local media. It is no coincidence that virtually all contributors to this book started out reporting on local politics. Remember that both journalists and politicians often rise through the ranks from the council chamber to Westminster.

Chairs of local constituency parties are rarely a good source of stories. They have a part-time, unpaid role, largely focused on overseeing the local office, retaining and attracting members, and raising money. They come into their own when the party selects new candidates.

Key people are the agents. In constituencies where a party has a strong presence, there will usually be an agent, a party official who runs the office, organises campaigns and coordinates all local activities. Beware: like whips in Parliament, they are loath to being quoted by name or position and they are totally loyal to their party. Although, after a few drinks (their pay is fairly meagre, so may welcome any hospitality), they can be encouraged to hint at their contempt for most of their local elected representatives. But they also know what is going on whether it is the likely timing of selecting a parliamentary candidate or hints of a new campaign.

Selection process

The ups and downs, the rows and the in-fighting all make the selection of candidates worthy of attention.

For council candidates, the local party office will usually invite applications and interview those interested in standing. One controversial aspect which can generate good stories is the assumption of those already serving on the council that they will be automatically reselected to stand again. Yet, often the local party will think that councillor is past their sell-by date or that it's time for 'new blood'. This has become a bigger issue as, under Tony Blair's reforms, councillors have been paid a far more generous allowance, which successfully attracted a more diverse range of candidates. One unintended and largely unspoken outcome is that elderly councillors come to rely on their allowance as a sort of pension and fight any attempt to encourage them to stand down.

A jealously guarded role for local parties is the right to select a parliamentary candidate. This is limited. The usual system is for the national party to hold an approved list, those who have been interviewed and vetted as potential parliamentary candidates. Those on the approved list will be sent regular lists of constituencies looking for a candidate. Once the national and local party have looked through applications, there will be a round of interviews and meetings – often called 'hustings' – of paid-up party members before a new candidate is voted in. Local journalists can usually unearth stories about friction between the personalities involved, especially if local activists are resentful when an outsider is chosen. Political journalists find stories in rows between the national and local party, attempts by the party HQ to 'manage' the process, or in accusations that candidates favoured by the leadership are being 'parachuted in'. All national parties have introduced initiatives to have a more diverse group of candidates selected for winnable seats, especially more women and more from the ethnic minorities. (Please take care in reporting such initiatives as so often it reads as if women, rather than forming the majority of the electorate, are also a 'minority'.) Such interference is not appreciated by local parties.

An example of the string of stories which can erupt from this process was the selection of a Conservative parliamentary candidate to fight Slough in the 2005 general election. The local party had picked one candidate who was then deselected by party HQ after some rather unfortunate photos of him with guns were circulated. The next candidate was similarly deselected for promoting alleged anti-Catholic conspiracy theories. The local association was put on 'support status', meaning it was suspended. It was not considered a 'winnable' seat for the Tories, but it was important that the party came a good second to Labour and put up a decent fight.

Five weeks before the election, I was called by the party's deputy chairman and 'made' the candidate (as the media and opponents liked to point out, I was the third Conservative candidate in so many months) achieving a swing of nearly 5.5 per cent from Labour to Conservative and invaluable experience in these rather difficult circumstances.

Candidates come in all shapes and sizes, but those really intent on becoming an MP will usually fight a hopeless seat before trying for a winnable one. Either way, candidates want regular and positive media coverage, particularly in the local media which influences the voters in their constituency. Long gone are the days when candidates and MPs were rarely seen in the constituency and knew little of local issues.

Today's candidates are regarded as a sort of super-councillor, running campaigns on local issues: perhaps about post office or hospital closures; cuts in services by the local council; or showing how a national policy would benefit a local community. Expect a constant stream of emails, phone calls and literature – some of which will be of interest. Do bear in mind that these odd people are doing all this for no money. Being a candidate is an expensive pastime (maybe this is one of the reasons why some expected to recoup the expenses when elected) and that only a small percentage will actually make it onto the famous green benches. Why some of us do it is perhaps a subject for another book. In the meantime *So You Want to be a Politician* offers more guidance on the processes involved.

The routes to the House of Lords

Nothing could be more different than the current peerage system. Most peers arrive on the red benches through some sort of patronage. The Queen has to approve new life peerages, but nearly all the recommendations come via the Prime Minister and have been quietly vetted. Regular lists of new peers are announced and there is generally some media speculation about who will make it. Those involved in the vetting will not usually leak details to you, but I have found peers willing to listen to my list of suggested names – and then, by their silence, indicate whether I was not wrong. This way they can genuinely claim that they have not leaked any names.

Occasionally a political journalist picks up information that Downing Street has put forward a name which is not welcomed by senior peers. Once I picked up information that Margaret Thatcher was keen to ennoble Jeffrey Archer, her former deputy party chairman, but that the then Lords scrutiny committee had warned No. 10 very quietly that this would not be wise. Unusually, she backed down. Archer, who had been a useful contact, was understandably livid at my subsequent front page story in *The Times* – and banned me from his famous Krug and shepherd's pie parties. He was later made a peer by John Major. It was a while later that he was sent to prison.

The honours lists for new peers come in different forms:

Her Majesty's birthday honours: people who have made a significant, non-political contribution to, for instance, medicine, science or charities.

Working peers: drawn up by the PM in consultation with other party leaders. These peers take a party whip and are expected to be 'active' participants.

Resignation honours: an outgoing PM can recommend a list of those, often his closest friends or confidantes, to be made peers.

Dissolution honours: at the end of each parliament, names are put forward for new peers – most of them are former MPs.

Prime ministers also announce new peers on an ad hoc basis with some regularity. A good example is the GOATs (government of all talents): as part of Gordon Brown's government in 2007, he gave peerages to figures such as Digby Jones and Admiral Alan West.

As the House of Lords is now full to bursting, something will have to give soon. In the meantime, speculation about what's next for the House of Lords, new peers and who is on which list adds to the gaiety of life and fills the column inches. An excellent subject to return to in otherwise quiet political times.

Covering by-elections

Party Spokesman 1: 'Governing parties rarely win by-elections but we are delighted at the performance of our candidate – and there was a clear lack of support for the opposition, which polled 2,000 fewer votes than at the last election.'

Party Spokesman 2: 'This is a severe blow to the government and we are delighted at our victory.'

Party Spokesman 3: 'The result illustrates the voters' lack of confidence in both the governing and main opposition party.'

These three statements are fairly typical of the reaction of those representing the main political parties. They will put the best possible gloss on the outcome, whatever the results. You are sometimes left wondering who won and who lost, for they will comb through the results for the merest hint that it is not all bad news.

Imagine some quiet corner of the British Isles going about its business when the local MP dies, resigns or is disqualified between parliaments. It suddenly becomes the focus of not only the main political parties, but of a significant tranche of Westminster-based journalists.

A local resident is trudging innocently along the road when she comes face to face with a phalanx of aggressive individuals, namely a very senior politician surrounded by men with guns (his armed Special Branch officers) who give you funny looks, a media scrum complete with metal ladders (photographers), many walking backwards, and overexcited young activists with garishly logo-ed t-shirts, placards and balloons. The central figure descends on you with an unnaturally bright smile shining out of a dog-tired face.

Yes, by-elections keep journalists and politicians occupied but, strangely, the turnout from the local residents remains depressingly low.

One attraction is to connect with senior politicians otherwise shut in their Westminster eyries. The experience of facing members of the public in circumstances which are not totally under control can produce great stories – both verbally and visually. Why? Maybe it reminds these politicians why they came into politics in the first place and they cannot resist the urge to say what they think. This explains why the old regime of holding daily press conferences has largely disappeared. The comment at such an event during the 1993 Newbury by-election by the then Chancellor, Norman Lamont – 'je regrette rien' – about Black Wednesday is part of Westminster folklore. And since this is a party political activity, the usual army of civil servants no longer exercise any sort of control.

Covering general elections

Much of this book shows how journalists can cover politics using their own initiative, finding ways to bypass various obstacles and judging each and every event by the key principle: 'Is this a good story?'

Two extra principles intervene during a general election campaign: political coverage is magnified by a factor of about twenty for three or four weeks; and there is a group of people far more important than politicians or journalists – the voters.

Just as you are faced with thousands of politicians and their armies in Westminster and Whitehall, general elections present you with 650 constituencies (planned to be cut to 600) each fielding between three and thirty candidates. Then there are the national party machines which, from being tight, focused entities, swell to gargantuan proportions. Then suddenly, Westminster – the centre of your universe – swings between being virtually empty of politicians to being a mass of near hysterical individuals at key times and points.

The main media outlets spend time and money planning their election coverage. Who and how do we cover the party leaders? Do we focus on particular seats, particular polices, particular personalities? How do we keep our audiences interested and informed?

An outrageously brief description of a political journalist's campaign diary would include: paying the closest possible attention to every nuance of the main political leaders – from policy statements to their wives' asides; identifying and monitoring opinion in around fifty key seats where elections are won or lost; relying on your antennae to twitch, indicating a change in the political wind; and unearthing those odd, quirky events which say so much about our politicians.

Coverage is a mix of personalities and policies – together with those unexpected dramas which bring joy into the life of a journalist. We may not have a presidency, but the activities of the party leaders dominate a campaign. The main media will usually assign particular journalists to the three main leaders. The parties themselves will have spent months, if not years, planning their campaigns with military precision and terminology. Ground war, air war, war books, ammunition, targets – this is the language of campaign planners.

Under the first past the post voting system – otherwise known as 'winner takes all' – much of the campaign will focus on influencing voters in what are variously called by politicians and journalists alike as key marginals, swing or target seats. This describes those seats which will make the difference between the party winning or losing. It will be based on complex computer models covering such elements as majority, swing needed, changes in demographics, specific characteristics of the constituency and the candidates.

Keep an eye out for inappropriate behaviour of individual candidates, however obscure. Before the 1997 general election, and with the words 'Tory sleaze' a mantra, a senior Conservative official warned all candidates and MPs standing again to assume 'there is a *Sun* photographer behind every bush'. One MP clearly forgot and was snapped in a compromising position with a young lady in a park by *The Sun* from behind a bush. Modern communications now make it painfully simple to transmit unfortunate comments or actions around the world.

Another way of analysing a journalist's job is to examine the official and unexpected events. A chronology of the 2010 general election, while unusual in its aftermath, contained many of these elements.

April 6: Gordon Brown asks the Queen to dissolve Parliament

This was widely predicted, but the actual physical act of a Prime Minister leaving No. 10, climbing into his car, being driven up the Mall, 'sweeping' through the gates of Buckingham Palace is highly symbolic. There's a 'this is it' feeling. The starting pistol has been fired.

April 6–8: Wash-up period to finish parliamentary business

Do not forget that there are all these uncompleted Bills swishing around Parliament. Some may be lost altogether, most are fast-tracked through with all manner of deals behind the scenes. Mainstream political journalists do not pay enough attention to this, because they are focused on the forthcoming election campaign. There may be the odd article about various Bills being dropped or watered down, but there are many more stories for specialist journalists in the wheeling and dealing which goes on during these few days before the election properly starts.

In this case twenty Bills were passed or, in some cases, fast-tracked, by Parliament and became law.

April 8: Parliament prorogued

A horrible word, but prorogation merely means the formal end of the parliamentary session.

April 12: Parliament dissolved

Labour launch manifesto
Writs issued for all 650 constituencies
Campaigning officially starts

After the end of the session, MPs are given a few days to wind up and empty their offices. After this, they are no longer MPs, but candidates. The Palace of Westminster is virtually deserted. But ministers are still ministers. In effect, the civil servants may be said to be running the country until a new government is in place. They will not make any changes in policy and will still give their senior ministers a red box or two every day for signature or approval.

Manifesto launches are serious media events, setting out the 'promises' and agenda of the party if elected. Political journalists will do the big picture stories while specialists will gut the relevant sections. 'Promises' is in quotation marks because it is slowly dawning on the media and the voters that in a coalition government, these commitments no longer stand. While this has long been accepted elsewhere, particularly on the Continent, it is a shock for the UK which is accustomed to one party in government with an overall majority.

The writs are notices to the acting returning officers, who oversee the elections in each constituency, that a general election has been called. They are also a signal that the campaign is on – and the main parties in each constituency will step up their strategies.

April 13: Conservative & Lib Dem manifestos launched

Again, plenty of column inches analysing the launch events and the contents of the manifestos. The main party leaders will be holding events or rallies, hoping particularly to attract good pictures for the TV, press and online news.

April 15: First leaders' debate (ITV)

A UK first: a televised debate between the three main party leaders. Joy Johnson describes the strategy and tactics in her chapter. One impact was that it totally absorbed the party leaders, their camps and the political journalists, distracting from usual campaign visits and events.

April 16+: 'Cleggmania' as polls show Lib Dems beating Labour and almost level with Conservatives

Media obsessed with post-mortems. Opinion pollsters and the various party-affiliated websites go into overdrive, analysing and commenting on the outcome.

April 20: Deadline for candidates' nomination papers

If someone wants to stand in the election they must hand in, and have accepted, their nomination papers to the returning officer, who is usually a senior executive on the local council. For journalists, this confirms who will and will not stand – and they should publish this.

April 22: Second leaders' debate (Sky)

Speculation about, coverage and analysis of the debate totally dominates the media.

April 27: Deadline for applying for proxy vote

This is the last date for those who want to nominate someone else to vote in their place, usually because they will be away.

April 28: Bigotgate: Gillian Duffy questions Brown

Anecdotes from many of the contributors to this book demonstrate that political journalism is a mix of the daily grind and those moments that become a part of history. What was planned as a well-orchestrated walkabout for the Prime Minister in Rochdale was one of those moments. A longstanding Labour member, a pensioner who spoke about the unspeakable: the impact of East European immigrants on local job opportunities; that those claiming benefits were not the vulnerable, and those who really deserved help did not receive it.

A perfectly reasonable exchange which the PM handled stoically, calling her a 'very good woman ...who has served her community all her life'. Not much of a story at this stage.

Gordon Brown and his aides deserve some sympathy. Canvassing with John Major trying to talk to voters while journalists are thrusting microphones between the two was not enjoyable. The 'pooling' system of arranging for a discreet microphone to be attached to the lapel of the PM or party leader – and its output then made available to other media – makes sense. In this instance Brown forgot about it when he retreated into what he clearly thought was the private sanctuary of his official car.

His description, relayed by the microphone, of Mrs Duffy as 'a bigoted woman' and his implicit attack on Sue Nye, one of his most loyal aides, were a gift. Before the election, many a column had been devoted to criticism of Brown's language and man management techniques in private. And many a journalist had been castigated for these stories. So such a vivid, undeniable confirmation of the 'real' Brown greatly added to the impact of his comments.

His subsequent reaction on Jeremy Vine's BBC show, made that much worse by the photograph of him with his head in his hands, added yet more oxygen to the drama. Then, ill-advised, he compounded the agony – or ecstasy, if you are a journalist – by subjecting Mrs Duffy to a 45-minute 'apology' in her own home. Within hours the story had gone from being a problem, to becoming a drama to turning into a crisis. A worthy case study for many a political or journalism student.

Most elections have something called a 'defining moment'. This was it.

April 29: Third and final leaders' debate (BBC)

Given the previous week's events, this was something of an anti-climax – probably because it had lost its novelty value.

April 30: Tony Blair joins campaign trail

It is hard to judge Blair's intentions. But his relaxed style, the well-tanned and toned features at this stage in the campaign were interpreted as those of someone who felt he was well out of it. A gift for sketchwriters.

May 1 & 2: *The Observer* and *The Guardian* come out for Lib Dems; the *Sunday Telegraph* for the Conservatives

None of this came as a surprise. But the 'coming out' of newspapers for political parties are now stories in their own right. While this should not affect the *news* coverage – as opposed to the editorial line – it inevitably has an impact on the selection and priority given to news and news features.

May 6: Polling Day: voting from 7am to 10pm

Something strange happens on election day. Journalists suffer from a severe case of constipation. It is wrong for them to speculate about the outcome. While print media is not subject to the same restrictions as broadcast media, this is a very thin day for political news. It is the voters' day. A key focus is the standard photographs of the leaders going to vote in their own constituencies. After that, communications between journalists and the party machines suddenly go quiet – until after the polls close.

Much has been written about the final message given to readers of the main newspapers, advocating how they should vote. Can they coerce or scare the voters into putting their cross in a particular box? Hopefully not. In any case, this should not be the concern of the working journalist.

Where do you plan to be on election night? One assumes that you will enjoy little sleep that night so it is worth pacing yourself on polling day itself. Those aspiring to be a political journalist should try at some stage to attend a 'count' – the place where the ballot boxes are brought in from the polling stations for counting. It is usually a community or sports hall. But you must apply in plenty of time to the local council for a pass to attend as a bona fide journalist.

As the big, black boxes come in, they are distributed among rows of people around long trestle tables who will sort and count them according to the wards, i.e. the areas within the constituency. Please be very careful how you behave. No loud noises, microphones or tape recorders unless specifically allowed by the officials in certain areas. This is one time when you must keep quiet, gain a sense of how each party is doing as you see how the piles of votes mount up in each ward. Those representing the parties may try to persuade you that they are doing exceptionally well. None of this is of any interest. All you are waiting for is the result.

You are likely to see little clusters of officials, usually the agents, from different parties in consultation with the returning officer at some point. What they are doing is agreeing which votes are 'spoiled'. Amazing as it may sound, there are UK voters who are incapable of grasping the concept of putting an X in one box. Odd as this may seem, these agents rarely argue and reach agreement without too many problems.

Apart from drinking gallons of caffeine-laden drinks, you need to gauge the likely time of the result and arrangements for interviews afterwards. Nationally, there is a competition to announce the first results – which tend to be in safe Labour seats, i.e. urban areas – by midnight. Otherwise it is a process that goes on all night long and, in the remoter parts of the UK, throughout the next day. But the fate of the main parties can generally be predicted by around 4 o'clock, though this varies in close-run elections.

Many people think that the candidates do not know the results until the returning officer goes to the microphone to announce them. That is not actually true. The returning officer will very quietly tell the candidates and their agents the results before the formal announcement. You are likely to be kicked out if you try to intervene. This is not your moment.

As you see on TV, there is a certain formality to the announcement with the returning officer declaring the results in the same order as they are on the ballot paper, i.e. alphabetically. The winner will make a short speech of thanks. Others may also say something. Once they leave the stage, that is the time for interviews.

May 7: Results show no party wins overall majority

Con 306; Lab 258; LD 57; Others 28

An overall majority means that one party has more seats than the other parties put together. If there is no overall majority, then the main options are for the party with the most seats to try to govern as a minority government or for that party to do a deal with other parties.

In spite of widespread speculation that no party would win an overall majority, there was something akin to panic among some commentators when this scenario emerged in the early hours of Friday morning. A few remembered the uncertainty following the first of two elections in 1974. But for most, this was a new ball game for which they had not planned.

May 8+: Negotiations start between the parties

In normal circumstances, the leader of the party with the most seats will go to Buckingham Palace where the Queen will ask him or her to form a government. This usually happens around 12 noon.

All serving prime ministers, however optimistic, are expected to pack up their belongings and order the removal vans to take them out of Downing Street if they lose the election. Certainly the UK system is dramatic – and may appear brutal, even hypocritical.

A departing PM and his or her family will walk down the corridor between the Cabinet Room and the front door. The staff lining will say their goodbyes – usually with some tears. These people will have all been working together closely during the good and bad times.

Less than an hour later, a new Prime Minister will turn up at the front door with his or her family. After all the photos outside, they will take that same path from the front door towards the Cabinet Room. The staff will line the corridor and welcome the new incumbents with plenty of smiles and congratulations. It is symbolic in that they serve the office of Prime Minister, irrespective of who holds the title. In most other countries, there is a transition period and a greater change of staff.

But the 2010 election was not as usual as there was no new PM on 8 May. While Gordon Brown was then given a hard time in the media for staying on as PM, constitutionally, the poor man had no option. Until someone else could go to the Palace, Brown had to stay in office. There is no provision for leaving the UK without a PM.

May 10: Brown resigns as Labour leader

Many political journalists were now showing signs of near hysteria as they were expected to report virtually around the clock and yet they had little knowledge of what was happening. The main focus was on the party leaders and negotiating teams going in and out of the Cabinet Office on Whitehall and their party HQs. Helicopters hovered overhead and College Green, the lawn opposite the Lords on Millbank, was a mass of scaffolding and TV paraphernalia as the channels resorted to pretty meaningless interviews with almost anyone who wandered by. The one real story which did emerge was that, with Brown as leader, there was no scope for a Lab–Lib pact.

May 11: Brown steps down as PM

David Cameron becomes Prime Minister

Eventually a deal between Cameron and Clegg appears possible. By now Brown had had enough and went to the Palace to resign formally. As the Browns left No. 10, Cameron was at the Palace, accepting the Queen's invitation to form a new government.

May 12: Senior ministerial team announced; Cameron & Clegg hold first joint press conference in Downing Street garden

Political journalists are now in ecstasy. A new PM will usually have carefully choreographed the appointment of his Cabinet and key posts. This time, this took a little longer as deals for dividing the spoils between Tory and Lib Dem MPs and peers had to be done. Coverage of the winners and losers are all good fun.

This is followed by the press conference: an event which all journalists attending are likely to talk of for the rest of their lives. One of those times when they can justifiably claim that they were part of history.

May 18: New Parliament assembles

Do not forget the new MPs. They start arriving in the Commons and swearing the oath of allegiance to the Queen. The only angle which tends to be mentioned is the absence of the Sinn Fein MPs as they refuse to swear the oath. The first business is the election or re-election of The Speaker, who is then traditionally 'dragged' to The Speaker's Chair. There is also a symbolism in the new seating arrangements. Suddenly, all those Labour MPs who had occupied the government benches were now a rump on the opposite side. The extra dimension this time was speculation about where the Lib Dems would sit.

May 25: State Opening of Parliament

The final event, officially marking the change of government, is the Queen's procession and speech, opening the new parliament.

Conclusion

As the above illustrates, the challenge for a political journalist lies in careful preparation and research before the start of the campaign, together with quick reactions to sudden events. While campaigns are physically tiring whatever role you take, do try to escape the constraints of Westminster for at least part of the time. There is nothing quite like being out on the road covering tours by party leaders and touching the voters' pulse in target seats.

24: A senior politician is coming to your town…

Sheila Gunn

At this stage, either you will be determined to become a political journalist or are quite appalled at the idea. In either case, you may want to consider your options. How do you get there if that's what you want? How do you channel your original ambition? As the personal stories in this book make clear, there are those who decide on their path early on in life and follow it doggedly; many others are less sure, but toil away until they see what doors open.

For my generation – and for many of the contributors – the traditional route was to work our way up through local or regional media outlets. Gaining experience at the local level and, inevitably, making mistakes, is still a brilliant training ground. Increasingly, large media organisations run their own graduate training schemes – another excellent way in. Either way it is unusual to cover Westminster politics without some sort of grounding at a lower political level.

One experience which can make a decisive difference to your view of political journalism is your first experience of meeting a senior politician. So imagine that you are working on a local or regional paper or broadcast channel when you learn that the PM is paying a visit to your patch. It is perfectly possible that the PM will sweep in, move from helicopter to car to building, back to car, helicopter and whirred away. All you've gained are a few glimpses of him through the circle of security, aides, some national media and guests. Not only is this a personal failure but you would have to rely on quotes and pictures fed to you by others, mostly those with a vested interest in putting a particular gloss on the visit. It needs good planning.

You are likely to be given no more than forty-eight hours' warning. This is rarely because of any sinister motive but merely because of today's demands for tight security. The good news is that the PM's office is likely to want media coverage for the visit, particularly in the regional media, and will approach local editors and producers offering interviews and operational details.

Contact with No. 10

Do not be afraid to contact the No. 10 press office (www.number10.gov.uk gives you the details). Generally, they would much prefer helping you than most national journalists. To your more obvious questions, such as why is he visiting a particular place and why now, they will have answers which have been prepared well in advance. Such as: 'The PM is very keen to see for himself the ... hospital. It has been a beneficiary of his patient premium strategy to focus extra funds on...' etc.

Do not be too cynical – all this helps towards your coverage. At least it means you can do some investigating yourself about the hospital and the impact of the strategy. Has it really received extra funds? There will always be those who will grumble about their local hospital! What about other health services in the area? For instance, is this hospital benefiting while another is losing its accident and emergency service?

Ask about logistics, although they may be cagey about travel arrangements. You can usually negotiate with them: remember that they want your media coverage, especially good pictures! They can usually slot in an interview time and place as well as giving you contact details of the press officer accompanying him. Clearly they would much prefer an interview at an organised time and place rather than have a microphone suddenly placed under his nose. What they will not want you to do is contact his opponents or those who may want to protest in some way beforehand. Some care has to be taken in passing on details to others for obvious reasons.

The press office often offers a local newspaper an article under the name of the PM for publication on the day of the visit. It is unlikely to be exciting stuff, but as it will include local references and help develop a good working relationship, it is worth accepting. For balance, it is a good idea afterwards to offer his opponent the same space to counter his arguments.

There is a convention that local MPs are told whenever other MPs, particularly ministers, go to their constituencies. So, if the local MP is in the same party as the PM, you can expect him or her to be involved in the visit and to try to milk it for all it's worth. If the MP is in the opposing party, he or she will also be told of the visit beforehand and will give you quotes along the lines of: 'I'm delighted he is coming here so that he can see for himself the damage that he and his government is doing to our...' They may also stage some kind of stunt, such as driving around a van with a billboard attacking the government.

Find out if the PM is visiting any other places. Often a private meeting with local activists is fitted in. No. 10 will not want to give you details, but you may have more luck with the press office at party HQ.

Hopefully you will have contacts within the local party and any other venues. Their press officers or officials are likely to be hesitant about giving you any details – and have probably been firmly told to refer journalists to the No. 10 press office. But you should be able to guess the identity of some of those likely to meet the PM, such as key executives or representatives. You could try to arrange in advance for them to give you an interview or quote straight after the visit. In some cases they will be happy to be quoted or interviewed, but sometimes they will only give non-attributable quotes. Annoyingly these are generally the more interesting, that is, critical, comments.

Your big interview

Trying to dig out a scoop by asking the PM about a topical political issue is tempting. And you should certainly be up to date on the current running stories. But do not forget your audience and make sure that you have some quotes that are relevant to their particular concerns, such as proposed closure of a factory or plans for a high-speed rail link through the area. Do not be worried about whether he has been briefed or not. He would have been given information by his aides on all likely issues that may be raised.

Try to keep the questions short. You are not Jeremy Paxman or John Humphrys: this is not the time to interrupt constantly, to be aggressive or rude. The PM will be used to that. Thorough research and knowledge of local issues and time spent preparing your questions is likely to produce far better results. How you handle yourself may also help you at a later stage when you are dealing with the PM and his aides. You would be surprised how well they remember the behaviour of individual journalists.

Afterwards...

Once the ministerial entourage has swept off, you may be under pressure to file or record your story immediately. If at all possible, gain a little extra time so that you can talk to some who met him. These interviews are often the most productive – especially from 'ordinary' people. Modern PMs are loath to confine these events to meeting 'the bosses'; they always want to meet some of those working at a lower level in the front line. Please deal gently with such interviewees: they will not be used to dealing with journalists and may be worried that they will be in trouble with their organisation if quoted by name. Just make clear where you are from and what you are asking. Stitch up the politician who says something unfortunate, especially if they think the microphones are off. But think carefully about how you treat someone who knows little about how politicians and political journalists operate.

If that visit has gone well, it is not a bad idea to email or ring through your thanks to the press officers or officials you have dealt with. You never know when you may need them again. The number of times that quite casual acquaintances in politics lead to decent stories many years later is quite amazing.

25: Reporting the town hall

Richard Osley

The first career stop for journalists is often a place that they hardly considered important before joining their first local paper: the town hall.

In fact, it would be interesting to know how many new starters professing to be dead set on forging a career in political journalism actually know the name of their own local councillor. I didn't when I started.

For many, the local authority is just an institution that makes sure the bins are emptied, collects council tax and squabbles with you over parking fines. Yet the council has a key role in nearly every aspect of life, from schools to housing to social services, and the skills acquired patrolling the corridors of local government can be replicated on every rung of the journalism ladder. It is here where the fundamentals can be learned and perfected.

It's not just journalists who couldn't tell you who represented them at local government level. Most people in Britain have no idea who their councillors are. Turn-out figures confirm that three quarters probably didn't even bother to vote in local elections.

Yet, when you write about the decisions they take and how they spend public money, interest pricks up. Tell readers the local council has just spent hundreds of thousands of pounds on a broken fountain or an unimpressive piece of public art and it becomes the chief conversation in every local greasy spoon over the morning bacon and eggs. That could get us three teachers!

The trouble is, while all of this sounds simple, and there are tricks and hints for reporting local politics, there is no quick shortcut. To do it properly takes time and devotion to develop contacts and a full understanding of how each authority works with its different committees and decision-making processes.

There are long evenings spent in council meetings listening to local politicians use fifty words when four or five would do. That's tough when your friends are in the pub watching the Arsenal match.

Only with experience do you gain the confidence to pick and choose accurately which ones are worth going to and which personalities – like the grown-up counterparts at Westminster – will cause the biggest stir. With reliable contacts, you will know when something major is about to break.

Do your homework

A great starting point when you begin work on a local newspaper in this role is to take a file of back issues going back three or four years – more if you are really keen – and get a feel for what stories make the prime pages and what news agenda runs through it.

See which issues have been important to the area, generate letters and interest your editor. You need to be able to work out how it all fits together.

Most councils are set up with an executive system where an inner cabal of around ten councillors have the final say on policy. Backbenchers supposedly feed into the direction of the council during private meetings. If the party leadership ignores them – and if they trust you – they may turn to you with their grievances, opening up the true debate within the authority.

There are two approaches that journalists take at this stage: the inside route or the outside. Both are profitable, both will get you hard-hitting front page stories and which strategy you use largely depends on your character.

The 'inside' is where you almost involve yourself in the council political bubble. You make sure the mobile phone number of every councillor is in your contacts book. You might get a few senior officers on that list too. You meet with them, go for drinks after meetings with them, call them regularly for stories. A two-way relationship develops where they trust you to let them talk off the record or in complete confidence, and they feel comfortable passing on leaked information – often the source of the best stories – without fear that they might be implicated in the release.

You become their first port of call. It is mutually advantageous. They get the coverage, you get the exclusive leaked memo. It's easier than rooting through the town hall bins every day.

The 'outside' approach is where you play hardball with the top table of councillors at all times. You don't want a private briefing or trade-offs, you want them to answer your questions. Now!

This is often the approach taken by reporters who may feel they don't want to stay on the local paper for more than eighteen months to two years. They want to get in, hit the politicians like Jeremy Paxman, grab the splashes and get out. Your contacts will not be councillors, they will be community complainers with a shared distrust of local authorities. Here, the reporter takes up personal crusades and one-off cases. Councillors may refuse to talk to you – but who cares if you have them banged to rights?

Whichever tactic you take, a healthy level of scepticism of what happens behind the front doors of the town hall must be retained.

Go for a beer and gossip with the housing chief of the council, but do so with the accepted understanding that if the housing department messes up, the newspaper will challenge him on every failure it has made.

The best councillors will have thick skins. Those who ignore local newspapers completely unsurprisingly tend to get the worst headlines.

Information channels

There is an obstacle: the council press office. Its staff would rather all of the things that you do to obtain your best articles didn't happen. They wish you wouldn't speak off the record with councillors and senior staff. It is effectively charged with controlling the message that comes out of the town hall, protecting the council's reputation. In most areas, staff will be explicitly prohibited from talking to the press without permission.

Funnily enough, the stricter the communications department plays it, the more likely a climate of leaks from within will develop. More fool them. The best bet is to bypass the press office for anything other than factual information. As much as some press officers think otherwise, it is not for them to answer political points or to justify a controversial policy. It should be the heads of department answering those questions. Arguments over stories with council press officers will eat up your time.

Communications departments are good for points of information: i.e. an explanation as to why a parking fine was issued on a parochial story. But they should not be a shield for a political party.

In Westminster City Council, reporters are often asked to go through the press office if they want to speak to a politician. It's far healthier to have a direct line to the top than to go through a series of middle men and women. And do not fall foul of the 'false campaign', especially around election time. This is when a mild threat to the closure of a service or a change in policy is ramped up into something inexplicably urgent by candidates and councillors looking to make quick political gain.

For instance in Camden's Kentish Town, campaigners who protested against the closure of Victorian swimming baths were later revealed to be Liberal Democrat election candidates who had helped themselves to weeks of free coverage and spots in newspaper letters pages without declaring their interest.

At least in that case, there was a genuine threat of the Victorian baths being sold off by the then Labour controlled council. A beautiful building may have been bulldozed. On other occasions, there won't even be that defence. They will claim that police stations and post offices are to close, at the slightest suggestion of a change in policy. These are naff stories and should be avoided at all costs. The parties who peddle them won't ask for permission when they rip photocopies of your headlines and stick them on election literature, trying to prove to the local electorate they saved something that didn't need saving.

During elections scour the mountains of party literature. Look for inconsistencies. In Camden, the Liberal Democrats sent different messages to different parts of the borough on Middle East politics. In the northern areas like Hampstead, which has a large Jewish community, there was a soft approach to the issue of Israeli bombing of Gaza. In the south of the borough, with a large number of Muslim residents, an election candidate called on Britain to stop arming Israel.

Once elected, councillors start to enjoy the to and fro. The full council meeting – usually held once every month or two – is the perfect forum for a bunfight. Sadly, as much as they may protest otherwise, deep down they know nothing much gets achieved as they shout at each other across the council chamber. It is the simplest thing in the world to get a 'Labour said this but then Conservatives said that' story here, usually starting with the tired, clichéd 'a huge row broke out at the town hall last night'.

But the better stories are the ones you pick up in the corridors outside. All of those councillors in one place; it is a gold mine for off the record briefings. Of course, you shouldn't miss key speeches or contributions inside the chamber, but it is a cardinal sin to stay rooted to your press box seat like a human Dictaphone.

Where the money goes

In the end, council politics all comes back to the money, even though around three quarters of it comes from central government coffers rather than council tax. These politicians, many of whom will be hoping to move up the political ladder and maybe even become an MP one day, are trusted to spend our money. They must be held accountable. They should be able to justify each cheque.

The local press is vital in this respect. If you can spot wastage, you have the kernel of a story. Check agendas for quirky expenditure and hiring of expensive consultants, particularly for aesthetic services like designers or providing frills where taxpayers don't want them. If vague terms are used, ask the executive members to explain them. If they can't, that in itself is a story.

Hidden Scoops

Much of the best information will be tucked away in what is called 'part 2' of council meetings. This is where the press and public are ordered out of the room so confidential matters, usually involving important financial deals and contracts, are discussed. Again, you need a trusty leak to tell you what's been said, maybe bend the rules and slip you a document or two. If you can 'double source' the nature of these private discussions, you will have a clear idea of the most important decisions being taken.

Councils, as public institutions, are subject to the Freedom of Information Act. This should in theory be another mine of stories. You get to ask for what you want. They send it back in twenty days. If only. Sadly, the tone of responses to requests made under FoI has changed significantly since the law was introduced. Local authorities once handed over almost anything you asked for, perhaps fearful of the legal consequences.

In the first year of this legislation I was literally carting away files of information on trolleys. Embarrassing emails and minutes fell into my lap without doing any work. The same went for other local institutions like hospitals and museums.

But I don't think I am alone in thinking that the mood has changed as time has gone by. Councils now frustrate journalists by calling on exemptions of all kinds. If they say the release of information affects 'candid negotiations' – the private talks you want to know more about – the info stays locked away. You can appeal. It, almost as a matter of course, will be rejected by an internal judge, leaving you with the only option of going to the higher adjudicator, the Information Commissioner, whose workload is so large that if you win the case the story may no longer be relevant by the time you get the information.

Perversely, all of the stories that critics attack FoI (for silly stuff like how many loo rolls the town hall ordered in the last three months, and how many biscuits were eaten by staff during coffee breaks) are to a large extent products of this stand-off. The important information, so much of it justified on good public interest grounds, is protected at all costs.

Still, one can still score some satisfying successes. I did manage to discover the actor Sir Christopher Lee's personal request for Earl

Grey tea and for nobody to mention horror films after he gave a talk in a library in Holborn. And also the shortlist of celebrities drawn up at the town hall to switch on the lights in Camden Town. It's interesting to know who else was considered before they plumped for John Fashanu.

If you do strike it lucky and prise figures out of the council a good tip is to have placed an identical request with a similar authority. That way you can make a proper judgement on whether the £10,000 spent on away days and conferences is a lot of money. It gives you a point of contrast, a safety net for describing something as a 'shocking massive spending spree on staff jollies' when it might actually be the lowest figure in London for conference bookings.

Where you might hit a brick wall with FoI, the Audit Commission Act usually yields better results. It's just not used that often because it isn't well publicised. There are no real limits on the release of this information available here. Every year local authorities are legally obliged to set up what is generally called an 'audit window'. For four weeks, the books are opened up for public inspection. They will place an advert in a newspaper, possibly the one you are working on.

During this spell, you can ask for nearly anything. You can see contracts signed by the council, ledgers of air travel payments, hotels booked, expenses for particular projects, compensation payments and money spent on those costly consultants. The list is endless.

It isn't used enough and your local authority may be surprised when you send a list of requests. By law, they must deal with them. You won't get the information straight away but when it arrives it is often the best insight of spending by the council, figures you will never see in public agendas. At the *New Journal*, one of the quirkier stories we uncovered this way was finding a shopping list for products used to decorate show homes on council estates.

It takes a bit of commitment and dedication to trawl through the financial books. If you don't understand every line of the spreadsheet, your newspaper's accountant should be able to help.

Get to know your local council!

This is the kind of material local newspapers must be scrutinising.

Sadly, in the near-decade I've worked on the *Camden New Journal*, we've seen local papers step back from council reporting. Reporters on papers across London and beyond no longer attend meetings so religiously. Under strain from financial cutbacks and lack of staff, there is a risk that sound bites and press releases win over proper analysis.

Maybe if every ambitious new starter who says on their CVs that they are passionate about journalism justified that claim by showing their commitment to reporting local politics at first base, the politicians spending your money would not have such an easy ride.

The low salaries and long hours often dampen that initial enthusiasm. But if we don't hold them to account, who will?

Richard Osley is the deputy editor of the Camden News Journal.

26: Another layer of government: the devolved administrations

Sheila Gunn

Tony Blair can be thanked by journalists for one particular innovation in his first government: the establishment of another layer of government for them to cover. Devolving power to two of the nations of the United Kingdom, namely Scotland and Wales, together with the transfer of powers to the Northern Ireland Assembly, has created a new class of politicians and all the paraphernalia that comes with them. Whether on personalities and their foibles, money and how it is used or abused, policies, elections or the wheeler-dealing, they are perfectly designed to supply the enquiring reporter with plenty of ammunition.

This may not, of course, have been the former Prime Minister's motivation. In moving to set up the Scottish Parliament, he was primarily fulfilling the ambition of the late and lamented Labour leader, John Smith. Once he had decided to allow the Scots some degree of independence, he had to think about satisfying demands in Wales for something vaguely similar. The situation in Northern Ireland was different as the rough road to the relatively stable functioning of the Northern Ireland Assembly is partly a result of the Belfast Agreement of 1998.

In his autobiography *The Journey*, Blair admits: 'I was never a passionate devolutionist. It is a dangerous game to play. You can never be sure where national sentiment ends and separatist sentiment begins.'

He could have added that no one would have predicted back in the heady days following the 1997 general election that the new structures in Scotland and Wales would uncover such a rich source of 'scandals', 'crises' and 'sleaze'. Initially these focused on such issues as Labour's attempt to dictate the leadership in each country's new elected body and the spiralling costs of the new buildings to house them. But, largely as a result of using proportional representation voting systems, it must have been fairly obvious to him and his colleagues that their elections were almost certain to result in either coalitions or minority administrations.

Reporting the different decision-making systems these throw up will have provided wonderful experience for journalists who have more recently been coming to terms with reporting the Cameron–Clegg coalition in Westminster.

Setting up the office of the Mayor of London, Greater London Authority and London Assembly also suffered teething problems. Again, Blair did not want Ken Livingstone to be the first Mayor and made a hash of the first elections by putting in Frank Dobson as the official Labour candidate. (Livingstone, of course, totally thrashed 'Dobbo'.)

Common features

The devolved bodies in all three nations mirror to a large extent the Westminster system. There is an elected body of politicians. From these are drawn the executive or 'government' of ministers, supported by civil servants who carry out the policies. The elected members meet either in the equivalent of the Commons' chamber or in committees. There are regular question times, debates and, to a more limited extent, the scrutiny and passing of legislation.

Elected members are almost always active members of a particular political party. They will be expected by their party's leaders to be loyal and vote as directed. But there is a far greater preponderance of those in a nationalist party, such as the Scottish Nationalists or Plaid Cymru, who advocate a greater degree of devolution or independence. In Northern Ireland, most of the parties are linked to particular communities.

However a key feature which is again very much under review in 2011 is the limitation of the powers of these bodies. Tony Blair was reluctant to devolve – or transfer in the case of Northern

Ireland – decision making affecting the overall economy and the international standing of the United Kingdom. They all basically have powers over the domestic issues of health, education, farming and the environment. The macro issues of foreign affairs, international development, the economy, tax and benefits remain with Westminster.

The future of these bodies should look clearer after the May 2011 elections (and the 2012 London mayoral election).

Scotland and Wales

There is many an editor or producer who will assert that a journalist who can survive Scottish politics is fit to report on politics anywhere in the world. In fact they may claim that the Scottish political scene is a far tougher and rougher working environment than Westminster. It is certainly no coincidence that so many seasoned political journalists 'down south' learned their trade in Scotland.

Many of the most successful journalists also started out in Wales. Again, it can be a tough working environment, but one where one's elbows do not need to be quite so sharp as in Scotland. In both cases you are, of course, covering 'national' politics. Nothing irritates Scottish and Welsh journalists more than being lumped together with 'regional' media.

What to do about Scotland? It was the question that many a Prime Minister posed since the union between Scotland and England came into being on 1 May 1707. Back in 1979, moves towards devolution helped finish off the Labour government of James Callaghan. His successor, Margaret Thatcher, wrote in *The Path to Power,* 'for the moment, devolution was dead: I did not mourn it'. She showed little enthusiasm for changing her attitude throughout her eighteen-year premiership. This is not to say that the issue itself was dead and it played a small part in her eventual downfall. For while she could justify her stance against setting up a Scottish Parliament, the decision to trial the poll tax (officially called the community charge) in Scotland a year before it was introduced in England and Wales now looks indefensible.

Her successor, John Major, came to feel – if anything – more strongly against Scottish and Welsh devolution as he warned that it was a gamble that could and, probably, would lead to the break-up of the United Kingdom. That has not proved to be the case; not yet, anyway. But the tensions remain.

Post-1997

Since the first, uneasy years, the Scottish government (originally called the Executive) and the Scottish Parliament settled down to work on a reasonably stable basis. Inevitably there are tensions between Holyrood and Westminster, particularly on budgets. Relations between Blair/Brown and Alex Salmond, the Scottish Nationalist First Minister and one of politics great survivors, were never happy. Nor do they look like improving with the coalition government. The May 2011 elections are unlikely to change that. But then Scottish politics are never ever boring.

Two issues which continue to cause tensions between Westminster and the devolved bodies are the Barnett formula and the West Lothian question.

The Barnett formula, named after Joel Barnett, the then Labour Chief Secretary to the Treasury, dates back to the late 1970s and determines the public spending per head of the population in the four nations of the UK. It means that about £1,600 more is spent per head in Scotland than in England. Wales and Northern Ireland also receive more per head than England. Not surprisingly, this convention is being looked at again.

The splendid Labour MP Tam Dalyell is the creator of the West Lothian question. In the late 1970s, he pointed out that after devolution, Westminster MPs would no longer be able to vote on issues such as education in West Lothian while Scottish MPs would be able to do so in West Bromwich. It has not been solved and there were times during Blair's premiership when he relied on the votes of Scottish MPs to push through reforms that applied only to England and Wales.

One other subject exemplifies the loss of some of Westminster's powers and has provoked national and international disputes: the decision in 2009 to release Abdelbaset al-Megrahi – the man found guilty of the UK's greatest single act of terrorism, the bombing of Pan Am flight 103 over Lockerbie in 1988. The decision was taken by Kenny MacAskill, the Scottish Justice Secretary, leaving the then Prime Minister Gordon Brown powerless to influence it. It was made on health grounds, as al-Megrahi was not expected to live for more than a few months. After his 'triumphant' return to Libya, he seemed to make a remarkably good recovery.

Among the 270 victims were thirty-five students from Syracuse University, flying back to the US after six months studying in London. For most it was their first trip away from home and their families were waiting to welcome them back for Christmas. I am reminded of them every year when I say goodbye to my own wonderful students at Syracuse's London faculty as they return home.

Devolution in Wales has not thrown up so many problems. The West Lothian question does not arise to the same extent because most legislation covers England *and* Wales. In the referendum on 3 March 2011, the Welsh electorate voted 63.5 per cent to 36.5 per cent in favour of giving the national assembly direct law-making powers in twenty devolved areas, such as education and health. However the turnout was only 35.4 per cent – showing a muted interest in increasing the Assembly's remit. May's elections could provide a better test of the standing and influence of the Welsh Assembly government's leadership and the Assembly itself.

Northern Ireland

In covering politics, how we communicate – the language we use – is obviously central to our work. In reporting politics in Northern Ireland, the correct choice of words is paramount. Quite literally, people's lives and livelihoods could depend on it.

Whether one talks about the United Kingdom or Great Britain; Ulster or the six counties; paramilitaries, terrorists or murderers; Derry or Londonderry; Catholics or nationalists; Protestants or unionists – journalists need to think extremely carefully about how their words will be interpreted. There will always be those who see conspiracies behind every statement, every action. Even your choice of background, your tone and body language will be meticulously scrutinised. It is no coincidence that many reporters who reported in Northern Ireland during its darkest days went on to become notable correspondents in war zones.

The more optimistic news is that, following the Good Friday

Agreement of 1998 – now more commonly referred to as the Belfast Agreement – signed by the British and Irish governments and all but two of the Province's political parties, Northern Ireland has made slow but discernible progress. Certainly it no longer hits the headlines across the UK with such regularity, if that is taken as an indicator of its political environment.

Official figures show that between 1969 and 1999, deaths arising from what was dubbed 'the troubles' totalled 3,326. Both John Major and Tony Blair are among those who deserve great credit for the relative calm of recent years. That does not mean that the tensions have evaporated. Remember that the majority of the population, mainly Protestants, want the Province to remain part of the United Kingdom; a minority, mainly Catholic, want 'the six counties' – to be part of the republic of Ireland. Sectarian violence still continues to blight the different communities on a daily basis, as does more commonplace criminality and intimidation.

London politics

As mentioned elsewhere there is a small room in the Commons where, traditionally, lobby journalists are briefed by No. 10 press officers most afternoons. It is up a spiral staircase in a tower in the south-east corner of the Palace of Westminster. From there myself and colleagues watched an extraordinary firework display diagonally across the Thames marking Margaret Thatcher's abolition of the Greater London Council. It is said, hopefully not entirely correctly, that the then GLC leader, Ken Livingstone, spent what money was left in his coffers on the sparklers.

This was in 1986. Until 2000, the capital had no pan-London authority. There were – and still are – thirty-two local authorities and various pan-London government agencies. A return to a London mayoralty with limited powers was part of Blair's constitutional reforms. The then PM did not want the mayoralty to be a massive power base with the powers of, for instance, New York's Mayor. Frank Dobson, the former Health Secretary, was Labour's candidate. In his memoirs, Blair rather meanly says: 'The truth is that Frank had about as much chance of beating Ken Livingstone in a contest to be London mayor as Steptoe and Son's horse had of winning the Grand National.' And he certainly did not want the office to be occupied by Ken Livingstone. That, of course, is what he got.

Another unguided missile succeeded 'Red Ken' – Boris Johnson. The jury is still out on whether the journalist – with an undoubted presence and extensive grasp of the classics – is delivering on behalf of London's residents. But both Ken and Boris bring their own kind of jollity to political journalism. With little respect for the restraints on other elected representatives, you never quite know what they are going to say or do. That's always good news for the media.

The mayor acts as a sort of 'ambassador' for London although his (there is yet to be a woman) real powers focus mainly on transport and crime. Whether these will be expanded is still under debate. But that would mean taking more decision making away from central government and from London's local councils. These bodies would fight tooth and nail to defend their territory.

Of the London Assembly, the least said the better. The powers of assembly members are limited. There is a regular question time with the mayor and scrutiny committees in City Hall, situated on the south bank of the Thames. But it is hard to generate too much enthusiasm. On a more positive note, the assembly members are pathetically anxious to be interviewed. Sadly the results are rarely impressive.

Conclusion

It is fair to say that, if you are competent in covering a large council, you will be able to adapt those skills fairly quickly to covering a devolved body. And then adapt them a little further to cover Westminster.

But please remember, there are many excellent and contented journalists covering local and devolved politics. You may even achieve a reasonable work–life balance – and could possibly enjoy a social life which is not dictated by politics. You do not have to think about moving to London. With benefit of that amazing thing called hindsight, most of us who took the local to regional to national route in journalism like to reminisce about the fun we had in the 'early days' on local media.

Part VI:

The roads to Westminster

27: An unplanned journey

Chris Moncrieff

'You must be bored stiff...' Those are the words invariably addressed to me when I tell people that I work in the House of Commons. But, for a journalist, nothing could be further from the truth. More stories are created within the precincts of the Palace of Westminster than any other single building in the country, possibly the world. It is never boring.

My first job was on the *Harrogate Herald*. After completing my national service I worked as a general reporter on the *Coventry Evening Telegraph* and the *Nottingham Evening Post*. Late in 1961, I applied for a job as a general reporter at the Press Association. After a brief interview I was told there were no general reporter vacancies, but they offered me a job as a parliamentary reporter. It came like a bolt from the blue. I had never been interested in politics and the thought of working in Parliament frankly appalled and daunted me. But you don't turn down the offer of a job which takes you into Fleet Street for the first time.

When I arrived in January 1962, my fears appeared to be well grounded. It was even worse than I had anticipated. Here were Hugh Gaitskell, the then Labour Leader of the Opposition, and Prime Minister Harold Macmillan going at it hammer and tongs during PMQs. I thought to myself: 'I am never going to be able to cope with this. I am going to apply for a transfer to general news.'

But I never did. The House of Commons gradually grows on you. I know of people who went to work there for two weeks as a holiday relief reporter and who were still there thirty years later.

Admittedly, there are turgid moments in the Commons chamber itself, but these are more than offset by the excitements and dramas that occur virtually every week. What is more, especially if you have lobby credentials, you are at the hub of the nation's affairs. You are right at the heart of sometimes cataclysmic events which can change the face of the country, even the world.

Let me describe some of the things that have happened to me over the course of more than forty years working at Westminster.

When an MP is thrown out of the House for some act of parliamentary disobedience (such as calling an opponent a 'liar' and refusing to withdraw the epithet) reporters are forbidden to talk to that MP in the short time that exists between the Speaker's decision to eject him and his departure from the precincts.

On one occasion when a Labour MP was ordered off the premises, I was waiting on the pavement in Parliament Square outside Carriage Gates. A taxi was just leaving the premises and I looked inside it and saw the very MP at the centre of the storm. Fortunately, the cab-driver had to stop momentarily for passing traffic, and I ran up to it, opened the door and uninvited jumped inside, to the MP's utter surprise. I got an interview with him and he dropped me off when I had finished. I hadn't the faintest clue as to where I was (it was Highgate, actually) but I filed an exclusive story before making my way back – on the bus this time.

On another occasion, I bumped one morning into a glum-looking Bob Mellish, the Labour government Chief Whip, in the members' lobby. I asked him what the problem was and he complained that he was not receiving the support he felt he deserved from the Prime Minister, Harold Wilson. I said cheekily, and half-joking, 'Why don't you resign?' To my utter amazement he said: 'That's a good idea', promptly gave me a statement and rushed off to write out and deliver his letter of resignation to 10 Downing Street. I had a huge story to myself!

The Press Association story had not filtered into Downing Street when, a short while later, political reporters were gathering there for the routine morning briefing. When the Prime Minister's press secretary was asked about the resignation, he looked blank. He hadn't a clue what the reporters were talking about, not having seen the PA tapes. So they actually rifled through the in-tray and found the letter sitting there, still unopened!

So what had been a splash story in the evening papers that day, was also splashed in the morning papers the following day. Wilson had pleaded with Mellish to withdraw his resignation, which he did. That shows that a chance meeting and a chance remark can yield huge dividends for the reporter.

I also may have played an unwitting and very minor role in the eventual downfall of Margaret Thatcher. There was some muttering within the Tory parliamentary party that a change was needed at the helm, and there was also talk of a 'stalking horse' candidate to oppose her, not with any prospect of beating her, but as a means of testing the water.

The name of Sir Anthony Meyer, an obscure Conservative backbencher had been mentioned, so when I saw him in the members' lobby, I put it to him. He said he was certainly considering it, giving me a story based precisely on what he had said, and using his own quotes. That story was splashed in the *London Evening Standard* that night, and when he saw it, Sir Anthony approached me in a rage, saying that he hadn't actually finally decided to stand, but now this story had appeared he had no option but to do so. In fact the story had said no more and no less than what he had told me. And since I was standing in front of him, writing it down in my notebook, he must have been aware that I intended to report it.

Needless to say, Thatcher won hands down, with 314 votes. But thirty-three Tory MPs voted for Sir Anthony and a sizeable number abstained. It could hardly be described as a resounding endorsement for the Prime Minister from her own party. After that episode, things went downhill for her and she finally had to throw in the towel. Some time after that Sir Anthony approached me again, apologising for administering that dressing down. He said that if the story had not been written, he might well not have stood, adding: 'It changed the course of history.'

On another occasion, one Saturday night, I was drinking in a Fleet Street pub. The telephone rang: it was 10 Downing Street (they always knew where to find you!) to tell me I was going to the Falkland Islands there and then with Prime Minister Thatcher. I had to be at the Ministry of Defence in an hour to take a coach to RAF Brize Norton where the journey began. It took twenty-four hours in those days, on two aircraft, including a stopover on Ascension Island. There were many incidents in that brief trip but one that stands in my mind was a childish 'stare-you-out' contest the Prime Minister had – with a penguin. Needless to say, Thatcher won the bout, leaving the penguin to waddle away defeated and disconsolate.

That little, innocuous incident goes to prove the fact that whatever grave events are going on in the world, the newspapers – and the broadcasters, too – still love the off-beat, quirky stories, of which there is always a profusion in the world of politics. It also demonstrates the importance for a reporter to carry his passport around with him at all times. You just never know when you may, like that, be suddenly yanked off to foreign climes.

Another tip I would offer to reporters is always to come to work soberly dressed. This means you are able to cover any event from a pop rave-up to a royal funeral. No newsdesk would ever send you to a solemn church service if you were sporting a Mickey Mouse t-shirt.

I travelled the world with Margaret Thatcher and John Major when they were Prime Minister. When I was operating, mobile phones were either non-existent or, later on, very much in their infancy – and ones which operated overseas, unheard of. And it was before the days when laptops came into general use. Therefore getting the story was the easy part of the operation. Getting it back to Fleet Street was often the problem.

Mostly, the telephones in the United States and Western Europe were fine. But in Eastern Europe (Moscow in particular) as well as in most parts of Africa, trying to get through to London was often a nightmare. That is why, after spending the day, effectively clutching the coat-tails of Thatcher and Major, you often had to spend the rest of the time trying to get through to London.

With Margaret Thatcher especially, we saw none of the sights. She was not interested in having fun. Whereas some people find it difficult to walk by a public house without entering it, so Mrs Thatcher was unable to resist the lure of a ball bearing factory whenever she came across one. I have, for that reason, probably been inside more ball bearing factories than I have had hot dinners. On one occasion, we spent the best part of a boiling hot day opening a new sewage farm on the outskirts of Cairo. It was bliss for her, slightly less so for the rest of us.

Luck can, of course, play a big part in a reporter's success – or otherwise. Once, I was doing an interview with Margaret Thatcher in 10 Downing Street when there was a call from downstairs: 'Michael has arrived!' This was a reference to her new grandson whom she had not, at that stage, seen. The interview was broken off and we all trooped downstairs. A Press Association photographer was also there for the interview. We had an exclusive series of marvellous pictures of the Prime Minister cradling her grandson outside and inside No. 10 – as well as that historic remark: 'We are a grandmother…' These were moments, and stories, to cherish.

Within the chamber of the House of Commons, there is often a verbal rough-and-tumble, with plenty of mud-slinging and noise from both sides. It is built like a cockpit and it should be healthily rowdy. Some recent Speakers get enormously fussy about the noise that is often generated. But it is natural when you have two sets of political enemies glaring at each other. And let us not forget that the distance between the two frontbenches, government and opposition, is officially classified as 'two sword lengths' – an indication that trouble is to be expected.

Outside the chamber, however, there is a wide measure of camaraderie. In some cases you will see an Irish Republican MP talking amiably to an Irish Loyalist MP – something neither of them would wish their constituents to see.

Sometimes however there is genuine friction – and worse. Fists have been deployed in the members' lobby. Inside the chamber once the fiery Ulster MP Bernadette Devlin (as she was known then) rushed across the floor of the House and physically attacked Reginald Maudling, the then Tory Home Secretary.

On another occasion, I remember a party being held in the lobby room high up in one of the parliamentary towers. Among the guests were Neil Kinnock, one-time Labour leader, and his wife Glenys, who was to become a member of the European Parliament and later still a life peer and a minister in Gordon Brown's administration. When she heard that Margaret Thatcher, then Prime Minister, was due to arrive at the party 'any time now', she said: 'I cannot bear to be in the same room as that woman' and immediately ran hell-for-leather through the door and down the precarious spiral staircase, leaving her drink undrunk. That was real hatred. I have often thought since it was a great shame (from a journalist's point of view) that the two women did not collide on the stairs.

There are so many things happening, so much splendid tittle-tattle and gossip, sex and drinking, gaffes and pratfalls as well as stories of international moment that any political journalist probably has enough material for a book after only working a year or two in the place. But that is only if they are prepared to deal with the flesh and blood of politicians, rather than spending the day staring at a computer screen.

28: A winding road

Carolyn Quinn

My route into political reporting was a circuitous one. I'd taken a degree in French and then, because I enjoyed the subject, thought I would like to teach it. I was accepted onto a PGCE (Post-Graduate Certificate of Education) course at the Institute of Education in London and completed the course, including several sessions of teaching practice. However it soon became apparent that, while I hugely admired my fellow teachers, I could not imagine pursuing that career path for the rest of my working life. I had to make a momentous decision. I held the qualification – yet have never been in front of a class.

What to do? I had to earn money, of course. During my year at the Institute I taught myself to type, so sought out secretarial work to tide me over. I got a job as a ward clerk in Charing Cross Hospital, shortly afterwards being promoted to a secretarial/administrative job. And it was here that my life changed.

As a hobby I started going along to Charing Cross Hospital Radio to help out, gathering requests and broadcasting them – badly! I loved the work and the thrill of being on air. But I assumed that to work in radio news I needed a journalism qualification. I applied to a couple of newspaper training schemes. No joy. I started to write freelance articles for whoever would take them. I applied for job after job on papers and magazines – all the while still working at the hospital.

Learning the ropes

My breakthrough came when I contacted Brendan Mac Lua – sadly now deceased. He was the editor of *The Irish Post* – a paper my parents had always taken. I asked if I could write ANYTHING for him, or whether he would take on a trainee reporter? I'll always remember his reply: he didn't have a job for me as a journalist but he did need a secretary. Why not come and work for him and he'd give me tips on journalism along the way as well as letting me loose on a few articles?

I gained huge insight and advice from Brendan – bleeding him dry for tips and for chances to write even an odd paragraph for the paper. Then I saw an advert for the BBC – asking for applicants for its local radio trainee reporter scheme. I was given a first interview, then a second, then… a rejection letter. Fortunately within days someone had dropped out and I was given their place.

The one-year course taught me all I needed to know about the technical side of radio reporting as well as the necessary journalism skills – legal, shorthand and the rest. I worked for several happy years at the BBC's local station in Southampton, BBC Radio Solent. Then I applied for an 'attachment' to London – to the regional unit of the BBC's Westminster office. And it was here that politics took hold.

Moving on to Westminster

I loved covering life at Westminster, feeding back news to each region about the activities of their particular MPs. I joined the parliamentary unit at the end of 1989, as part of a wave of new employees to coincide with the project to televise Parliament. The place was full of big characters. Margaret Thatcher was about to embark on her last year as Prime Minister. And I grew to love the theatre that is the Commons chamber.

In 1992 I became a parliamentary correspondent, reporting and presenting for BBC Radio 4's *Today in Parliament* and *Yesterday in Parliament* programmes. Then in 1994, as Tony Blair became leader of the Labour Party and BBC Radio 5 Live was launching as a continuous news service, I joined the ranks of political correspondents – a very junior figure in a team that included Huw Edwards, Jon Pienaar, Jon Sopel, Lance Price, Jeremy Vine and Steve Richards. I learned a lot from them, building up contacts among MPs across the parties, feeling my way on national radio, then national television – many's the time I've stood outside No. 10 doing a live two-way for a TV bulletin.

I spent the 1997 election with the Paddy Ashdown campaign bus; 2001 with Tony Blair. By now, I was doing the odd bit of presenting – on 5 Live and on Radio 4 when they needed a stand-in for their regular presenter. I started to fill some slots on Radio 4's *PM* programme – all the time continuing my work as a political correspondent. I spent twelve years as a political correspondent before moving into presenting full-time, including four years on the *Today* programme. But still the Westminster link remains. On big political days I'm *PM*'s 'woman on the scene' and I present the political programme, *The Westminster Hour* on Sunday evenings at 10pm as well as Saturday *PM* and some weekday *PM*s.

Your road

My best tip to aspiring political journalists would undoubtedly be to demonstrate your commitment – through voluntary work, offering to help out in spare time, asking to shadow someone already doing the job you'd like one day. Show that you have initiative and that you are prepared to work extremely hard. Show too that you understand that journalism is not a glamorous job – that you are not expecting to swan in and present programmes without putting in a lot of hard grind. Examine the writers/broadcasters you admire and learn from them. And don't despair if it doesn't all go your way at first – as I know only too well, a bit of patience and perseverance can pay off!

Carolyn Quinn is a presenter on BBC Radio 4 and chairman of the Parliamentary Press Gallery.

29: Starting out early

Jonathan Isaby

Based on my experience, to make it into political journalism – or journalism of any kind for that matter – requires bags of energy and enthusiasm, a willingness to start off by toiling away for little or no reward while you earn your spurs, an ability to make and cultivate a variety of contacts and a degree of luck.

I spent much of my time at the University of York working on the student newspaper, *Vision*, and YSTV, the campus television station. Student media is a brilliant way of immersing yourself in that environment, gaining experience of all aspects of how a paper or TV/radio station is run, honing the necessary skills and learning from the mistakes you will doubtless make along the way.

I cannot emphasise enough the value of doing student journalism, not least because it also has the capacity to help open further doors, as it did for me. During my second year at university I went to a weekend conference for those working in the student media. I got chatting to someone from the BBC who had been speaking at one of the seminars, explained where my interests lay, and she gave me the name of someone she thought it worth my contacting about getting some work experience.

I was offered that (unpaid) work experience the following Easter holiday, during which I took every opportunity to demonstrate my relevant knowledge and expertise, and set about any tasks I was given with zeal. I was invited back for every following holiday until I graduated, at which point I was offered a permanent job.

I was in the lucky position of coming from London, so was able to live at home during those university holidays and commute into the office on a daily basis (for which I was latterly able to claim travel expenses). Clearly this puts anyone with a base – or at least access to a couch – in London at an advantage, since so much of the national media is concentrated there. That said, there is no reason why you shouldn't be able to seek similar opportunities at regional and local media outlets.

Once ensconced at the BBC, I continued to make it my business to get to know many of the other journalists around Westminster as well as lots of the politicians, spin doctors and other characters who inhabit the political world. Not only are excellent contacts vital for getting stories and just being a good journalist, but you never know who might be in a position to open doors for you as your career progresses. My 'in' at the *Daily Telegraph* initially came from a chance meeting with a columnist through a mutual friend in a Westminster pub.

Do I have any specific tips for success? Being trustworthy, decent and able to keep confidences have always stood me in good stead. And the earlier that you can show a flare for journalism and get some experience on your CV, the better. Websites such as my own are always looking for contributors and the beauty of the internet now is that anyone can begin to get themselves known by starting a blog of their own and putting their work out there for the world to see. But please remember that anything you put there could come back to haunt you one day, so take care.

The hours for an eager political journalist can be quite long. For most of my twenties I worked in an office throughout the day, with much of the real work – of contact-making and story-getting – being done during the evening over drinks in bars, at dinners, book launches, receptions and the like. It therefore helps to be quite a social animal.

So work hard and take every opportunity that comes your way – and be aware that sometimes they arise by just being in the right place at the right time.

Jonathan Isaby has been co-editor of ConservativeHome.com since November 2008. He was a political analyst for the BBC at Westminster before becoming a reporter and then deputy diary editor at the Daily Telegraph.

30: The joy of writing

Sam Macrory

Even when I was young, very young, I wanted to be a journalist. I avidly followed the work of my role model, a reporter who travelled the world and yet, only once in his many adventures, was summoned to see the editor. Tintin, the Belgian comic book hero, seemed to have the perfect life.

I found myself writing from an early age, about almost anything. At secondary school I naturally joined the school magazine's editorial team and, on arriving at York University to read history, I applied to join one of the two student newspapers. After a hard-fought election – candidates: one – I was appointed sports editor, eventually earning promotion to become the paper's news editor.

The sedate pace of life on the university campus didn't provide a steady drip of scoops. But I learned how to write good (and bad) headlines, put in phone calls to people who didn't want to speak to a spotty student hack, and write copy to deadlines, even it meant being holed up in the newspaper's cell-like offices for forty-eight hours. It was fun, exciting, and fulfilling. But although I enjoyed my embryonic efforts I carelessly gave little thought to mapping out a realistic career plan.

The string of low-paid holiday jobs on my CV didn't offer many clues, bar one possible highlight: I'd spent a summer fortnight as a runner on a low-budget film set. After gaining my degree, I decided to find fame and fortune in the glamorous world of movie-making. Weeks of trudging around Soho with a bagful of CVs led to me being employed as the post-production runner on Richard Curtis's latest romantic comedy, *Love Actually*. I photocopied with gusto, booked couriers and brewed hot drinks relentlessly, eventually establishing myself to such an extent that Hugh Grant, the film's leading man, referred to me as the 'tea bitch' when he dropped into the office.

In spite of those heights, I soon realised that I had little flair for the cinematic world. To my slight surprise, I had also begun to miss the rigours of writing, once a time-consuming distraction as a student but now a gaping hole in my post-graduate days. Student journalism suddenly seemed like the best hobby and I began to kick myself for failing to look into graduate journalism courses or apply for a traineeship on a newspaper.

It was now eighteen months since leaving university and I worried that I had missed my chance. Around this time I met up with a friend who was working for a political think tank, giving me the incentive to adapt my writing skills. I set my sights on Parliament, and again, I was lucky. The Liberal Democrat culture and media spokesman, Don Foster, was advertising for an intern. Armed with a thin but first-hand knowledge of the film industry, I convinced Don that I was the expert he needed.

These were the days when Lib Dems were a lowly opposition party with no highly paid special advisers to call on, so my political education was of the hands-on variety. Despite his position on the frontbench, Don soon had me preparing press releases, drafting speeches, and, most importantly, drafting articles for a variety of niche publications such as *Coinslot International*, the UK's low-stakes gaming specialist publication, and a long-standing and rather earnest Westminster weekly called *The House Magazine*.

When the latter publication advertised for an assistant I applied – and I've been there, in a variety of guises, ever since, ending up as the magazine's political editor. Mostly I think I am incredibly lucky: to have a front seat during one of the most exciting times in modern British politics is something which I never take for granted.

At the start, my duties centred around commissioning – phoning MPs to plead for articles – and checking copy for spelling mistakes. Eventually I acquired a pass for Parliament and moved into the frontline. I learned some early lessons.

Always take two dictaphones or at least some spare batteries. An early interview with Michael Howard – an intimidating figure for a young journalist to meet – disappeared into the ether after my dictaphone let me down. After much heart-pounding and a grovelling phone call from me, Howard quietly forgave the slip-up.

Arrive for interviews armed with many more questions than you think you could ask. Just occasionally, you meet a politician who favours the one-word answer or, more likely, goes in for endless waffle. Both can be excruciating, but if you want something interesting to come from your interview, be prepared to try many different ways to get there.

Then, if you do find a line that makes news, beware the backlash.

During an interview with the deputy Labour leader Harriet Harman, I asked her about her constituency – where I lived – in an effort to get away from the rather bland policy-heavy answers. We discussed the bars and pubs which she claimed to like, comments which, unprompted by me, were picked up by a national paper and made a mockery of. Luckily I was out of the office when Harman called.

Finally, get reading. I've always followed politics, but I was never a student politician, a local campaigner, or even – including my stint with the Lib Dems – a party member. Most people inside Parliament are obsessive about politics, and have been from a worryingly young age. They know political history, they understand the often arcane and confusing procedures of Parliament, and they are up to speed on the seemingly never-ending array of legislation which spouts forth from the government of the day. It's easy to be caught out unless you do too.

So, for anyone aspiring to join this trade, here are a few suggestions. Practise, be it on the student paper or any other publication which you can help out on. And if you can't find one to join, then start one yourself. The rise of the blogosphere means everyone has an outlet for their words, and potential employers will expect you to be out there, however low your readership. Falling circulation and advertising revenue has left the traditional print media in a position somewhere between precarious and panic-stricken, so for future employment, experience of writing online is essential.

At the same time, take advantage of all the politics you can. You won't have the contacts and the sources which the veterans of political journalism have acquired. But anyone can – once you have made it through the airport-style security – enter Parliament and attend debates in the chamber and sittings of select committees. Every day, there's a story to be written.

Finally, think a little earlier than I did about acquiring a qualification. To learn the basics and widen your skills, an intense course in journalism can only help. In a sense I was lucky in that I stumbled on another route in. But if you are set on becoming a journalist, then a recognised grounding will stand you in good stead. Whether Tintin would agree is another matter.

Sam Macrory is political editor of The House Magazine.

31: The future role of the political journalist

Professor Ivor Gaber

'If we want everything to remain as it is, it will be necessary for everything to change.'
Giuseppe di Lampedusa, *The Leopard*

The view from here

To say that political journalism is undergoing rapid and dramatic change is to state the obvious. As the quote from Lampedusa illustrates, in a fast-changing world stability only comes through adapting to change. Political journalism is changing because the media, politics and society are all, themselves, undergoing rapid transformation. And as long as the democratic system continues political journalism will continue to survive and thrive – for without free, independent and robust political journalism, there is no democracy.

But the form that that political journalism takes can only be surmised. This is because the traditional media – newspapers, radio and television – have all been undergoing major changes in recent years. Newspaper readerships have been migrating from print to online, and finding a way to get people to pay for their news online – monetising the news – remains the great conundrum for the media industry. People are prepared to pay for entertainment on the web but, so far, they appear to be reluctant to pay for news (although media magnate Rupert Murdoch is trying to break this habit by putting his UK papers, including *The Times* and the *Sunday Times*, behind an online 'pay wall'). As for television, news and current

Shane Greer, Executive Editor *Total Politics* magazine and Conservative blogger

The future of journalism is far from certain. But clearly online journalism will come to play an increasingly important role. Ultimately, this question can only really be answered once we know how future media will be funded. For my money, I believe print newspapers will at some point, in the not too distant future, become a thing of the past as users migrate to handheld devices like the iPad. In that future environment making the most of atomisation will be the key: identifying a niche, filling the niche and exploiting the commercial opportunities associated with that niche. In the long run I think our current distinctions between television, print and online journalism will become a thing of the past. Technology will converge and journalism will react in kind. The journalist of the future will be multi-platform, multi-skilled and utterly specialist.

affairs viewing figures have been in steady decline as audiences, particularly the younger ones, spend more time online, browsing, blogging, but above all using social network sites such as Facebook and Twitter. Some of these sites do cover politics, in their own way, but with nothing like the breadth and depth of the traditional media. However, the televised leadership debates in the 2010 UK general election did give television's coverage of politics a massive shot-in-the-arm. As for radio, audience figures have been holding up well and, even though the majority of the audience listens to music stations, the BBC's speech stations Radio 4 and 5 Live have maintained their audience shares – during the 2010 election campaign these two stations attracted around 17 million listeners a week.

Whether politics will ever fully migrate online is one of the debates that, for the present, remains unresolved. Certainly, as a way of engaging activists and raising money, the political online revolution has been well underway for a decade or more. But the number of people using the web to access political information remains relatively small (around one in ten at the 2010 UK election). That might change. Certainly one thing that has changed is the rise of the political blogosphere. From the big beasts of the blogs, such as Guido Fawkes or ConservativeHome, whose sites attract up to 250,000 unique users a month, to the lone student furiously blogging on his or her laptop, the blogosphere has now enabled everyone to be a political journalist.

But change is not just impacting on the journalists. Politicians have also been affected; they no longer see press releases as their main means of communicating with their voters. Now they blog, they tweet, they set up Facebook sites and so on. In the 2010 election eight out of ten Labour and Conservative candidates had their own websites, as did more than nine out of ten Liberal Democrats, half of all candidates had Facebook accounts, a similar number blogged and six out of ten regularly tweeted during the campaign.

On the ground, politics is changing fast. Party membership, across all parties, is in decline, while single-issue campaigns are buoyant. Even the role of government is changing as the coalition government – the first in more than sixty years – seeks to reduce the role of the state in society at large. Will this all mean that there will be less focus on Westminster with political journalism becoming a more diffuse activity? Many, many changes afoot, and not too many pointers.

One way of penetrating this mist is to begin by looking at political journalism in the context of general elections. They might not be the 'be all and end all' of political journalism but in the few hectic weeks of the campaign it is possible to see a microcosm of political reporting as politicians and journalists fiercely interact – the good, the bad and the not so pretty – in ways that offer some clues as to how things might be in the future.

Back to (see) the future

Envisage a *Life on Mars* scenario. Our texting, tweeting, blogging political reporter, who has been covering the 2010 general election, has just been thrown back to 1979, the last time Labour was ejected from office. It's a time when there's no breakfast time television, no 24-hour TV and radio news, no mobile phones and the internet is just a twinkle in the eye of American military planners (and Tim Berners-Lee).

The first shock to the system for our time-travelling reporter is an early – very early – start. For the campaign day begins with a series of party press conferences, the first at 7.30 at the Liberal Party HQ (no Lib Dems then) and then, after thirty minutes of pronouncements and some desultory questioning, the hack pack moves on to Labour's press conference and finally to the Conservatives at 8.30am.

Why the early morning start? It's because the parties – and the media – need pictures; for after the press conferences, the party leaders and their entourages, used to go through the highly staged process of boarding the campaign 'battle bus' and setting-off for the day's campaigning. The press conference and this daily photo opportunity were designed to provide the lunchtime news bulletins which were (in an age pre-breakfast TV and no 24-hour news channels) the first bulletins of the day, with some pictures to illustrate the start of campaigning.

The rest of the day continued to be based around the broadcasters' news bulletins. Pictures of the press conference and battle buses for the lunchtime shows, a newer story based, the parties hoped, on their various 'themes for the day' for the early evening bulletin and finally a story for the flagship evening bulletins, possibly featuring the leader speaking at a major rally of supporters.

Reporters, either those travelling on the campaign battle buses or under their own steam, would join the leader, or other senior politicians campaigning, but only file their stories (if they were newspaper reporters) – by landline phone – for use in the following day's paper. The reporters might also visit key marginal constituencies to pick up a flavour of how the campaign was going 'on the ground'. In the constituencies they would have walkabouts to report, set-piece and impromptu speeches to cover, door-to-door canvassing to observe and a host of other 'real events' to report, such as visits to hospitals, schools and so on. Their only other source of predictable news would be the party press releases, delivered twice a day by special messenger to their offices at Westminster or Fleet Street.

Fast forward

So much for the past, what about the future? In the absence of a reliable crystal ball the best way of predicting how things might be, come the 2015 (or whenever) general election, is to look at what happened in 2010, for change in these matters is incremental and organic, rather than sudden and dramatic.

In the 2010 election, when there were virtually no early morning press conferences, battle buses were rarely seen and very few set-piece speeches were delivered. Most political reporters covered the campaign from home, from their office or at the various locations of the leaders' televised debates.

The election reporter's day began by turning to the BlackBerry, iPhone or iPad to catch-up on the news from the parties, from the major news sites, the Facebook groups, the key tweeters and political bloggers, not to mention the messages and queries from the office – and that's before even getting up. In the bathroom he or she might flick between BBC Radio 4's *Today* programme (one of the few remaining vestiges from 1979, although in those days it only began broadcasting at 7am) and the 5 Live Breakfast Show. Over coffee and toast our reporter will be keeping an eye on Sky News and the BBC's News 24 with another eye on the laptop, checking out the updates and reading emails from the party press offices. In fact, on the days when no leaders' debates were taking place, the election reporter could stay at the breakfast table, keeping abreast of all the campaigning news and information. At the same time he or she could start filing copy, be it an update of the main news of the day, a new blog, some Tweets, something for a Facebook group or record a podcast.

The occasional press conference didn't need to be attended in person because Sky and the BBC carried them live, and provided instant analysis as well. The same went for major speeches by the party leaders. The only thing pulling the reporter away from his or her desk was either the need to get some local 'colour' or to attend the leaders' debates. These debates, which in 2010 were held in three locations outside London, might, or might not have illuminated the electorate, but they did at least force reporters to leave their desks for the lure of the so-called 'spin rooms'. These makeshift press offices, based at the debate locations, were used by the parties for face-to-face briefings with the journalists after, and even during, the debates, to convince the waiting reporters that their man had been the victor.

Adam Boulton, Political Editor, Sky News

Media coverage of the 2010 election was transformed by the debates. For the first time TV was allowed to do what it does best – take a live event to millions of viewers simultaneously. This process coincided with the structural decline of UK newspapers, confirming that they are no longer the public's primary source of election information. And I do not expect newspapers will ever again be the primary and dominant force of political coverage – the electronic media will not give up that role.

While on the one hand reporting elections is becoming easier – in terms of reporters' ability to access information and to file stories – it is also getting more complicated. In 1979 campaigns were straightforward and visible, that is no longer the case. Parties now distinguish between what they call the 'air' war – fought out in the national media – and the 'ground war' – the hand-to-hand combat in the constituencies (involving direct mail, phone canvassing, emailing, text messaging and so on). The 'ground war', while being highly visible to those being targeted, is almost invisible to political reporters, particularly those not locally based. And not only is this campaigning taking place away from the national stage, there has also been a significant reduction in terms of local campaigning events. Senior politicians are doing fewer walkabouts, partly for security reasons and partly because, in the context of ever more highly managed campaigns, fears of a 'Bigotgate' moment (when Gordon Brown's encounter with an 'ordinary voter' in Rochdale went drastically wrong) loom large. In an age when mobile phones are capable of taking pictures and recording audio and video, the parties now rightly fear that the slightest deviation from the party norm will result in an embarrassing posting on YouTube, Flickr, Facebook or Twitter.

Justifying why parties prefer the 'ground war' to the 'air war' Lord (Philip) Gould, Tony Blair's polling adviser, said:

> Four years ago the national campaign mattered, now it's the ground campaign that deals with individual voters that is central. That's because the electorate are now cynical about national messages, they don't believe them. But they do believe messages from local sources especially their local MP.

This sense of the real campaign taking place elsewhere was strongly felt by the journalists. Andy Bell, Political Editor of *Channel Five News* wrote:

> I was based in Westminster throughout the campaign and by the last ten days that became uncomfortable. It was like sitting in a command bunker far removed from the battle while ever-more interesting rumours filtered back from the front line.

This trend will continue and intensify. But while journalists might suffer from too little information gleaned from the local 'ground war', it is more than compensated by their receiving too much information about the 'air war'. Terabytes of news, analysis and information about the parties, the policies and the polls inundate journalists' desktops, laptops and mobile phones on a minute-by-minute basis. Most goes unread and unused. However, polls are regarded as 'real' nuggets of useful information – a doubtful proposition at best. (The general assumption is that polls 'predict' the winner; they don't, they simply tell us what those polled thought about a particular issue at a particular time.) Notwithstanding, during the 2010 campaign, ninety-three opinion polls were published in the national media, providing an almost hourly supply of 'horse race' material for journalists. But sorting useful polling information from the dross has become increasingly problematic for non-specialists (although websites such as UK Election Report and Political Betting do an extremely good job at decoding trends and indicating which polls should be regarded as reliable and which should not).

The whites of their eyes

Elections are the high point of political reporting but what of the daily grind of politics in what journalists call 'peace time'? The Westminster village – Parliament, government departments, party headquarters, think tanks, lobbyists and of course the media itself – will probably remain central but will it retain its current pre-eminent role?

> **David Walter, former BBC political correspondent and Liberal Democrat 'spin doctor'**
>
> I think political journalism is on the whole rather behind the curve. Consensus politics and the politics of coalition are rather alien to the trade, and not all political journalists have caught on to the way it works. A narrow focus based on stories about 'splits, spin and sleaze' is not adequate to explain what is going on any more. I believe political journalists have always suffered by being pushed down the silo known as the Westminster Village.

For many years lobby journalists (covered elsewhere in this book) have been in a privileged position. The 'L' on their parliamentary passes being the magic sign that gave them access to the members' lobby and surrounding corridors where there was a good chance of button-holing passing politicians and gaining information at first hand. But that power has decreased and will continue to decrease. One of the reasons for this is that the lobby have lost one of their key assets: the ability, in theory at least, to be able to contact MPs and ministers in and around the Palace of Westminster.

Returning to our time-travelling reporter thrust back to 1979 – he or she would have discovered that, even with a lobby pass, there were only a limited number of ways of making contact with an MP. First, there was hanging around the central lobby hoping for a chance encounter. Second, phone calls could be made to the MPs' or ministers' office – but then, what to say if the MPs were not there (which was usually the case)? 'Hi I'm in the lobby and I will wait here for eternity until you show up' or 'Hi I'm in my office and I am going to sit by my (landline) phone for ever in the vain hope that you might return this call.' Finally, a message could be scribbled on a piece of paper and then handed to a so-called 'Badge Messenger', who then strolled around the various committee rooms and other corners on the off-chance of finding the MP. When that didn't happen the message would be left in a pigeon-hole, to be collected many days later.

That all began to change with the introduction of pagers in the 1980s, followed by mobile phones, email and all the other means of online communication. MPs are no longer elusive; they can be contacted, messaged and interviewed, all without any face-to-face contact. Thus the vital access that made the members of the lobby so dominant is now available to all. Even the lobby briefings themselves – held twice a day and open only to members of the lobby – have been partially opened. Summaries of the briefings are now published on the Downing Street website and non-lobby journalists are allowed to attend the morning session. The afternoon briefing remains exclusive to the lobby – but for how much longer?

The other advantage of actually being in Westminster is the ability to attend debates and committee hearings in person; but now, thanks to the BBC's Democracy Live website, at any one time, live or recorded, feeds from eight separate sources can be viewed and, even better, audio-searched. These sources include the chambers of the Commons and Lords, select and other committees, Westminster Hall debates, the Scottish, Welsh and Northern Irish devolved assemblies and parliaments, the Greater London Assembly and the European Parliament. So the question has to be asked, is there any great value in actually having staff based inside the Palace of Westminster?

Chris McLaughlin, Editor *Tribune* magazine

The future of political journalism is both exciting and worrying. It is now common practice for lobby journalists to email questions to a group of MPs and await a response. Face-to-face contact is diminishing and with it the practice of looking politicians in the eye and judging their inflections of speech and demeanour.

A torrent of information

Information about politics in general, or specific policy areas, is now much more widely available and in the future this trend can only continue. Not too long ago the main source of information about government activity could be found on one very large table situated at the back of the parliamentary press gallery. On this table messengers from government departments would place press releases, official reports, statistical summaries and so on, for political reporters to browse. At any one time there might be up to fifty piles of such documents and sorting the proverbial wheat from the chaff was no easy task. In fact it has been surmised that government departments, looking to 'bury bad news', to coin a phrase, would leave their press releases on the table on a Friday afternoon when virtually no reporters were around, and then have them removed on the Monday morning before the reporters arrived. Should they ever have been accused of covering up damaging information they could say, with all the honesty that they could muster, that the releases had been made available to journalists and it was not their responsibility that they had not been used.

Another aspect of the information tsunami relates to the fact that journalists are now making growing use of the Freedom of Information Act (FOI) to ferret out stories that the authorities would prefer to remain 'unferreted'. This trend is bound to continue. Research suggests that journalists are one of the major users of the FOI Act, accounting for 16 per cent of all requests to government departments in 2007. Some journalists have used requests to launch fairly pointless 'fishing trips' – for example, asking every local authority in the country how often they flew the 'Union Jack'. But for the most part, FOI requests have produced a number of significant stories. For example the fact that 'Traffic cameras earn Treasury £21 million', that 'Hospitals in North Essex have paid out nearly £13 million in three years to settle clinical negligence claims' and that 'Lord Levy (Tony Blair's Middle East Envoy) visited the leaders of Israel, Syria, Jordan, Egypt and the Palestinian Authority eleven times', wouldn't have been known were it not for the Freedom of Information Act. Little wonder that Tony Blair records in his autobiography that passing this legislation was one of his biggest regrets.

Bogged down in the blogosphere

One of the most important trends that has developed in recent years has been the rise of the political blogosphere, now a major factor in the reporting of politics and one that is unlikely to diminish. The size of the political blogosphere is difficult to estimate as new sites appear, and old sites die, on an almost daily basis. According to the magazine *Total Politics,* which monitors the blogosphere closely, there were in October 2010 some 1,859 active political blogs in the UK. These included 435 that they described as 'non-aligned', 327 Conservative-supporting, 221 pro-Labour and 199 pro-Liberal Democrats. A number of these need to be monitored on a regular basis, some daily, if not more often, and some just occasionally checked. Either way it has massively increased journalists' access to information, but also their workload. It has also increased their opportunities of reaching an audience; *Total Politics* identifies ninety-seven journalists' blogs.

David Hencke, former *Guardian* political correspondent

Political journalism is going to be increasingly dominated by the 24/7 agenda with journalists darting from one thing to another and being influenced by stories breaking in the blogosphere. There will also be a change as newspapers are unable to keep such big staffs – and more freelancers will start breaking stories. This is already being shown in the membership of the parliamentary press gallery, with not every newspaper using its full quota and organisations like the ConservativeHome blogsite getting a pass.

Most, if not quite all, political reporters are now obliged to either blog themselves or contribute to a 'team' blog. Indeed some political correspondents now appear to be more influential in the blogosphere than in print – Benedict Brogan, a *Daily Mail* journalist, is a notable example. Adam Boulton, Sky News Political Editor, and his opposite number at the BBC, Nick Robinson, both run lively blogs; but it is the print journalists that have experienced the real liberating force of the political blogosphere.

In the pre-blog days a political reporter, working for a newspaper, had to wait once every twenty-four hours to make his or her contribution to the debate. Now he or she can blog on an hourly basis, if not more. Clearly, at a time when information is moving that much more quickly, and when the notion of a 24-hour news cycle seems as quaint as a manual typewriter, the ability to keep blogging can be an immense liberation, though it can, at times, feel like an immense burden as well.

And this is the downside. There used to be a joke in journalist circles that a newspaper foreign correspondent having just arrived in an international trouble-spot, and required to file a story immediately, would begin dictating their copy with the immortal words, 'I stood and watched in horror as ... *take in agency material*.' Now political journalists can find themselves under similar pressure. They might return from a press conference, debate or whatever to find urgent requests from their paper's website, to tweet, to blog and then to record an audio or video piece – and, by the way, write 1,500 sparkling words for tomorrow's paper. On top of the sheer impossibility of meeting all these tasks in the time available, there's a great loss in the time for reflection, to make a few more phone calls to check out some half-understood information, or to have a brief conversation with a wise head back in the office. There is clearly a great deal more political news flying around, but what of the quality?

Michael Crick, Political Editor BBC TV's *Newsnight*

One of the dangers of this surfeit of information is the overwhelming pressure to pluck the low-hanging fruit of immediate, personality-related stories on easy subjects, at the expense of longer-term, detailed, sometimes investigative work, about policy and other issues which might be hard for journalists and audiences to comprehend.

In addition to social media, political journalists can now access vast amounts of data through the web, not just from official government websites but from a whole host of other sites. The official Hansard site has become more user-friendly and easily searchable and, with databases of electronic cuttings available online, hours are saved compared with the time that used to be taken manually searching cuttings libraries. But the downside of this surfeit of information is all too clear. For a start there is the wood for the trees argument. For example, in 2006 the Department of Health and the Home Office (in the last year before it was downsized) produced 803 press releases – an impossible number for any journalist to track, and that's just the output of two departments. In addition there are all manner of news and specialist websites, political and other blog sites, Facebook groups, Twitter feeds and so forth, all pouring out vast quantities of information.

Ah but that's for the 'commentariat' I hear you say. Editorial Intelligence, a commercial firm that tries to keep track of newspapers columnists and political bloggers – and coined the term 'commentariat' – estimates that there are now over 200 writers whose columns appear regularly in the daily press, much of which is political. The political commentator can, and usually does, work well away from Westminster, at home and in bars and restaurants, and his or her stories do not need to be sourced. It is their opinion that the newspaper is paying for, and this will be fed by conversations, briefings and observations. For newspapers, despite the high salary of some columnists, this is good business. Commentators, despite their experience, represent rich pickings for the spin doctors. They have thousands of words to file every week, don't have to follow the daily news agenda and are free to opine in any direction that catches their fancy – and 'catching their fancy' is what spin doctors are good at.

Political comment does not require armies of reporters and can fill half or a whole page. Hence, the continued rise of the commentariat seems inevitable, especially until newspapers solve, if they ever do, the problem of making news on the web pay – the single biggest challenge facing newspapers today. For until the issue of 'monetarising' news online is solved, newspapers are going to be forever in search of cheaper ways of filling their pages.

The implications for political journalism are threefold – ever greater use of political columnists, more use of freelancers or greater use of news agency copy. And while news agencies do a good job of covering politics, they are constrained. They have to demonstrate the rigorous sort of neutrality which can drain political coverage of its flavour and thus make for unspectacular copy.

Spinning into the future

The future of 'spin' is one of the most fascinating areas of speculation when it comes to predicting the future pattern of political journalism. The days of Downing Street seeking to control the media, in the way that was the case under Blair and Brown, appears to be fading, with David Cameron and his coalition government taking a more relaxed view of media management. There are three possible reasons for this.

First, because it was seen to unravel; this began with the famous 'Jo Moore incident' on the 11 September 2001 – the terrorist planes were striking the twin towers in New York and one of Labour's chief spinners, Jo Moore, was sending an email to her colleagues advising them that 'today is a good day to bury bad news'. That email was leaked, Moore lost her job and Labour spinners began to lose confidence. Subsequently, one of Labour's chief spin-meisters, Peter (now Lord) Mandelson, has admitted that New Labour placed 'too great an emphasis on managing the media at the expense of managing policy' and Blair's Press Secretary Alastair Campbell has acknowledged that in office New Labour 'obsessed about every headline, every bulletin, every statement made by anyone in Labour ranks who might make news'.

Second, the growth of the blogosphere has undermined spinning. Not only does the political blogosphere monitor spin closely but it has, in some cases, cut down spinners in their prime. Right-wing blogger Guido Fawkes has two such scalps to his name – the first was Derek Draper, a former adviser to Peter Mandelson and the second was Gordon Brown's spinner Damien McBride. Guido Fawkes revealed that the pair were plotting to set up a website dedicated to spreading smears and rumours about Conservative politicians. (Although it has to be said that the political blogosphere might not be averse to a little spin itself, indeed some would argue that it consists of little else.) But the blogosphere is a constant source of media monitoring and as soon as it spots 'spin' it shrieks.

The third factor – not unrelated to the previous two – is that once spin is revealed it loses its potency and the public are turned off. There is polling evidence that suggests that just as the Conservative government of John Major came to be associated with 'sleaze' so the Labour governments of Blair and Brown came to be negatively associated with spin. In the public mind this was also linked with the notion of trust – or lack of it – and this in turn was closely associated with the two major issues which have blighted contemporary politics – the Iraq invasion and the revelations about MPs' expenses.

Spin was perhaps seen at its worst in the attempts by the government of Tony Blair to defend its invasion of Iraq in 2003. Whether direct lying was involved or not, there was undoubtedly a great deal of spinning employed in an attempt to convince the British public that Saddam Hussein possessed weapons of mass destruction that justified the invasion. There were no such weapons and the spin that was employed to try and convince the British public otherwise was fatally tarnished. Meanwhile the revelations about MPs' expenses not only seemed to encapsulate public distrust of politicians, but the story itself was so big, so impactful, that no amount of spin could minimise it. Former Labour MP Chris Mullin writes vividly about how the Parliamentary Labour Party, in 2009, was consumed by the impact of the MPs' expenses scandal and how it felt powerless to do anything to calm the issue down.

However, the notion that spin will cease is fanciful. Wherever politicians seek to stay in power there will always be spin. It was not something that was invented by New Labour – merely taken to new heights – but is it a permanent fact of political life? Lance Price, a former BBC political correspondent and Downing Street spinner, suggests that the Conservative–Liberal Democrat coalition, which in its early days was remarkably free of spin, will eventually succumb to its temptations. 'Cracks will appear in the coalition – cracks must appear – and when they do the spin will become more obvious' he suggests.

Until they do, some observers are seeing the 2010 election, and the subsequent formation of a coalition government, as heralding a watershed for political journalism. And they suggest that whatever difficulties political journalists might have had in the past, the future, on- or offline, is rosy. This is because, notwithstanding the problems of spin, information overload, more demanding workloads and increased competitiveness, those writing, broadcasting, tweeting or blogging about politics have more outlets available to them, access to more sources of information and audiences that are now more interactive than ever before.

Gone are the days when the lofty political correspondent could sit in one of Westminster's numerous bars or restaurants, safe in the knowledge that while enjoying the facilities of 'the best club in London' none of his colleagues would do anything as dastardly as seeking to scoop him (always a 'him' then) with an 'exclusive'. Now political journalists have to be on their mettle all the time – it might be exhausting and stressful but in terms of the functionings of our democracy, it can only be a good thing.

Ivor Gaber has worked as a political journalist for the BBC, ITN, Channel Four and Sky News. He planned and initiated the coverage of live political events for Sky News and for Radio 5 Live, and devised the televising of the House of Commons' and Lords' committees. He was a member of the Westminster lobby during the premierships of John Major and Tony Blair and currently directs the MA in Political Journalism at City University London.

32: So you still want to be a political journalist

Dear aspiring political journalist,

By now you have read – or at least scanned as journalists do – the offerings from a wide range of contributors. Hopefully you have gained a lot of practical advice. Perhaps you have enjoyed some of the anecdotes which demonstrate the sort of unexpected and even ridiculous situations political journalists find themselves in.

If you have reached this point, there are likely to be different reasons why you are still considering a job in political journalism. I hope they are the right ones. As you can see from those who tell of their different roads to Westminster, a mixture of determination plus a bit of luck at the right time is required. But, as long as you are making progress in journalism, honing your skills, contacts and experience, the most amazing opportunities should come your way.

I make absolutely no excuse for the occasional whiff of nostalgia in this book. There is some sort of lesson in each of the anecdotes. Yes, it is easy to stand back and see the tremendous changes there have been since many of us started out. No more searching for a working phone box and striking matches as you dictate copy from your notebook in the middle of the night. No more full pages of parliamentary speeches. Very little deference for those in authority.

As Ivor Gaber, my colleague at City University, makes clear, there are new challenges today. Yet there are eternal themes running through the contributions. Doing your homework. The importance of spotting and pursuing 'the story' you want to communicate. Meeting your deadlines. Being naturally curious. Asking questions, lots of questions. Sitting through gatherings where you need to understand and translate the proceedings, whether it is a local council committee, a debate in Parliament, a select committee hearing or a party conference speech. Making and keeping your contacts, ever more contacts.

One of the changes is the ease of access to information. A click of a button will bring you televised proceedings, access to all the written materials, information about the processes and technicalities. You can also arrange to meet MPs, for instance, in Portcullis House or at 4 Millbank (where the broadcasters have studios), or a peer in the peers' lobby. Investment in a publication, such as *Vacher's*, tells you who does what, plus all the contact details, at Westminster and Whitehall – and beyond.

As you know, I'm in this odd position of having been involved in politics from six different viewpoints: mainly as a political journalist, but also as a prime ministerial spokesman (or 'spin doctor' if you insist), local councillor, party activist and parliamentary candidate, political and media consultant at home and abroad – and as a lecturer. I do not have a rose-tinted view of either politicians or political journalists. But perhaps the balance and influence between the two is slightly out of kilter.

It is not healthy, in my view, to start from the premise that all politicians are crooks and liars. Certainly a few are – and your job will be to suss them out. Yet the basic job of finding out what government, local and central, is doing – how taxpayers' money is being spent or misspent; how elected representatives are carrying out their roles – never changes.

Nor do I believe that political journalists are coerced by self-seeking proprietors into reporting what they know to be untrue. Do political reporters commonly make up quotes? No. Well, maybe occasionally – but those do not usually survive for long. Do politicians and political journalists have very different concepts of what makes 'a story'? Definitely, yes. Perhaps that is how it should be.

Please take it from me that, when working with political activists and presidential candidates in the developing world, they all look with envy at our democratic systems, all the things we take for granted: the relative lack of corruption, the independent judiciary and the freedom of the press. If in doubt, study Michael White's comments. And while the reputation of our Parliament and political system has sunk to a depressingly low level in recent years, there is little indication that the general public has any more respect or trust in political journalists.

I would not be as presumptuous as to pen a recipe to repair this. But I am hoping that, now you have heard the different voices in this book, you will still consider playing your own part.

Good luck!

Yours sincerely,
Sheila

THE PRIME MINISTERS WHO NEVER WERE

A collection of political counterfactuals

Edited by Francis Beckett

Back in the days of the smoke-filled rooms, the Tory grandee Lord Salisbury, who could not pronounce his Rs, invited the Cabinet into his room one by one and asked: 'It is Wab or Hawold?' The smart money was on them all saying Wab...

Had J. R. Clynes pipped Ramsay MacDonald to the Party leadership, the millworker who'd left school at ten would have become Labour's first Prime Minister. In the dark days of war, Lord Halifax had first refusal on the premiership ahead of Winston Churchill. Both Hugh Gaitskell and John Smith would have been Prime Minister but for their sudden, early deaths.

Each of the chapters in this book of political counterfactuals describes a premiership that never happened, but might easily have done had the chips fallen slightly differently.

256pp hardback • £14.99 • Available now

www.bitebackpublishing.com

SPEAKING TO LEAD

How to make speeches that make a difference

John Shosky

As a speechwriter and consultant, John Shosky's credentials are impeccable. During the last twenty-five years he has worked with people at the highest levels of government and business, including three presidential administrations and many top executives from Fortune 500 companies. In this book Shosky distils his incomparable know-how into an accessible practical guide to the essentials of his art.

Speaking to Lead teaches the importance and use of speech as action: a tool to fix problems and push issues forward. As the title suggests, from the boardroom to the podium, this is a book for leaders.

288pp paperback • £14.99 • Available now

www.bitebackpublishing.com

SO YOU WANT TO BE A POLITICIAN

Edited by Shane Greer

So You Want to be a Politician is a must read for any first time candidate or anyone looking to put together and run an effective campaign at any level of public life. This accessible, practical guide offers common-sense advice for almost any scenario.

Featuring contributions and advice from some of the leading names in contemporary British campaigning, *So You Want to be a Politician* is an essential resource that some of today's serving politicians could make good use of.

304pp paperback • £14.99 • Available now

www.bitebackpublishing.com